GOD'S
FAITHFULNESS
Stories from the China Inland Mission and OMF International

GOD'S
FAITHFULNESS
Stories from the China Inland Mission and OMF International

ROSE DOWSETT & CHAD BERRY

GOD'S FAITHFULNESS
Stories from the China Inland Mission and OMF International

© OMF International 2014
Hardback ISBN: 978-0-85363-160-6
Paperback ISBN: 978-0-85363-161-3

Published by OMF International

Printed in Singapore by Mainland Press Pte. Ltd.

www.omf.org

Contents

Acknowledgements

An anthology of stories covering 150 years is a complex project requiring input from numerous people. It would be impossible to name everyone who has contributed to this book. The Bibliography lists sources—books and articles written by scores of authors, as well as a large number of personal letters and conversations.

Initial ideas for the book were developed during 2011 by OMF's International Directors in Singapore. In the IHQ Media team, Charlotte W. did important work in planning, research and writing. At the same time, Chad Berry (OMF U.S.), worked on other research and wrote several stories.

In August 2013, the portfolio was passed to Rosemary Dowsett, who worked tirelessly for the next eight months to flesh out the bare bones of over 35 stories. She also wrote the historical section, basing some of it on work done by David Huntley. We owe a huge debt of gratitude to Rosemary for taking on this challenge and completing this task with such skill and efficiency.

Major editorial work and the cover design were done by a team in the U.S. led by Communications Director Gwen

Hanna, including Chad Berry, Megan Sarian and Michelle McCorkle.

Above all, we recognize and give thanks to our faithful God, under whose direction this volume has come to completion. It is testimony to his grace, his strength and his inspiration. It is an example of his body at work—different parts with different functions at different times.

We pray that God will use these stories to inspire you and be a powerful reminder that he is faithful—forever. All glory be to him!

GLENYS GOULSTONE
OMF Project 2015 Coordinator

Foreword

The Bible is packed with a vast array of stories: those of exuberant joy and deep pain, of remarkable success and regrettable failures, of unbelievable miracles and unbearable disasters. Yet, the greatest story of all is not about man, but God: his extreme patience when his people strayed, his bountiful provision when his people were in want, his embracing care when his people were hurting.

The Bible instructs us to tell God's story to the next generation: "Since my youth, O God, you have taught me, and to this day I declare your marvelous deeds. Even when I am old and gray, do not forsake me, O God, till I declare your power to the next generation, your might to all who are to come." (Psalm 71:17-18)

Moses instructed God's people to remember the faithfulness of God: "Remember the days of old; consider the generations long past. Ask your father and he will tell you, your elders, and they will explain to you." (Deuteronomy 32:7)

The Bible records stories of personal lives touched and renewed by God's love and power, sometimes in the most tender of ways: the healing of Simon's mother-in-law (Mark 1:30), breakfast with downcast disciples (John 21:12), hope in the starless night and raging storm (Acts 27:19ff). Stories such as these are not on a grand scale, impacting a huge number of people, yet each one reflects the tender father heart of God, who is also Yahweh—the eternal, sovereign and creator God, Lord of the universe.

This book is a book of real stories about real people. Every encounter recorded in these pages testifies to the powerful work of God in the lives of each OMF worker —ordinary people like you and me. Read about the transformed life of an angry father whose daughter went to serve in Taiwan; the courage of a young Canadian worker who spoke the truth fearlessly to the rebel leader in a lawless environment; the compassion of a Dutch sister to reach out to those in prostitution; the loving testimony of a family who set up their home in a former brothel, reaching out to others in the dark corners of Bangkok; the journeying of Christians with those who searched desperately for missing loved ones after the Indian Ocean tsunami. In every story, we catch a glimpse of the light and hope found in Christ. May you find inspiration in these stories just as I have.

Patrick Fung
OMF International General Director

Introduction

In 2015 OMF celebrates 150 years of service. Such an occasion is a good moment to trace the organization's story from a small seed of faith sown in 1865 in order to seek to understand what God is doing in the present and discern where the wind of the Spirit may be blowing for the future.

OMF began as the China Inland Mission (CIM). It was not until 1951 that it became clear that at least for a time further ministry in China would not be possible. A name change was in order, and the Mission became the Overseas Missionary Fellowship of the China Inland Mission. Later, the "China Inland Mission" part of the name was dropped since the Mission was no longer in China and now ministered to unreached people throughout East Asia." Later still the name was changed to OMF International.

Even more impactful than name changes have been the changes in the world since 1865. Then, ships still operated under sail, large inland areas of the continents were unexplored or too unhealthy to inhabit, many languages had no written form and extensive swathes of the world were entirely untouched by the gospel of Jesus Christ. In today's world of instant communication, air travel that takes us around the globe in little more than a day and of a worldwide church, it is hard to grasp what life was like just a century and a half ago.

However much the world may have changed, the God whom we love and serve has not changed. The Lord Jesus Christ "is the same yesterday and today and forever" (Hebrews 13:8). The words that the Holy Spirit has inspired and given us in the scriptures are unchanging. The very nature and character of the Triune God is utterly reliable. He is the faithful one. A Christian's seed of faith may be small, but the one in whom that faith is placed is the sovereign Lord of the universe.

It is the faithfulness of God to one community of his people, down through 150 years, that this book wishes to celebrate. The men, women and children who have been a part of this story were—like us—fragile human beings, many of them with names scarcely remembered, though securely recorded in heaven. Despite their weakness, it was their desire, generation after generation, to bring glory to God through seeing the gospel take root in East Asia and East Asians coming to a living faith in the one and only true God. Both gospel-bearers and gospel-embracers have become part of the far larger story that stretches back to the dawn of history. From creation to the present, we see the grace and faithfulness of God to his children.

The work of God through OMF represents just one small evidence of the living God at work in his world: small, but by no means insignificant. God delights to bless those who, though weak, depend on God to accomplish his purposes. The growth of the church throughout East Asia is awe-inspiring evidence of God's faithfulness to bring harvest out of the sowing of the gospel seed—seed that has often been sown in tears and suffering, sometimes taking decades to bear fruit and whose full harvest we do not yet see. A much-loved hymn echoes our prayer: "We'll praise him for all that is past, and trust him for all that's to come."

Reading this Book

Readers may like to jump straight in to the many stories in this book or may prefer to begin with this brief history that explains how OMF came into being and how God guided the ministry through many changes to the present.

The history provides a condensed background for the stories that follow. It is of necessity only a brief sketch. Many important parts of the story have been omitted in the interest of brevity.

The main purpose of the book, however, is not to provide a systematic history but to tell the stories of particular individuals, events and experiences. It is only a small selection. Many more stories could have been told. What they all have in common is that they testify to God's faithfulness to one community of God's people. That faithfulness has been experienced in tragedy and triumph, in sorrow and joy, in provision on a huge scale and provision in some small but precious way. The stories tell of answers to prayer. They tell of human weakness and God's power. They show ordinary men and women struggling to tell the story of Jesus across cultures and the grace of God in using stumbling words and flawed lives to bring people to faith. They show what love for God and love for East Asia's peoples can achieve in the life-creating hands of the Holy Spirit. They show the timelessness of the Good News of a Savior who lived and died and rose again out of love for a broken world.

The stories are all true stories of real people. Some come directly from the pens of people still living and able to tell their stories themselves. Some are stories from the past, recorded in letters and journals and other documents. They are drawn from many decades, from many countries of service and from a variety of ministries.

This book goes out with the prayer that it may bring glory to the God whose faithfulness we celebrate. May it also inspire many more to join in with the great adventure of seeing the church in East Asia continue to grow, numerically and in outreach, but even more in depth and likeness to the Lord Jesus Christ. It is the promise of God that one day there will be worshippers of every tribe and tongue and nation gathered around the throne in heaven. What a vision that is! There will be countless East Asian faces among them!

> "To him who is able to keep you from falling and to present you before his glorious presence without fault and with great joy—to the only God our Savior be glory, majesty, power and authority, through Jesus Christ our Lord, before all ages, now and forevermore! Amen" Jude 1:24 25.

Through 150 Years
of our History

1. The Start of the China Inland Mission

In May 1832, a baby boy was born in Yorkshire, northern England. His parents named him James Hudson Taylor. He came to simple Christian faith as a child, and grew up nurtured in the then-vibrant world of Methodism. He later renewed his commitment to Christ at the age of 17.

At that time, Methodism was a powerful force in evangelism, especially among the poor, and had a strong tradition of discipling its people. Further, the denomination had a strong social conscience and engaged tirelessly in what is now known as holistic or integrated mission: education and literacy work, simple medical care for the sick, support for the vulnerable and help in breaking the chains of alcoholism.

The Industrial Revolution was changing both the landscape and way of life in 19th century England. Hudson Taylor grew up surrounded by all the energy and exploitation of the mills around his home and by a growing awareness of the wider world

*James Hudson Taylor as
a teenager*

with whom those mills traded. Even as a child, China fascinated him. Apart from a few seaports, little was known about the vast land of the Middle Kingdom. In particular, what lay inland? Had anyone there ever heard of the Lord Jesus Christ?

Gradually, fascination became conviction, and after a short time of medical training in London, Hudson Taylor sailed for China in 1853. He was just 21 years old. His initial experience under the China Evangelisation Society was disappointing. There was little interest in inland China and almost no information to be had about the inner provinces. The Society soon collapsed and Hudson Taylor found himself with no financial support.

In his first tenure in China, Hudson Taylor became increasingly convinced that most westerners living in the Chinese ports greatly hindered the gospel by the way they lived. He also learned lessons that later proved invaluable to his ministry. He made several independent journeys a little way inland; he became fluent in the Chinese language and began to understand some of

James and Maria Hudson Taylor

the intricacies of Chinese culture; he found that his medical knowledge opened doors; and he met and married Maria Dyer in 1858.

In 1860, the Taylors were forced to return to England for a while because of ill health. But the call of inland China would not be silenced. As they prayed and waited, and as Hudson Taylor did some more medical training, they became convinced that God was calling them to start a new mission, in faith and with the specific goal of reaching inland China. They did not wish to divert funds from other established Christian initiatives.

Would they dare to copy the example of George Müller? In 1836, Müller had founded an orphanage in Bristol, trusting the Lord to supply all the considerable daily needs to house, feed and care for hundreds of children at a time, with no regular support. The Taylors had already experienced the Lord providing for them as individuals and as a family. Could God do the same for a significantly larger group if Hudson Taylor initiated a mission for inland China? Was it presumptuous to think that someone like himself could pioneer such an enterprise?

He became convinced that it was not so much that he and Maria had to exercise faith as that they needed to hold on to the faithfulness of God himself. The Bible taught that "The one who calls you is faithful and he will do it" (1 Thessalonians 5:24). They were sure of their call to China and of God's heart for the Chinese people; now, they said to one another, God will do it.

Finally, one Sunday morning—June 25, 1865—as he paced up and down the beach at Brighton, England, Hudson Taylor crossed the last hurdles in his mind and heart, and prayed that God would supply him with "24 willing skillful workers," two for each inland province of China and two for Mongolia. If

God was in it, he would answer their prayers, supply their needs without any appeal for funds and take them where the Spirit led them. Willingness to trust in the faithfulness of God and commitment to prayerful dependence on him would be required of anyone who wished to join this new venture.

The China Inland Mission was born. Hudson Taylor was still only 33 years old.

2. The China Years

One by one, the Lord brought an initial group together, and gradually others followed. Trust in God was sorely tested. Some of the early workers decided that they could not cope with the challenges of pioneer living and adapting as closely as possible to Chinese diet and dress. Some succumbed to illness. Some simply did not like being directed by Hudson Taylor. Some discovered that neither the Chinese they had loved from a romantic distance, nor their colleagues, were so easy to love up close. For all of them, there was the unnerving reality of living surrounded by a totally alien religious

Taylor family

and cultural environment, of being foreigners and therefore the natural object of hostility and suspicion, of not being able to communicate until they could learn some language and of simply living in a sinful, fallen world. The first years of the organization were especially difficult. For Hudson Taylor himself, there was the added grief of losing his beloved Maria, along with four children within a few short years of one another. Still, he repeatedly urged his fellow workers, "Have faith in God!"

Gradually, progress was made. Hudson Taylor had learned some valuable lessons from his earlier time in China and from his experience in the now defunct Chinese Evangelisation Society. He decided that unlike other mission organizations at

CIM Headquarters, Wusong Road, Shanghai 1891-1931

CIM Headquarters, Sinza Road, Shanghai 1931-1951

the time, the headquarters of the growing mission would be located in China, not in Europe or anywhere else thousands of miles away. Decisions about policy and practice must be made as close to the action as possible, and as swiftly as possible, by the people who best understood the context of the ministry. As the CIM grew, the most influential councils were all based in China, although with good rapport with the growing number of homeside offices around the world. For almost all the China years, the CIM's headquarters was in Shanghai, a thriving port close to the coast but ideal as an entry and exit point for most missionaries and communications hub for all of China.

As the CIM grew, and quite differently from Hudson Taylor's first assumptions, it became international, with sending bases in a growing number of countries. These homeside

VOLUME 1, NUMBER 1: THE LAUNCH OF
CHINA'S MILLIONS

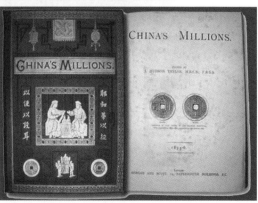

*China's Millions
Vol 1, No.1
– 1875 and
China's Millions
book – 1875*

offices' task was to stir up prayer based on accurate, up-to-date information sent from China. As such, producing informative magazines and books soon became an important part of their role. The home bases also screened candidates for suitability and compatibility with the CIM ethos. They ensured that any funds given were carefully accounted for, faithfully acknowledged and then transferred to China.

The CIM was interdenominational from the start, with Hudson Taylor insisting that those who loved the Lord and the gospel, and were called by the Lord, should be eligible to join, whatever their denomination. Such a stance was radical in an era when most Christian enterprises were fiercely denominational. It was also radical that Hudson Taylor was less concerned with formal educational qualifications and much more concerned with the spiritual caliber of those who came. Were applicants passionate about winning people to Christ? Did they trust God to keep the promises made in the Bible? Were they prepared to live sacrificially and prayerfully? And so carpenters, housemaids and shop assistants rubbed shoulders with teachers, doctors and professors—equal before God in the task to which each were called. Perhaps even more radical still at that time in history was that women, married or single, were accepted as missionaries in their own right. Over the years, single women proved to be wonderful pioneers and team members in the ministry.

Hudson Taylor was adamant that as churches were planted they should be indigenous, that is, not tied to any denomination elsewhere in the world. Neither should they be dependent on foreign funds. Help might be given to acquire or build a suitable church building once a group was firmly established, but it would reflect local architecture (often very simple) and local believers would be responsible for maintaining it.

Missionaries would rightly pay language teachers and house helpers, but would not pay the salaries of pastor. Since local churches appointed the pastors, it would be the responsibility of the local group of believers to pay the pastors. In this way, the churches would be self-supporting and not in the control of the Mission or any outside body. Some early experiments in directly employing pastors showed that this led to problems and made relationships with missionaries difficult. The only flexibility to this principle came later on when Anglican work began in inland China and some CIM personnel were allowed to work in partnership with the denomination.

Over the nearly 90 years of the CIM's work in China, through famine, war and disease, a swelling number of men and women poured out their lives to tell the Chinese of the Savior who loved them and had died for them. More and more, as the Chinese church grew and matured, local evangelists, pastors and Bible women, all eager to spread the Good News of the gospel, worked alongside the CIM missionaries. Many of them—both men and women—walked hundred of miles to visit one city, one village, one home, one after another, or traveled on rickety boats along the rivers. How else do you reach the unreached? It was a long time before they had bicycles, let alone motorized transport, to ease their journeys.

Along with perhaps a thousand independent churches planted, and many more embryonic small gatherings of believers, the CIM started schools and Bible colleges, hospitals and clinics, and refuges for opium addicts to detoxify. CIM workers cared for orphans and abandoned babies. They brought love to abused women, to rejected leprosy sufferers and to the outcast. They challenged every power of darkness, the breadth and length of the vast country of China. They often buried their children, their spouses or their colleagues, as so many diseases simply treated today were then beyond the scope of contemporary medical knowledge. Some died a martyr's death, such as during the Boxer Rebellion of 1900, when many Chinese Christians also lost their lives. Many served year after year, trusting that God who is faithful would one day bring a harvest, whether or not they lived to see it.

Increasingly, inland China was impacted by events in the wider world, including two world wars and the Russian Revolution. Internally, the final imperial dynasty fell in 1912, a civil war erupted between Nationalist and Communist forces in China, and competing warlords vied for control of large areas of China. Eventually, much of China had to give way to Japanese occupation. Japanese expansionism had been going on for decades, including nibbling away at parts of China, but from 1937 until the atomic bomb in 1945 ended Japan's all-Asia dream, China suffered greatly.

Many CIM missionaries, together with about 120 children and 30 teachers from the CIM Chefoo schools for missionary children, were interned for years in prisoner-of-war camps during World War II. Nearly 200 more children had been sent back to their families before the school was taken over, with some of those families leaving China for home leave before their area was overrun. Others were taken into other internment camps as the war progressed and more countries outside China became involved in it. As many workers as could stayed at their posts as long as possible, encouraging their Chinese friends and continuing in evangelism and service.

It was a hard time for Chinese people, Christians and unbelievers alike. It was also a time when Chinese Christians often showed great endurance and faithfulness to the Lord in

Arthur Matthews & Rupert Clarke

the face of suffering. They also showed compassion for their neighbors, which probably contributed to the extraordinary growth of the church in the period after 1945, the last years of CIM's ministry in the country.

On October 1, 1949, Mao Zedong declared the founding of the People's Republic of China; Communist forces had won China's civil war. As Communism took hold, it became clear that the best way foreign missionaries could serve the Chinese church at the time was by leaving. Missionaries might have to leave, but God did not.

With heavy hearts and many questions about the future, the CIM missionaries steadily left China. Most had left by the close of 1951. The last ones to leave, after imprisonment, were Dr. Rupert Clarke and Arthur Matthews in July 1953. The "reluctant exodus" from China was complete.

3. Starting Again: A Renewed Vision

For some years before the exodus, there had been discussion about reaching out to the large Chinese communities that had migrated out of China into surrounding countries. There were also several tribal groups that spilled across the border of China into Thailand, Laos and Burma. As senior CIM leaders met to pray for wisdom in discerning the way ahead, it became clear that CIM missionaries who were willing to do so could be deployed to other locations. This possibility was confirmed by Christian Chinese leaders in Singapore who begged for the CIM's help in reaching the Chinese in Malaya (now Malaysia). Most of the Chinese there had not yet heard the gospel. Could the CIM help?

As surveys of various countries were carried out, other invitations followed, although in some places there were not believers to issue such an invitation. The surveys also showed that there was an acute need to take the gospel not only to the Chinese communities (which were at first assumed to be the

Senior CIM leaders meet in Bournemouth

Lord's place for CIM to go), but also to many other ethnic groups throughout East Asia. Much of the region at that time was poor, much had suffered greatly through World War II and many nations were vulnerable to ideological take-over by Communism. In many countries, the church was quite small or virtually nonexistent. The window of opportunity for the gospel might be very short. It seemed that God was expanding the heart and vision of the Mission. If China was to be closed to foreigners for the foreseeable future, there were others who equally needed the gospel. It would be disobedient to ignore them.

The political map of East Asia was very different in 1952 from what it would become over the next few decades. Several countries were in the throes of civil war; some either had recently become independent from former imperial powers or were about to become so; some were under military rule and most were to suffer an extended period of great instability. In some countries, external aid to help rebuild areas damaged by war was welcomed. In most countries it was still possible to gain entry for explicitly Christian activity, but in some places it was educational or medical help that was mostly accepted. In all countries the new post-imperial and post-colonial world meant that government permission must be gained for foreigners to be allowed to enter, and in some cases that permission came with considerable restrictions or could be withdrawn at any time. Sometimes, for instance in Indonesia, visas had to be sponsored by an existing recognized local denominational board, to ensure that no new denomination would emerge.

The newly named Overseas Missionary Fellowship of the China Inland Mission was once again challenged to look to God's sovereign rule to find where doors would open for further ministry. Some of the earliest work was in Malaya (now Malaysia), where the government was settling many Chinese in New Villages to prevent them from being impacted by—or becoming allies to—Communist guerillas. Chinese-speaking missionaries were especially  welcome, since it was supposed that their influence would be particularly significant, and around 150 OMF-CIM members served there. Some years later, with political change in Malaya, fewer foreigners were able to gain visas, though some specialist invitations still came, particularly in theological education.

Other former CIM personnel found their way to Taiwan (then named Formosa), Hong Kong and Singapore with their large Chinese populations, as well as to the minority Chinese communities in the Philippines, Indonesia, Vietnam, Laos and Thailand. In North Thailand there was continuity in work among tribal minorities that spilled across political borders (e.g. the Lisu, Karen etc.). CIM members had already worked among many of those groups in China.

Alongside the work among ethnic Chinese and the tribal people, there was also almost at once the opportunity to work with many other nationalities and groups. The Mission was committed not to compete with other agencies and so deliberately went to areas where no other group was working. Where there was a national church already in place, it was (and is) important to consult with local leaders about where service would be most acceptable. For example, in Thailand the Mission was directed to Central Thailand where there were almost no known believers at the time. In addition, because there was then no government medical provision for many miles around, first a clinic and then a hospital were set up at Manorom. Both there and in South Thailand, where another small hospital was established, leprosy was widespread and greatly feared. OMF International medical personnel developed effective treatment, including reconstructive surgery. Many successfully treated leprosy patients not only were rehabilitated back into their communities but also responded to the gospel and became the backbone of a number of rural churches.

Japan was another country entered into for service after the organization's withdrawal from China. It has also proved one of the most difficult within which to see people come to faith in the Lord Jesus Christ. For the foreigner, it is incredibly difficult to learn the Japanese language sufficiently to be able to engage in good communication. It is a context where long-term service is essential and where a gospel-bearer may need years of disciplined prayer and trust in God so that his ministry is not a waste of time. It may take years for someone in Japan to progress from first hearing the gospel to the point where he or she becomes a disciple. Most churches remain small in number; in many towns there are still no known believers. Why is it so hard? It stretches our faith, but God remains the faithful one, and we trust him.

Cambodia by contrast has been a very different story. There was a brief opportunity for evangelism before the terrible genocide under Pol Pot and the Khmer Rouge. Most believers were killed or fled the country at that time. OMF personnel were able to minister to traumatized survivors in the refugee camps, especially in Thailand. When it was possible to re-enter Cambodia, many workers were able to establish different types of compassion ministries, help rebuild education and medical services, and develop care for orphans and for those deeply scarred by their traumatic experiences. Profound love offered in the name of Christ is powerful, and the church has grown quickly. Why should rapid growth of the church occur in one place but not another? That, too, stretches our faith, though in a different way, and again we look to God who is faithful.

Both literature and radio ministry have also been important in East Asia as means of sharing the good news. OMF personnel have been seconded to the Far East Broadcasting Company (FEBC) to help create programs in numerous Asian languages. These broadcasts have often reached communities where the actual presence of a person to share the gospel is forbidden. Literature ministry often began with the need to prepare simple tracts and gospel portions. Step by step, literature work has developed in a number of countries into publishing a full range of evangelistic and teaching materials, books written by local authors and the printing of new Bible translations. Today's new technologies offer exciting new possibilities.

Today many OMF personnel serve under or alongside local Asian leadership. Since the early days of the CIM, such an arrangement has been a deliberate goal. The Mission is the servant of the Lord and of those to whom he sends us. Many pioneer church-planting efforts and student ministries established by OMF workers have now been passed into the hands of local East Asian Christian leaders. Workers have also established many Bible and theological colleges to serve the churches and contribute to the training of local leaders, but many of these, too, are now under local leadership. In some countries, expatriates are still welcomed to join a student ministry team or teach at a Bible or theological college. Of course, there are also still places where pioneer church planting remains a pressing need.

Over the years, as political and religious shifts have swept through East Asia, some countries that once were open to missionary presence are no longer so. Yet in such contexts, there is often openness to many kinds of professional service offered by expatriates. It is important that such professional service is performed with integrity and to the highest standards possible, but Christians in such roles also have many opportunities to pray for those they work with or teach, and to share their faith in informal contexts.

It is now more than 60 years since the CIM left China. The Chinese government itself recognizes that there are millions of Christian believers there today. This growth is a miracle that only God could perform. It is not only in China that the gospel has taken root. In the grace of God, there are now well-established and mature churches throughout much of East Asia.

By 1965, Asian Christians were clamoring to be allowed to join OMF. World mission was no longer (as it should never have been regarded) seen as "the West to the rest," but increasingly seen as the task of the global church in all its multi-ethnic diversity. Mission is not a task for just one particular part of the world church, but is central to the very nature and calling of the church everywhere. And so joyfully, and recognizing the goodness of God in the growth of the church in many parts of East Asia, OMF welcomed a growing stream of Asian brothers and sisters into membership. Today, more than one-third of the membership comes from the region or from Asian communities already settled in other parts of the world.

In 1951, the decision was first made to follow Chinese migrants across other parts of East Asia. Since then, migration has accelerated from many East Asian countries to the rest of the world. East Asians who relocate to other countries are known as "the diaspora." Some settle long term in another country, some are economic migrants or refugees, some are only temporarily overseas for study or work. A growing band of OMF workers partners with churches and other agencies in discipling diaspora people. Most recently, African church leaders have asked for help in reaching out to the many East Asian migrant workers now living among them. East Asians are no longer only in East Asia.

4. Peering into the Future

In some countries and among some specific ethnic groups, there remain many millions who have not yet had any contact with the Christian gospel. OMF's aim is to see a church movement among every people group of East Asia. Each of those churches should be committed to reaching out with the gospel to those around them and beyond. In much of East Asia, that has become an increasingly complicated task; but it is the calling of a healthy, faithful and obedient Christian community.

Why is the task of church planting in East Asia increasingly complicated? Several major factors in Asia itself stand out.

The first of these is the population explosion. Nearly one-third of the world's over seven billion people live in East Asia. Population growth and demographics sometimes create unique challenges to ministry among East Asia's billions. While Japan's falling birth rate leads to an increasingly older population, in countries such as Thailand or the Philippines the majority of the population are children and young people.

Second is rapid urbanization. In 1952, the large majority of East Asia was still rural rather than urban, agricultural rather than industrialized. It was in that context that many of the early OMF-CIM personnel were deployed to small towns and villages since that was where people lived. Today the situation is far different. Thirty out of the 100 largest cities in the world are in East Asia. East Asia's cities are growing at a phenomenal rate as people pour in from the countryside that is often increasingly poor and marginalized. This migration presents both challenge and opportunity for the church. Urban populations can be extraordinarily complex, with people of many different cultures, languages and backgrounds living alongside one another. Squalid poverty may exist alongside obscene wealth, illiteracy alongside a burgeoning community of the highly educated. In China, it is projected that 60 percent of the population will live in cities by 2018, and 70 percent by 2035.

The vigor of other religions and philosophies in East Asia is another factor. In particular, both Buddhism and Islam have seen renewed strength in Asia. On the one hand, old and familiar social ways are being challenged by the speed of development and of engagement with the wider world. On the other, security amidst such upheaval is sometimes sought in more radical commitment to historic religions. Sometimes national identity is bound up with a particular religion. It can be costly to change one's allegiance to become a follower of Christ.

Costly but not impossible, because the God we serve has final authority over his world. In the stories that follow readers will find time after time how this God of grace and love has intervened powerfully in people's lives. For now, we see only a little part of the whole overarching story of what the Lord is doing in East Asia. The whole story is known to God and he is the faithful one. He will write the future as he has the past.

We invite you to join us in this great adventure of faith, hand in hand with the one and only living God.

"Then Jesus came to them and said, 'All authority in heaven and on earth has been given to me. Therefore go and make disciples of all nations, baptizing them in the name of the Father and of the Son and of the Holy Spirit, and teaching them to obey everything I have commanded you. And surely I am with you always, to the very end of the age.'" (Matthew 28:18-20)

"After this I looked and there before me was a great multitude that no one could count, from every nation, tribe, people and language, standing before the throne and in front of the Lamb. They were wearing white robes and were holding palm branches in their hands. And they cried out in a loud voice:

'Salvation belongs to our God,
who sits on the throne,
and to the Lamb.'"
(Revelation 7:9-11)

To Strengthen the Weak

God's Faithfulness to Strengthen the Weak

The Apostle Paul struggled with a recurring problem that he wished the Lord would take away. We are not told what the problem was, only that Paul believed that it hindered his ministry. The Lord responded lovingly, "My grace is sufficient for you, for my power is made perfect in weakness" (2 Corinthians 12:9). Our human weakness displays the glorious power of God, and takes us deeper into the experience of God's grace. Paul goes on to say, "Therefore I will boast all the more gladly about my weaknesses, so that Christ's power may rest on me. That is why, for Christ's sake, I delight in weaknesses, in insults, in hardships, in persecutions, in difficulties. For when I am weak, then I am strong" (2 Corinthians 12: 9-10).

The apparent weakness of Christ in being crucified at the hands of his persecutors is revealed as something else: not weakness, but "the power of God for … salvation," endorsed by the triumph of the resurrection (see Romans 1:16).

Missionaries are not superheroes. They are very ordinary men and women. Most struggle with learning new languages and with trying to understand and then live in an unfamiliar culture. Most experience fear, discouragement, anger and homesickness at least some of the time. Some find their faith challenged at deep levels. Some just want to quit. There are tears as well as joy—and sometimes the joy seems in short supply.

Yet the promise of God still stands: "My grace is sufficient for you …" It is often in the hardest times that we discover in fresh ways something more of the height and depth and breadth of that grace.

5. The Pilgrim Life

One might think that continually moving to a new place would make moving easier as time goes on. Not so for Mary Welander, who first went to China with the China Inland Mission in January 1946 and then started afresh in Malaysia (then called Malaya) in 1952. Over the course of many years, Mary found the Lord moving her to new places over and over. She also found that his presence remained strong with her no matter where she went.

In the early 1950s, Chinese Christians implored CIM leaders to bring ex-China missionaries to serve in Malaya. This provided the "Macedonian Call" for the CIM to redeploy outside China. At the same time, British General Templar posed a question: "Where are the missionaries from China, who will come and live in the new village resettlement areas with these one million

Chinese we are bringing in from the jungle?" Later, as he was bidding farewell to Malaya after the work of resettlement was largely completed, he declared: "This is by no means the end of the problem; in fact it is only the beginning. We are now faced with the human problem, and the human problem can only be solved by methods which spring from the heart, rather than from the mind."

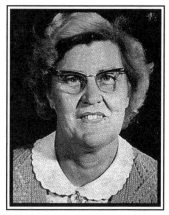

Mary Welander

CIM-OMF had answered the call and first sent workers to Malaya in 1952. Having been there a number of years, the Malaya field council was now considering a new venture. They believed the Lord was leading them to start work in the 5,000-strong Hokkien community around Ulu Yam, Malaya. Whom could they send? The council wanted someone with experience in the country, who understood the complex cultural and linguistic mix of Malaya, who might have already learned a little of the Hokkien dialect and who could be a wise, yet passionate, pioneer evangelist. "Let's send Mary," they said, "but we don't know who else to send with her yet."

Mary felt the Lord nudging her to agree, but the fact was that moving to a new place would not be easy. She might have done it many times, but somehow it was always scary. She wrote to her circle of praying friends, "Can you imagine what it will be like to move to a completely strange village, to settle into a house where every move is watched by curious spectators, to go out into the street to buy something and be followed by children, discussed by adults as one passes their shops, to be the subject of village gossip, never to be left alone, never to show any sign of irritability in the heat and noise, not to grow weary of answering endless questions in Mandarin about my age, white hair, eating habits, and family history before being able to get in a word of witness for my Lord? Where shall I begin? By going from house to house? Dare I stand alone in the street and gather a crowd which could so easily get out of hand and overwhelm me? These are some of the things that occupy my thinking and praying these days. One thing I know: all of these people need the Savior, and I can introduce them to him."

The villagers seemed to be willing to listen when she told them about Jesus. They would accept literature, too, and she discovered that those who took it not only read it themselves, but also passed it on to neighbors. Gradually, curiosity was turned into interest, and in some precious lives interest was transformed into faith. It did not take away the daily challenges she had to face as a foreigner, but it did make them worth the cost.

It was not the first time that Mary had found herself in circumstances different from those she might have wished, but she knew that the Lord had his loving hand on her life and that she could trust him. She had grown up in a loving home, but had been a complete rebel as a child and, to her mother's chagrin, was expelled from school twice. Mary hated school and resented any authority figure or anyone telling her what to do. Rules were made to be broken. One night, in utter desperation, Mary's mother said to her, "If Jesus comes back tomorrow, you'll be left behind!" It might not have been the best choice of words for just anyone, but it was exactly what Mary needed to hear. One night, she even dreamed that Jesus did come back, taking her parents but leaving her behind. She asked the Lord for forgiveness and from that day on, trusted him and found him changing her uncontrolled bad temper into self-control and joy.

Mary trained as a nurse and loved the work, but became convinced that the Lord wanted her to go to China. When in China, she soon discovered that there were many rules (with good reason, usually), and many people were telling her what to do. How wise of the Lord to tame her youthful rebellion! During her years in China, Mary served in the Borden Memorial Hospital in Lanzhou.

Borden Memorial Hospital

She traveled hundreds of miles and had many adventures, some of them quite frightening. On one journey, she traveled along a stretch of the Yellow River on a fragile raft made of inflated animal skins lashed together: not very robust for navigating around jagged rocks and down surging rapids. On another occasion, she had to ride for several days on an old Russian truck, perched on top of a load of rock salt, in temperatures at 20 degrees below freezing.

Mary was sad when it came time to leave China and wondered whether she would spend the rest of her life as a nurse back home. However, as the call for workers to go to Malaya went out, she knew that the Lord was asking her to uproot once again and to face yet another country and culture. Malaya, at the time, was struggling with Communist insurgency, and Mary dreaded being caught up for a second time in that situation. However, when the Lord calls, obedience and trust are the only option, so she went.

Arriving first in Singapore, the humidity and heat hit her hard. "Lord, am I supposed to live in a climate like this?" she prayed. "I don't think I can do it." Sure enough, her first assignment was indeed "in a climate like this."

Almost halfway between Singapore and Kuala Lumpur, the train stopped at a village of resettled Chinese rubber tappers, made in a jungle clearing called Bekok. Inside the high double-width of barbed wire which surrounded it lived about 3,000 people, many with Communist sympathies. Some of the 200 or so terrorists outside were their friends and relatives. "Malaya was at the height of its emergency and war was at our door," Mary recounted. "Fighting between police patrols and the terrorists was a daily occurrence. My co-worker and I lived in a one-room house on the main shopping street. We were always in the public view. To close our windows was total darkness and the midday temperatures were most often over 100 degrees Fahrenheit. Attached to our shack was the government clinic where we worked."

It was not an easy place to live as witnesses for the Lord, yet gradually a handful of people came to faith, then some more. Finally, a church was established and leaders appointed. A few years later, Mary was asked to go up north where a nurse was badly needed. It was another change, but she was in her element now. She had ten clinics a week and taught the Bible for 30 minutes or more after each clinic. Mary felt deeply happy and fulfilled. After one year, she contracted pneumonia and was sent by the doctor into the hills to recuperate. To her dismay, the Lord told her that after her recovery, she should go back down to South Malaya again. How could she start all over again in yet another new place? Yet again, it was a matter of responding to the Lord's calling in obedience.

Over the next years, during which time Malaya became a newly independent nation, Mary was to make her home in a number of different places as circumstances and needs changed. It was never easy to make each fresh adjustment, but her constant desire was to be where the Lord lovingly put her. "I have long since learned," she wrote, "that service motivated by anything but sheer love of the Master is fruitless drudgery."

Through all that moving, she discovered the ministry that would be her chief occupation until she left Malaya: literature ministry. In the earliest years of CIM-OMF work in Malaya, there had been a great urgency to produce and distribute tracts, booklets, scripture portions and Bibles. Chinese dialects are different in speech, but use a shared written form. For those CIM workers coming from China initially, confronted with dialects they could not use or understand, literature was a blessing.

Often, Mary would visit a school and set up a book stand. In 1968, she reported visiting 108 schools, one with 2,000 students. That year she recalled 66,000 students visiting book exhibitions and book stands and spending 16,000 Malaysian ringgit (5,033 US dollars) on the Gospels and larger books. In 1969, Mary took one display of books to a school with 3,000 students. The 44 classes came through one after another to see

Mary with a group from church in Johor Baru.

the books between 8 am and 6 pm One boy bought 20 Tamil Gospels, saying he wanted to sell them to people on the estate where he lived. The young people were reaching far beyond where missionaries or local believers could go.

During Mary's last three years in Johore Bahru, she was asked to take over leading the Christian writers' correspondence course in 10 countries of Southeast Asia. It was a satisfying ministry, with far-reaching results.

Before leaving Malaysia (renamed from Malaya in 1963) and retiring, each course was established within a local literature ministry. Mary handed over her final course to the Asian Beacon magazine in Kuala Lumpur.

This time it was the books, not Mary, going to new places. The rebel tamed by the Holy Spirit could trust the literature to do the traveling. To God be the glory.

6. Let the Little Children Come

Jesus loved children. They were not an annoying distraction from his ministry, as his disciples considered them to be on more than one occasion. They were precious to him. "Let the little children come to me, and do not hinder them, for the kingdom of heaven belongs to such as these," Jesus said (Matthew 19:14). The following two stories tell of God's love for Thailand's children displayed through his workers. Grace Harris joined the China Inland Mission in 1946 and went on to Thailand soon after work started there in 1952. Erwin Gröbli from Switzerland arrived in Bangkok in 1985 and began an outreach to street children shortly afterward.

Grace Harris grew up surrounded by tales of mission and missionaries: her parents had been missionaries in Japan. She was just seven years old when she trusted the Lord Jesus for herself, asking him to forgive her for her naughtiness and to help her to love him all the days of her life.

Perhaps it was that experience as a small child that gave Grace the deep conviction that even young children can put their trust in the Savior in a true and meaningful way. Whatever planted the seed, she was to spend most of her remaining days surrounded by children, telling them about the Lord. She was not foolishly sentimental about them—she knew they needed a Savior, however young they were—but she loved them, and she longed for them to know of God's love for them. In turn, they loved her back.

Grace first went to China in 1946 and quickly became known for her love of children. When it was no longer possible to work in China, she humbly offered to serve wherever she might be directed. She joined the new team in Thailand and started the arduous task of learning another language.

"This time we had no language school or fellow workers who knew the language and we had to pick it up as best we could," Grace recalled. "This was difficult as I am not good at languages, and after struggling to learn Chinese for five years, the thought of starting another language was daunting. I was very conscious of my weakness, but God is faithful and raised up Thai friends to help.

"Our first friends were the children," she said. "They followed us everywhere because they had never seen a foreigner before—those were before the days of tourists! Some of the children had hearts to respond as we tried to tell them of God's love in our stumbling Thai. Some went on to become leaders in the Thai churches."

Armed with some choruses translated for them by a Thai teacher in Bangkok, and with a painstakingly memorized Bible story, Grace and a colleague would find a tree where they could stand in the shade and begin to teach. The children were drawn to them like magnets, full of curiosity. To add to the attraction, Grace had a piano accordion. The children watched her busy fingers, fascinated. On foot, on her bicycle or on one of the riverboats, Grace went to village after village, town after town. Wherever she went, the children gathered.

One of the first people to profess faith in Central Thailand was one of these children. "The day after she first heard the gospel she shyly handed me a letter saying she wanted to believe in Jesus," Grace said of this first believer. Although

Grace Harris with 3 Thai children

years later that girl seemed to drift away as she worked in a staunchly Buddhist environment in her young adult years, she was a great encouragement at the time to those wondering whether they could ever communicate the gospel in a way that Thai could understand.

Before long, some of the parents began hovering over the children during lesson time, trying to find out what their youngsters were so excited about, and Grace had the opportunity to teach them, too. Grace became greatly loved. In one town, a colleague later wrote about the favor Grace received from her neighbors, one of whom was a Thai head of police. His wife, too, was very friendly. The husband and wife considered it their responsibility to protect Grace from harm. When her rural Thai friends came to visit, the policeman would hide in the bushes to make sure the men in particular were not drunk or trying to steal from her. Grace received Thai language lessons from the wife, and they went through a study called The Way of Salvation. After many months, the wife felt she now understood the difference between Buddhism and Christianity. "Christians receive forgiveness of sins, but Buddhists never do," she said.

Soon, Grace not only set up Sunday schools, but also children's clubs during the school holidays. These gatherings drew increasing numbers of children. Later, there were children's camps, with help from students from Phayao Bible College, and openings to go into schools. Through the years, Grace's greatest joy was in seeing children and young people come to faith, often after a long period of faithful teaching. It is hard to break away from the Buddhist worldview that dominates Thailand and hard for children to take a different path than their parents and community. Even so, the grace of God not only led many children to trust their Savior, but also led many of them to establish Christian homes, raising their own children to know and love the Lord.

Throughout her nearly 35 years of service in Thailand, Grace lived in many places. Whenever she moved, her first prayer was that she would be able to reach local children. The world might have seen them as less significant than adults, but Grace knew better. She passed that love for children along to many young missionaries who lived with her after they completed their initial language study or while they were waiting to get married. She inspired and encouraged many young women who struggled to adjust to their new lives and helped them learn that weakness could be the doorway to proving the Lord's strength. Grace's training took on very practical forms, too, like teaching someone to ride a bicycle—a vital travel skill. One new worker from the U.S. had never previously ridden one and never quite got the hang of it, despite all of Grace's patient instruction. The best she could do was fly at full speed down the road while shouting, "Watch out! Keep away!"

Grace was greatly loved by her colleagues as well as by Thai people. Because of her example, people no longer questioned the importance of reaching children with the gospel. The year before Grace left Thailand in 1986 for retirement, Swiss worker Erwin Gröbli arrived. Before long, he began a new kind of ministry to children.

Erwin was almost 49 years old when he arrived in Thailand, but he was filled with energy and passion to share the gospel. When Bill and Francoise Merry (from the U.S. and Switzerland, respectively) had to return to the States suddenly because Bill's father was dying, they asked Erwin to take over their role as house parents of a student hostel on the outskirts of Bangkok. Erwin had not yet completed his first year of language study, but he was single and able to move in. The hostel was in Hua Mark, where OMF was starting a church. The church had primarily consisted of student members and was close to a university with half-a-million students. Erwin wanted to work with students anyway; it seemed an ideal fit.

He transferred to the local university to continue his Thai language studies. Also, with help from some of the Christian students in the hostel, he established a book stand in a nearby shopping mall. They sold hundreds of Bibles and books, CDs and tapes and spent a lot of time telling people about the Lord.

One Sunday morning, a Catholic student from the university appeared at Hua Mark Church with four street children in tow. The children were only about seven years old, had no home or place to live and were surviving by begging for food and money. "Please, you must help these children!" the Catholic student told Erwin. Erwin would feed them and let them shower in the hostel, but the boys kept returning and pleading for help. He was at a loss for what to do next. What he did have were stories about Jesus and his heavenly Father's love. Erwin shared these stories with the children, but knew they needed practical care also. He tried to recruit help from the students in looking for a place to house the children, but they were reluctant to pitch in. Soon, they objected to dirty children hanging around the hostel and told them to go away.

The students' response made Erwin upset and rather angry. He knew that the children were at risk for getting caught in the prostitution industry or becoming cheap labor for those who would take advantage of them. If the students at the hostel and the church would not help, he would find a home where he and the boys could live. He found a suitable apartment that, while small, was good enough for housing the boys and beginning a small house church. During the day, he sent the children to a place where they were offered some basic schooling. He also took it upon himself to provide their food and clothing.

It was a confusing time for Erwin. He had been sure of his calling to work with students and now he was living with a ragtag group of small children. As he wondered about what to do, prayer partners back at home urged him to set up a ministry with street children. They even contributed to the ministry by sending him money for a house where he could take the boys and have space to invite more. God led Erwin to a suitable house not far away. A Thai friend told him to call it Baan Nok Kamin, which means "House for the bird that has no nest." The

Children housed at Baan Nok Kamin

name was a perfect fit. The house was even on a street called "Rodanan" which means "saved forever."

There were many answers to prayer as Erwin's ministry to street children expanded. A Thai friend had bought the house on Erwin's behalf since a foreigner could not do that himself. God also provided a local lady who came as a maid and cook, three Christian students who came to help and a primary school nearby that was willing to take the boys. Erwin started out with six children, all about seven years old. The number soon grew. The boys' school teachers were astonished to see the children's good behavior and asked what the hostel was all about. Erwin very happily told them about the Lord. The neighbors were equally curious and started visiting. Before long a church was planted.

Feeding and clothing so many children, plus employing some staff, cost a lot of money. Time after time, as Erwin and his friends prayed, the money came in. When they needed more houses, the Lord supplied the money for those, too. God also provided Christian Thai house parents so that, as the number of children grew, they could all be in homes with a dozen to 15 others. The groups of children became like family—albeit a large family—but family nonetheless.

During his first home leave, Erwin married Irene, who proved a fine companion in the growing ministry. They faced the next challenge together: What should be done about children who had no birth certificates and no official documents? Without these documents the schools could not allow them to register. Erwin and Irene discovered a workaround. In a northern province, the authorities were willing to let the children enroll in school while the search for documents continued. When it came to searching for a house in that area, Erwin found out that the governor of the province had a small weekend home on a large plot of land that he used for a farm. The governor had died in an accident, and because of superstition the Thai would not live in that house anymore; as a result, Erwin could buy the house and land cheaply. He sent all the children without documents to that house, and the teachers let them go to school. "That was a great help," Erwin said.

The work grew. Before long, there were 12 homes caring for about 200 children, both boys and girls. In addition to these, the ministry also established an old people's home, a drug rehabilitation center and several churches, while staff members planted and led many more churches. Many people became curious about the ministry as they witnessed the children's good behavior in school and saw how well the workers cared for them. This curiosity eventually led to people attending a Bible study with the workers. Over time, some came to faith and another new church was born. In addition, many of the children trusted the Lord. Throughout the journey, Erwin's main focus remained the same: "That the children would know our Lord Jesus as their personal Lord and Savior."

Indeed, children entered the kingdom of God because of the ministry that started in Erwin's small apartment. As the ministry grew, so did opportunities to help the children grow. Plans developed to provide trade skills for the children. This possibility was particularly appealing to youth who did not enjoy academic learning in a classroom and liked the idea of earning a good living with their skillset. For some of them, training to be a car mechanic was a dream come true.

The drug rehabilitation center produced fruit also. Some of the former drug addicts, after coming off drugs and showing a real lifestyle change, went on to Phayao Bible College and became pastors. The drug rehabilitation center provided the constant skilled care that enabled them to leave their addiction behind them and begin a new life.

Erwin and Irene left Thailand in 2008 for a well-earned retirement, but Baan Nok Kamin continues its mission: rescuing vulnerable children, sharing the gospel and building the church.

It is no wonder that Jesus told his disciples, "Let the little ones come to me."

7. Church Growth in Borneo

Whether dealing with children's health problems or spiritual warfare, Brian and Esther Newton often felt stretched beyond their limits. But God proved faithful. He was their strength in weakness and established a vibrant church in Borneo.

For Brian and Esther Newton, the calling to overseas mission work was clear, but the exact location was less obvious. Esther had long sensed a call to "her own people," the Chinese, while Brian's initial interest was Eastern Europe. In the September 1973 issue of OMF's East Asia's Millions magazine, however, an article outlining the challenges of church planting ministry in Japan caught Brian's attention. While Esther had often said she would go anywhere but Japan, she was willing to follow Brian's sense of leading—though she could not take her eyes off the island of Borneo, the largest island in Southeast Asia.

Brian & Esther Newton

In recent years, Borneo had been the site of a major revival starting with the Kelabit people in the Bario Highlands of Sarawak (the largest state in Malaysia) and spreading to the surrounding people groups on the island.[1] At that time, however, OMF only had missionaries in Kalimantan, the Indonesian part of Borneo, and even that work was in the process of being

---

[1] This revival is often called the "Bario Revival" and has been described in books such as Bario Revival by Solomon Bulan and Lillian Bulan-Doral.

passed on to the local church. There were no openings for new workers on Borneo. As the February 1975 Orientation Course in Singapore unfolded, the Newtons' designation to Japan was confirmed by leadership at OMF's international headquarters. Visas were obtained, and plane tickets to Sapporo in the northern part of Japan were purchased.

Then, returning from an evening out in Singapore one night, the Newtons found their one-year-old son John struggling to breathe due to a severe attack of asthmatic bronchitis. Brian and Esther immediately rushed the child to Singapore General Hospital. John's breathing was so labored that the doctor was amazed that he had not gone into heart failure. After the incident, OMF leaders had to reconsider the family's designation to northern Japan, a problematic location for asthma sufferers due to the area's long winters, air pollution and dusty roads.

With a deep sense of peace in their hearts, the Newtons accepted the closing of the door to Japan, but where did God want them to be? After several weeks of prayer, reading, talking with leaders at headquarters and looking at other needs across East Asia, the options finally seemed to narrow down to the possibility of serving in East Malaysia – on the island of Borneo. Only while the Newtons were at orientation course had this area become an official OMF field and thus able to accept new workers. The Newtons had never imagined that they would serve among the tribal peoples of East Malaysia on Borneo.

"The more we heard of the stories of revivals, and people movements emanating from the interior of Borneo, the more we marveled that God was leading us there," said Brian. "This experience confirmed to us God's faithfulness in leading, that he who calls us, not only equips but ensures obedient servants are positioned just where he is able to work his will most thoroughly through their lives."

God had indeed proven faithful, but more challenges awaited the Newtons in Borneo.

Ready to pack his bags

Having been designated to serve in East Malaysia, the Newtons arrived in Sarawak, on the island of Borneo, in August 1975. They tackled the task of learning the Malay language, while also studying some of the Iban language as well since the Iban people made up nearly a third of the population in the area and the Newtons had been designated to serve among them in the future. Soon, however, in early 1976, OMF's East Malaysia field leaders asked if the Newtons could help direct the work in the Sarawak town of Sibu for one year since the missionaries previously leading the work needed to go on home assignment. "Just a year," the Newtons were told, "and then you can move on into Iban ministry."

Recently, a Borneo Evangelical Church (also known as Sidang Injil Borneo, or SIB) church plant had begun in Sibu. The Newtons' responsibilities would include pastoring the English-language congregation,[2] overseeing the Malay-speaking tribal group that met nearby, managing a Christian bookstore, speaking at the many Inter-School Christian Fellowship gatherings throughout the district, and doing evangelism, literature work and other forms of outreach.

Attending their first meeting at the new church plant proved to be an experience that Brian and Esther would never forget. It was a Saturday night prayer meeting and the intensity of prayer was impressive, especially since this was a group

---

[2] English was the language used in schools in the area and thus often the best common language for a congregation composed of a wide range of people groups.

of young believers. Then, halfway through the meeting, a young woman began to manifest demon possession. Studying demonology and spiritual warfare at Bible college was one thing, but confronted with this stark reality was another. A glance across the room to their senior missionary colleagues led to them dealing with this situation, and the Newtons watched as the woman was delivered and set free from the harassing demon.

Similar scenarios occurred at almost every meeting over the next three weeks. Brian felt out of his depth spiritually. With other, seemingly overwhelming outreach and leadership responsibilities compounding the issue, he began to wonder why he was there. What did God have in mind? Desperate and ready to pack his bags and go home, the Newtons decided to visit their senior missionary colleagues.

"They had every right to sit us down and give us a good talking to," Brian recalled, "but they simply asked if they could pray for us. Describe it how you would, that evening of prayer proved a turning point as God met us there." The Newtons did not return home to England. They remained at their post and saw God do remarkable things in terms of deliverance, healing and hundreds of people coming to Christ over the ensuing years.

From one to 100

The Rejang River is the Malaysian state of Sarawak's longest river, flowing from the mountainous border with Indonesia to the South China Sea. The communities in the Rejang Valley are mostly rural. The people live in longhouses along the rivers and practice a type of slash-and-burn agriculture. Most of the small towns along the river also included small communities of Chinese who ran the stores, restaurants and businesses in the area.

The history of Borneo's interior had been dominated by inter-tribal conflict and headhunting. Many of the Iban longhouses still proudly display the skulls of those killed in earlier warfare. Although the British colonial authorities in the area had outlawed headhunting, they tended to turn a blind eye toward the practice during World War II as the people of Borneo resisted the Japanese occupation.

Prior to the arrival of the gospel of Christ, most of the people groups in Borneo practiced animism and lived in fear of spirits. In addition, there were a few Malay Muslims (especially in the coastal region) and some Chinese who practiced Buddhism, Daoism and ancestor worship. The Christian presence in the area included scattered congregations of Roman Catholics, Methodists, and by the 1970s, the evangelical SIB church of Borneo.

During their first term in Borneo (1975-1978), the Newtons became involved in three almost simultaneous church plants throughout the Rejang Valley. The churches usually started as small meetings for worship or Bible study in people's homes. Brian visited the fledgling churches regularly in order to teach and encourage the believers. Each church was unique and established with input from local leaders or even government servants posted to those towns. Also, a Mandarin congregation was begun in Sibu to offer a meeting place and worship center specifically for non-English speaking relatives of Chinese church members who were coming to Christ.

The reality of spiritual warfare, which the Newtons had experienced at those earlier Saturday night prayer meetings, was intense and perhaps the greatest obstacle to the spread of the gospel in the valley, where many people lived under the influence of animism and evil spirits. Yet, as Brian pointed out, the spiritual battle also created a context that allowed for incredible breakthrough and freedom. After all, to those living in fear of spirits and demons, the gospel was "good news" indeed! In fact, the level of spiritual hunger and readiness to embrace the gospel displayed by some of the people in the valley presented its own issues. "They were so receptive that the challenge was did they really understand what 'following Christ' meant?" said Brian.

By 1979, an outreach to the Iban had begun, as had a ministry reaching out to Fujianese-speaking Chinese in the area. In total, five SIB congregations had been planted in Sibu, with more established in three secondary towns in the Rejang Valley. Over the next six years each of these congregations became instruments in God's hands to plant other congregations or preaching points. The number of Chinese-language congregations grew, further Iban congregations were planted in nearby longhouses, and the work among the Melanau, another tribal group in Borneo, spread from one river to another. In 1986, when the Newtons had to leave Malaysia due to visa restrictions, there were at least 22 congregations meeting throughout the district, up and down the Rejang River and in the valley's scattered towns.

"What is humbling is that everyone knew it was God who was working these miracles of grace," Brian said. "The people had seen the measure of this young missionary couple, and knew it was not them! Thus, all the praise goes to God."

The task of the missionaries was to remain sensitive to God's leading in caring for, encouraging and "watering" this growing work. That it was all of God was underscored a further 10 years later. In the late 1990s, on a return visit to

Sibu, the Newtons learned that the 100th group of believers in the Rejang Valley had recently been established. In addition, the first congregations in the valley had begun sending out their own missionaries.

Since the turn of the century, the growth of the church in Sarawak has slowed due to a variety of factors, but according to the 2010 census, nearly half of the people in the East Malaysian state still identify as Christians. It is the largest Christian percentage of a population in all of Malaysia. God's work, through those who sometimes felt weak and even unfit for the task, has multiplied many times over.

8. A Sudden Boldness

> Robbers, political insurgents and religious extremists can present severe challenges for both expatriate and local Christians. Sometimes the border lands between two countries can be especially unpredictable. Robert and Ruth Erion lived in the far south of Thailand, a region that is different culturally, linguistically and religiously from most of the country. At times, fear threatened to derail their ministry, particularly on a day when Robert found himself cornered by Communist soldiers.

The sharp ring of the telephone pierced the quiet night at Robert and Ruth Erion's South Thailand home.

The couple was in bed, but Robert had not yet fallen asleep. He glanced at the clock before he got out of bed: 10:55 pm. He walked quickly downstairs, knowing from past experience that calls at this hour rarely brought good news.

"Robert, it's about Koos Fietje—he's just been shot ..." a panicked voice on the other line stammered. "He has gone to be with the Lord!"

It was Bob Joyce, OMF Deputy South Thailand Superintendent. Too shocked to respond, Robert listened as Bob told him what he knew. Koos had been leading a Bible study in a Thai home. Afterward, he had joined three or four from the group for some food and drink. While they were talking, a shot was fired at Koos through the slatted wall of the veranda where they sat. He died instantly.

Robert could feel his heart pounding so hard he wondered if Bob could hear it, too. Eventually, Robert found his voice to ask if there was anything he could do to help. Koos and his wife Colleen were friends as well as colleagues. They were around the same age as Robert and Ruth and had started working in Thailand about the same time.

After the conversation, Robert put down the phone. Grief and fear gripped his heart, restricting his chest so tightly he did not know if he would get another breath. *How could this happen to Koos? How could God allow this? He still had so much to give!* Thoughts and questions quickly swirled around in his mind, but one thought screamed louder than all the rest: *This happened to Koos—it could happen to you or Ruth, too.*

With his whole body shaking, Robert managed to rush back upstairs, climb into bed and pull the covers tight over his head. *It could happen to you, too* echoed in his mind, even as he tried to pray for Colleen, their family and their ministry in Central Thailand. He pulled the covers even tighter over his head. *What am I doing here? Why am I putting my pregnant wife in this kind of danger?*

"During that time in our ministry, I was really suffering from fear," Robert recalled. "I'd often wake up at night screaming. I'd be screaming so loud that Ruth would start to scream, too! Where we were living, we knew there were people around us who were watching us, not always in a friendly way. Even though we weren't consciously thinking about it all the time, we always knew and were always on guard. When I heard about Koos' death, the fear factor rose, and I recognized that we lived in a dangerous setting."

It was 1981, and Robert and Ruth were living in South Thailand working as church planters among the Thai and Chinese in an area called Betong. They had been married for nearly two years at the time, and Ruth was expecting their first child, Tim.

Robert & Ruth Erion

The Erions lived in a town close to the border between Thailand and Malaysia. In this area, safety could never be taken for granted: bandits attacked people on the roads, local people sometimes received extortion threats, and others were kidnapped for ransom. In addition to this, a large part of the Communist Party of Malaysia was based in the mountainous area a few miles from Betong. The Communists' presence and activities, such as demanding transport, food or medical supplies, had a strong impact on the community around them.

Kilometer Four was a particularly dangerous village, as it was a stronghold of the Communist Party and also a hotspot for bandits. However, Robert finally got permission to visit there for ministry purposes, provided he went accompanied by Thai believers. Ruth was not allowed to go. "We started going over to Kilometer Four because there were already two believers in that village and one of them wanted us to come and teach her extended family," Robert said. "It just grew from there, with a children's program and a Bible study for the young people."

About three months before Koos' death, Robert set off for Kilometer Four, along with two Thai believers. Robert planned to lead the youth Bible study, and his friends planned to teach the children. The youth group consisted of about 12 young people between the ages of 14 and 20. Previously, they had stood around watching the children's program, but now they wanted a study for themselves so they could learn about Jesus. Robert knew that the Communists were annoyed: they wanted the young people to work for them, not become Christians.

One day, as the youth study drew to a close, Robert looked up and saw a Thai friend, a deacon at their church in Betong, walking towards him quickly. "You need to come outside now," he urged. "As soon as he said that, I knew there was something very wrong," Robert recalled, "and my first thought was to get on my motorbike and go home as quickly as I could."

However, as he walked out of the house to get his motorbike, he was surprised to discover around 200 Communist soldiers in the street. Two of the men sat on his motorbike. When Robert looked over at the two soldiers on his bike, they stared straight back at him with a look of aggression and superiority. In that moment, Robert knew he would not be able to leave any time soon. He decided to return to the house and pack up his things, telling himself, "Don't get frightened, just act normal and pretend nothing is happening. Go get your things."

He then walked to the nearby shop house a few doors away where the children had been meeting in order to collect his accordion. Robert felt a tap on his shoulder. "We want to see you in the kitchen," the Communist soldier said.

Trying to swallow his nerves and remain calm, Robert put down his accordion case and followed the Communist soldier, along with the church deacon who was also told to come. Walking into the kitchen they saw four solemn-faced men sitting at the dining table waiting for them.

"I'll do whatever they say," Robert thought to himself. "I just want to get out of here!"

He sat down, the gaze of every eye beating down on him. The church deacon later told him that at least one of the soldiers had been carrying a gun. Robert was thankful he did not notice at the time. The leader of the group smiled at Robert with feigned friendliness and introduced himself. He spoke Thai, but Robert could tell from his accent that his first language was actually Chinese.

"He said they were from the Communist Party of Malaysia," Robert recalled. "They had been following me for a number of years and knew everything about me—they knew about my passport, they knew about my work permits, they knew everything."

"We've come here today to tell you that we don't want you here anymore," the soldier said.

Robert reflected back on the moment. "That was when I was going to say, 'Yeah, okay, I won't come here anymore.' Instead, when I opened my mouth, I said, 'You've got no right to tell me not to come here.' Completely different words came out of my mouth! It was a very strange sensation. It was like I had these thoughts that I was intending to say, but then they were cut off and the Lord just gave me these other words."

Robert's own words shocked him, but he saw that the Communist leader was also taken aback. The man had not expected to meet such strong opposition. The leader went on, telling Robert that it was not right for him to teach the children to disobey their parents.

"Have you ever read the Bible?" Robert immediately replied. The leader confessed that he had not. "Then you have no right to assume that you know what I am teaching the children," Robert said. He continued speaking boldly, amazed by the words coming out of his mouth—they were not what he had planned to say.

The leader, again taken aback by Robert's boldness, went on to tell him that Communists did not need religion and neither did the people of this village. As Robert sat listening to the leader, he felt his finger wanting to come out from under the table to scold the man for wearing spirit charms.

"In Thailand, it's really rude to point a finger. I knew that, so I sat there literally holding my finger down with my other hand so that it stayed underneath the table," Robert recalled.

After a while, Robert's strength gave way. He found himself pointing at the Communist soldier and saying, "You say you don't believe in any religion. But you're wearing all these spirit charms, and so you must believe in spirits, otherwise you wouldn't need to wear them.'"

The leader eventually stuttered, "I wear them because my friends gave them to me." Once again Robert found himself uttering bold words that shook even himself: "You're a hypocrite!

You're wearing those because you're afraid of the spirits. If you were a true friend you wouldn't wear those charms, you'd tell your friends you didn't need them and neither do they!"

Once the leader mustered up the words to respond, he told Robert that they knew about the work of the China Inland Mission in China. The Chinese Christians were the hardest ones to manipulate into following Communism, which is why they had stopped OMF from operating in the villages under their command near Betong. Robert, however, replied, "You can take my life today or you can give me my life. But whatever you choose, I'm going to live for Jesus."

Even though Robert knew that the Communists could have easily killed him on the spot, he had no fear because, for the first time in his life, he knew that the Holy Spirit was guiding his every word and action.

At the end of the conversation, the leader said he would go back to his commander and, within the week, let Robert know whether or not he could continue teaching at Kilometer Four. "As we left, I shook the leader's hand and told him I'd send him a Bible so he could see for himself what we were teaching. He told me that I was welcome any time to visit the Communist Party base in the mountains. I smiled at him but in my heart I thought, 'I never want to see you again!' That thought probably wasn't from the Holy Spirit!"

As Robert set off home, the time neared 9 pm—three hours later than he had promised to be away. Ruth would be worried. When he arrived home, a young missionary who was living with them rushed to the door. "Where have you been?" Doug asked. "Nowhere." Robert replied. Doug retorted, "You must have been somewhere, because for the last three hours I've had the strongest feeling that I needed to pray for you. Whenever I tried to stop, I couldn't, until just a few minutes ago." Together they thanked God that he had kept Doug praying through the precise period of Robert's need and danger, even though Doug had no idea what was happening.

A threatening letter from the Communists soon arrived for Robert. With a heavy heart, Robert accepted that he could no longer go to Kilometer Four. His heart ached for the young people who asked to learn about Jesus. Even so, he could also see that God had used this whole experience to encourage and strengthen him at a time when he was struggling with fear. When a number of mass killings from shoot-outs happened in their local area, God enabled Robert to stand courageously by affected families and to visit them when he would have otherwise been too scared. Doing so opened new avenues for ministry that had not existed before.

About 20 years later, Robert and Ruth found themselves in South Thailand again, but this time to join a conference for local believers. A man whom Robert did not recognize approached him. He explained how he had been one of the men at the kitchen table that memorable night. He asked for Robert's forgiveness. "My family and I are all believers now," he said.

9. His Eye is on the Sparrow

Transportation in Asia can take many forms, from Japan's famous, punctual trains, to Singapore's efficient metro, to Manila's jeepneys with dubious tires and manic drivers. Sometimes waiting for public transport can be a potentially dangerous undertaking, especially after dark, and even more so for a woman traveling on her own. Beth McFarland, who moved to Indonesia in 1998, found herself alone and without transportation options on her travel home one evening. She tells her story of God's provision below.

It had been a stressful day at the immigration office, and I was more than relieved to be on my way home with the paperwork all completed for my new visa—never something to be taken for granted.

At that time I was teaching English in the Christian university in the highlands of Toraja in southern Sulawesi. I could feel myself relaxing and was looking forward to getting back to my base there, a journey of five hours by bus. I made my way to Kilometer Two on the outskirts of Parepare, intending to hitch a ride on the night bus on the main national route north, heading up into the hills, as was my usual routine. This was a favorite pick-up location for many different forms of transport. Generally there were a number of buses coming up from the provincial capital after 5 pm, so I settled down to wait by the roadside on a little wooden bench by a roadside stand selling snacks and drinks.

It was rather strange for the local people to have a white-haired Western woman on their street and at first the questions flowed freely.

"Where have you been? Where are you going? Where do you come from?" they asked.

A teenage boy assured me with great certainty that there would be no buses heading north until close to midnight. I was reluctant to believe what I was being told, as this had not been my experience on other occasions, but I waited, and waited. Dusk was fading into night. Soon, the kiosk lady closed up shop and disappeared to her home.

Feeling more and more uneasy about the situation, I began to wonder what I should do. This city was a port and had a rather unsavory reputation. There were some small hotels available in the city center, but there was now no way of returning there with my small suitcase, as public buses stopped running after nightfall. Another option was taking a motorcycle taxi. There were several young men with their bikes, hanging around, laughing and chatting, revving up their engines. Everyone else had gone home. I enjoy motorbike travel if I know the person, but this was a different situation. Could I trust these boys? Maybe, maybe not. Would they rip me off or get angry if I bargained about the price to get back to the city? Worse, would I get mugged? After all, they probably saw me as a vulnerable, wealthy, white woman, completely alone on an isolated, dark country road.

As if my situation was not frightening enough, no one knew about my predicament. I had no way of contacting anyone. Cell phones were not commonly owned at the time. I did not know anyone who lived in the city. There was no sign of a bus coming soon. I felt panic setting in.

As I sat there on the bench, considering my non-existent options, I became aware of a few sparrows pecking at some crumbs close to my feet without any hint of fear. Had not my heavenly Father assured his children that not even a small bird's needs escape his notice or care (Matthew 6:26-27)? Surely he would look after me. As I was encouraging myself to trust him, I noticed a minivan setting down some passengers coming up from the city center. I heard a young woman's voice, and suddenly realized she was addressing me.

"Hello, Ibu (Miss) Beth, what are you doing here?" I was completely surprised, having no idea who she was or how she knew my name. Apparently her English teacher had taken her class on a school trip to our campus in Toraja some five years before, and she remembered meeting me then. Her name was Rini; I had no memory of her.

When I explained my situation, she became concerned. "It's not safe here. You shouldn't stay here," she insisted. "Why don't you come to my home to wait there? My village is about 10 miles up the road and we can get a taxi that will take us there."

A little while later, I found myself sitting comfortably in Rini's house, having a hot dinner (I had not eaten since noon) and meeting her father and her brother. She offered me a bed to rest on and invited me to freshen up in the bathroom. Rini was a bank clerk who lived and worked in the city. She only traveled home on Fridays, and it was a Friday when I happened to be stranded in a bad part of town. God's angels come in many forms.

At 11 pm, Rini accompanied me on the family motorbike back to a main road junction, where she waited patiently with me for an hour. Eventually a night bus came along and took me safely back to my home in Toraja. I never saw Rini again.

The experience reminded me again of the truth I quickly forget: that our God is the Lord who protects and provides for his children in the most unexpected ways.

10. Learning to Trust: Marginalized Women in Cambodia

One of the churches planted by OMF workers in Cambodia is among the urban poor of Phnom Penh, Cambodia's capital. It was started by Markus and Elisabeth Hirschi with the help of others, both foreign and Khmer. Whereas Markus concentrates on the church, Elisabeth is involved in counseling women who have come out of prostitution. Their stories are heartbreaking, but God is bringing hope and healing.

It happened in the middle of the night. Lina* and her two children aged eight and ten finally had fallen asleep in spite of their rumbling tummies. Lina woke up as she felt someone touching her leg and urging her to go to a nearby hospital. She was nine months pregnant. Lina looked around her hut made out of cardboard, material and tin—whatever they had been able to find on the rubbish dump. Lina could not make anyone out in the dark and decided she must have been dreaming. However, it happened twice more; the third time round she caught a glimpse of a face. So Lina finally decided to get up, cooked some rice for her children and then set off to the nearest hospital.

It was hard for Lina to make decisions like this on her own, but she had become used to it as her first husband, whom she married at 18, had died suddenly leaving her with two small children. She married again, but then her second husband passed away with AIDS just after she found out that she was pregnant with her third child, the one she was carrying now.

---

* Names have been changed.

Looking at Lina you could tell she had not lived an easy life: extreme poverty had taken its toll on her. She was a single mother with no formal education.

Sometimes, she saw no other way of getting food on the table than to prostitute herself.

Lina arrived at the hospital even though she was painfully aware that she had no money to pay the doctor. After a brief consultation and a reproach, asking why she did not come any earlier, everything went very fast. Her delivery was induced and soon after her child was born, slightly blue but just in time to prevent a tragedy. The mother was overwhelmed and confused by the events of the past few hours, but her two older kids were alone at home and she did not have any money to pay the hospital. She got up quickly and returned to her hut.

Life continued to be a fight for survival and often left Lina completely exhausted and barely coping. A few months after her third baby was born, someone gave her a tract. Since Lina could not read, she just shoved it into her pocket. When she got home she looked at it and recognized the face on the picture: was not that the man who had told her to go to the hospital in the middle of the night and saved her baby's life? Wanting to find out who he was and to thank him, she got up straight away and went from neighbor to neighbor asking who the man was. Finally, she learned his name: Jesus. She had never heard of him before and no one seemed to know any more about him.

Shortly after this incident Lina found work at a centre in Phnom Penh which offers training and safe jobs to women who want to escape from prostitution. It was there that Lina met Elisabeth Hirschi, who was working there as a counselor. Lina asked Elisabeth, "Do you know a man called Jesus?" She listened in awe to Elisabeth's response, wanting to know everything about him. Finally, Lina had found her two-fold Savior, the one who had saved the life of her child and the one who offered her new life—now and for eternity.

Elisabeth and Markus Hirschi have lived in Cambodia with their three boys since 2002. Five years ago, Markus started Stung Meanchey Church among the poorest of the poor in the area where many of the women who Elisabeth meets live. Quite a few of them have started to attend church and grow in their faith and relationship with Jesus. They are part of an expanding church family that includes male and female, old and young.

Connected to the church is the Hope for Life project. Through Hope for Life, children who are too poor to attend school are supported to get an education, and youth receive vocational training. Providing education is a powerful tool to

Markus and Sochea teaching Bible stories

help families out of poverty, keeping girls from sex work and boys (and girls) from becoming drug addicts. Other ways of trying to keep young people from getting on the wrong track include music lessons, sports training and a drop-in library and community center. Many of the young people who attend these programs also end up going to a Christian youth group that was started by a young Khmer man, Sochea, who loves the Lord deeply. Sochea can identify with the youth as he himself grew up an orphan, unloved and in severe poverty; however, Jesus found him and changed his life.

Hope for Life not only focuses on drug prevention but also helps addicted youth attend rehab and then find training and a job. Recently, it has opened a halfway home where these young men can support each other, avoiding the wrong old friends and sharing their struggles.

The Hirschis have found that wherever suffering is the strongest, we can also feel God's care most powerfully; the more intense the pain, the warmer his love. Many of the poor cannot read and write, or only do so on a very basic level. They do not trust others and do not believe that religion can help them. Therefore, God often reveals himself to them in a special way, as he did for Lina. When the Lord touches them where their pain is deepest, they can experience God's healing and supernatural help, his love, his mercy and grace, his justice and holiness.

Inner healing can be a lifelong process for those who have suffered deeply from a life of extreme poverty, whether they have experienced prostitution, drugs, violence or other hurts. Their problems do not just disappear when they decide to follow Christ, but faith gives them hope, they find forgiveness for their own sin and they feel cared for and carried by God. This enables many of those at Stung Meanchey Church to keep taking small and big steps to positive change, even though there are setbacks and weaknesses.

One other lady who experienced the Lord Jesus' help in a supernatural way is Sola.* As a small child, she was chased away from home because her parents did not know how to feed yet another mouth. Sola lived here and there; for many years she did not have a place to call home. She found food in trash bags or went begging for it. Later, she started collecting recyclable material such as plastic bottles and cardboard which she sold to a recycling store. However, one day she was assaulted by a group of five rich youth who raped her one after the other in the most brutal way possible. Many scars remind her of this event to this day. She did not know where to turn in her pain. Her already low self image practically vanished. Having lost her virginity, Sola felt destitute. Her self-worth as a woman had disappeared. Any hope of a better life with a husband was gone. She went into prostitution. She did not earn much but at least she had a place to stay and did not have to worry when she would have her next meal.

After a while, she became friends with one of her regular customers. When he offered to marry her she gladly jumped at the opportunity to get out of the primitive brothel. They had a simple common law ceremony. Sola had three children with her husband. Since he was an alcohol and drug addict, there was never enough money and Sola still had no other way to support herself and her family except to continue prostituting herself. Often she drowned all the pain and the memories of her suffering in alcohol.

Later, she came to know Jesus at the same Christain centre that enables women to leave the sex industry. Her life became

---

* Names have been changed.

a bit better although it was still very hard. What helped her to keep going was her strong love for her children. However, one day her husband went to visit his mother in Vietnam with their three children. As soon as he got there he called her and said he had planned the visit for a long time and that he would not return. He would stay in Vietnam with the children; she would never see their children again. Sola was devastated and felt absolutely worthless. She had never been to Vietnam and had no clue where to start looking for her children. She had no reason to live on: the rat poison was already bought and waiting for her.

At her workplace everyone tried to help. Many prayers were prayed but nothing seemed to help. Sola just sank deeper and deeper into hopelessness. Elisabeth prayed and prayed but she heard nothing from God; she had no sense of him leading her. Elisabeth was just desperately thinking: "Lord, if you don't do anything she'll kill herself!"

Then, suddenly—without really being aware what was happening—Elisabeth felt God giving her a vision. She started to paint a detailed picture before Sola's eyes of how God would intervene and bring her children back to her within three months. Sola quieted down while Elisabeth was talking and seemed to regain hope. Elisabeth herself was a bit frightened by what she was finding herself doing for the very first time. She just prayed that God in his mercy would do as she had described. In the following weeks, Sola and Elisabeth met regularly to pray that God would intervene and bring the children back. The more time passed, the more challenging it became to trust God. No word from her husband, no sign whatsoever. With just two weeks of the three-month period remaining, doubts started to creep in and the mind rebelled. In tears, the two of them cried out to God to help them and to teach them to trust him.

Then, just before the three months were over, Sola came running towards Elisabeth one morning, overjoyed. The Lord had answered their prayers and had done exactly as he had shown Elisabeth three months ago. He had rewarded their trust in him. The following weekend Sola picked up her three children at the Vietnamese border. Afterwards she said: "Now I can die in peace. I know for sure that God is trustworthy. He will look after my children also in the future. I have found my worth in him."

Elisabeth has talked to countless women who share heartbreaking stories, but each of the stories continues to touch her heart. "For me it's a privilege to peek over God's shoulder in the counseling sessions," Elisabeth said. "Again and again I find that God has prepared the hearts of these women—often long before I meet them. This motivates me to continue in the exhausting battles with the past and the life stories that are so heart-wrenching." It is challenging for Elisabeth to hear so many horrible stories firsthand and journey with these women in their suffering. Thus, Elisabeth said, it is crucial for her to plan significant time to be in God's presence on a regular basis. "I bring each one of these women I speak to before the throne of God. Knowing that the Lord never turns his face from them I entrust them into his loving care and can turn to other responsibilities in my family, OMF and church.

Elisabeth finds that through these times in God's presence he strengthens her character, heals her and gives her a clearer view of himself. "To truly bring hope and faith to these women I need a clear and biblical image of God and lots of grace to see him for who he really is," she said. "We can't ever bring someone closer to God than we are ourselves."

11. Beyond Our Strength

Thea* from Singapore was living in an East Asian city for her full-time language study. In trying to help a local young woman, she found herself stretched to the limit and beyond.

"Would you like some help packing up?" Thea asked her colleague, Monica, who was about to move. Monica accepted gratefully and was even more grateful when Thea offered to clean the apartment thoroughly before returning the keys to the school where she worked.

"Hey, this is May, one of my students," Monica told Thea. "She has offered to help with the cleaning, too."

At this moment of introduction, Thea's simple offer to help began one of the more demanding emotional and spiritual journeys of her life. Thea and May chatted as they cleaned out the apartment, but Thea did not expect to see May again.

One day, May contacted Thea. "Please can you help me? I'm so scared!" May said. Thea knew that May had recently become a Christian and been baptized. What could be wrong? They arranged to meet.

The story came out, bit by bit. May had gone to watch a local festival—a spiritually dark festival that had been celebrated as far back as anyone knew. While there, she began chatting with a local girl who, rather drunk, had talked openly about her past. Sadly, the girl's story contained details that brought back traumatic memories of May's own childhood. May struggled to release the thoughts. They would not go away. She felt trapped in her past and overwhelmed with a sense of guilt for the bad things she had done.

---

* Names have been changed.

May's father had been an unhappy and embittered man after being unjustly imprisoned for many years. After his release, he married and May was one of the two children he had. He was a teacher, and on two different occasions, one of his students had raped her. May's mother had gone away to find work, and May had nobody to turn to. Her attacker had threatened to harm her family if she told anyone about the incidents. By the time she became a teenager, May had begun rebelling as a way of dealing with her pain. She resented her father for giving most of his attention to her sister, who was chronically ill, and reacted by being disobedient. When May's father committed suicide, she became convinced that it was her fault—that he had taken his life because he could not control her.

All of the suppressed memories came flooding back as May listened to the girl's story, leading May to cry out for help. Thea scarcely knew what to say or do, but she knew she must reach out to help this young woman. As she read her Bible, Thea thought, "What are words without offering practical help? What can I do?" She felt she should ask May to come and stay with her for a few days for some concentrated prayer ministry.

Ten days later, May came. In the meantime, Thea had asked some of her praying friends back home to pray for the Lord's protection on them both and for deliverance from every chain of bondage for May. Thea knew that this would be a spiritual battle—and so it was, for two whole days without a break. By the end of the two days, Thea reported back to them, "I am exhausted physically, but victorious in the spirit. The presence of the Lord was so sweet and comforting." May had asked the Lord Jesus for healing and restoration, for forgiveness for the anger and bitterness she had clung to and for his power to cleanse and deliver her as only the Lord could. Afterwards she experienced God's peace. Not only that, she paid a visit back to her home village to tell those who had hurt her so badly that she now forgave them because the Lord had forgiven her.

A while after the prayer ministry took place, Thea moved to a big city. May had neither a job, nor anywhere to stay, so Thea invited her to move in until she could afford her own place. Thea realized the decision was probably not wise, as the authorities did not approve of locals living with foreigners, but Thea worried that May might move in with her boyfriend if she had no other options. May found a succession of jobs, but did not get along well with her supervisors and consequently quit one after another. When May had no work, Thea ended up supporting her financially, not just sharing her home. Then, May discovered that her boyfriend was seeing another girl, and she spiraled into depression. She locked herself in her room and became sullen and unresponsive.

By this time, Thea was at her wits' end. She became angry and frustrated. She often wanted to tell May to leave, but remembered that the Lord Jesus had told his disciples to keep forgiving those who harmed them. Still, she struggled to do that for May.

Things came to a head when May attempted suicide by cutting her wrists. Thea had not realized how ill May had become during her self-imprisonment in her room. May's boyfriend had told her that he wanted nothing more to do with her; he was going to stay with the other girl. This news tipped May over into a suicidal state. Immediately, Satan put accusatory thoughts into Thea's head: "It's your fault. You didn't care for her enough. You could have prevented this. You didn't mentor her properly." Round and round the ugly accusations swirled. What if May tried again to take her life and succeeded? What would the police say if they discovered the suicide of a local person in the home of a foreigner? Who else would get harmed?

Thea knew she was out of her depth and that May needed help far beyond anything she could supply. Thea, too, needed help. For her, that came through colleagues who quietly and repeatedly prayed with her and encouraged her. God's word spoke wisdom and love into her heart. Some friends pooled money to pay for May to go to counseling—if she could be persuaded to go. They found a good counseling center not too far away. Eventually, May agreed to go.

It took some time, but May recovered. However, during May's journey to recovery, Thea felt totally inadequate to help her at home. Much of Thea's emotional resources were drained, in addition to her time. She lost a lot of weight. Thea eventually went in for counseling also. She realized that she had absorbed some of the darkness that threatened to overwhelm May, and while the Lord had given her grace and strength, she had also been wounded in the spiritual battle. What had seemed a straightforward offer of help had become something profoundly demanding. Thea, too, needed healing.

Finally May discovered that her boyfriend had married the other girl, even while he was still seeing May. This realization gave May the motivation she needed to make a new start somewhere else. Her counseling had helped her greatly and to Thea's relief she seemed to want to trust the Lord for daily help. May moved to another city, where a local believer helped her find work.

Thea still wants to help others, but has learned that she must be very prayerful about what she undertakes. She writes, "I've realized that even as I reach out in compassion, wisdom is needed to know when to help and when to hold back."

God's Faithfulness from Darkness to Light

Ever since God created the world, there has been both darkness and light. Wherever you live on the planet, and in any generation, the rhythm of day and night is familiar.

In God's perfect plan, both light and darkness, day and night, were designed for blessing. Within the light of day, life is nourished and work accomplished. In the shelter of night comes rest and sleep. Darkness as well as light is benign in the loving hands of God.

However, with the coming of sin into the world through human disobedience, darkness takes on an increasingly sinister quality. In the night, fears magnify. Who will attack? What powers of darkness surround us, wishing us harm? What wickedness will take place "under cover of darkness"? Darkness becomes the metaphor for all that is evil and wicked, for human life that is alienated from the God who created us and for ignorance, disobedience or unbelief which keeps a person from glad submission to the Lord as king and owner of our lives.

In God's word, we see the gospel pictured as a journey from darkness into light. It is the good news through which the Holy Spirit brings men, women and children to know and love the Lord. God is faithful to keep his promise that anybody, however dark their background, can come into the light of restored friendship with himself when they put their trust in the Lord Jesus Christ. Indeed, it is Jesus Christ who is the light of the world.

Much of East Asia has grown to be very successful in economic terms and educational attainment. Even with this progress, much of East Asia and its peoples remain in spiritual darkness. Other religions cannot bring peace with God nor lead to light as the Bible explains it. People are held captive to fear of the spirit world or are overwhelmed by the darkness of tragedy. Others simply love darkness rather than light. East Asia is not alone in this, of course. Thankfully, all over East Asia there are those who have made the journey from darkness to light as they have come to put their trust in the Lord Jesus Christ. The stories that follow tell just a few of them.

12. Fertile Ground

> Displaced by the Communist takeover of China in 1949, China Inland Mission (CIM) workers dispersed to other parts of East Asia. Leprosy work in Thailand found a receptive audience to the gospel, leading to the transformation of a rebel soldier and his family.

As he lay near death in Thailand, David,[1] a former Malay Communist-turned-servant of Jesus Christ, called his youngest daughter Lydia over to him. "I am old and going soon," David told Lydia. "The acorns have dropped around the tree. Your job is to water the baby trees. That's where the future lies!"

On March 25, 1951—Easter Sunday—CIM missionaries Dorothy Jupp and Doris Briscoe taught a Sunday School class in China's Ningxia Province. The following week, they embarked on a long journey to Hong Kong. They were the last foreign missionaries to leave Ningxia as part of the "reluctant exodus" from China by all foreign missionaries in the wake of the Communist takeover of China in October 1949.

Upon arrival in Hong Kong, the displaced missionaries began hearing of open doors for the gospel in surrounding countries. Dorothy and Doris were particularly moved by an opportunity to start a work in Thailand, where perhaps they could use their medical skills in conjunction with gospel outreach. By the end of 1952, they had settled in an area with a large ethnic Malay population and near the coast of Thailand.

---

[1] Name has been changed.

As it was more than 30 miles from the nearest hospital, the area seemed like a suitable place to start a medical clinic. The clinic opened on April 5, 1955. Soon, approximately 100 patients were being seen every morning. As patients arrived at the clinic, they would look at the Bible pictures adorning the walls or listen to Bible stories or gospel songs on a hand-wound gramophone. Afternoons were reserved for home visits to those not able to travel to the clinic. Urgent cases were seen any time, day or night.

On January 1, 1960, the clinic was replaced by a hospital. From the beginning, people suffering from leprosy were among the patients. Gradually, the leprosy work expanded. The hospital's official leprosy program began in April 1966 when the first leprosy clinic was opened in a nearby fishing village. Taking a folding table and some chairs, workers held the clinic under a tree. A few months later, a rudimentary hut was built and clinics were held every two weeks. A small clinic was also held on Fridays at the hospital.

The leprosy work rapidly spread to other villages and proved invaluable in meeting urgent medical needs as well as opening the door for the love of God to reach many more. Two factors unique to leprosy work made the outreach a fruitful ministry:

- At the time, leprosy required a period of treatment lasting at least five years. This meant regular contact with the same groups of people who could hear the gospel on a regular basis.

- Leprosy often spread to other family members. Missionary doctors and nurses often had contact with several patients in one family and several families in one community, thus allowing for greater ease in the spread of the gospel.

The love of God

In 1967, a tall, well-built Malay soldier named David wandered out of the jungle into a Thai village that was the site of one of the bi-weekly leprosy clinics started by doctors and nurses from the hospital. David was part of a band of Malay Communist guerilla fighters based in a mountainous and remote area of Thailand. With deformed hands and deep ulcers on his feet, he knew he had leprosy and heard that he might receive help at the clinic.

In addition to having his wounds treated, David also heard the shocking message of God's grace many times as he visited the clinic. Eventually, he was admitted to the hospital, from where he sent word to his wife and three children to join him. As he spent more time with the foreign missionaries, David began to open up about his violent past. The combination of the spoken word of God and the loving, sacrificial care given to him by the nurses at the clinic gradually softened David's heart to the gospel. While staying at the hospital, he read straight through the New Testament and was taught the Bible on an almost nightly basis by one of the missionaries. David was eventually discharged from the hospital, but he left as a new man in Christ. He later returned and was baptized along with four other patients in January 1973.

Among the nurses who cared for David was Minka Hanskamp, a six-foot tall Dutch missionary who had grown up in Java (Indonesia) as the child of missionaries. Minka had worked at the clinics from the start and was fluent in Malay. Another woman caring for David was Margaret Morgan, a nurse from a Welsh mining village who had joined OMF in 1965.

In April 1974, Minka and Margaret visited a village for the usual bi-weekly clinic. Strangers who insisted that they knew of some patients needing help in the nearby mountains lured the two women away from the village. It was a trap. Bandits in the area kidnapped Minka and Margaret and demanded a 500,000 US dollar ransom. The women were kept alive for some time, but in March 1975, a Malay man confessed to executing both of them upon orders from his commander. According to him, Minka and Margaret remained calm when told that they were going to die, only saying, "Give us a little time to read and pray."

In May 1975, a funeral for the two women was held and attended by hundreds of Christians, Buddhists, and Muslims in the area. At the funeral, David read from Romans 8 and told the crowd about the impact that Minka's care had on him. "When Minka put my stinking foot on her lap to treat my ulcer, then I knew what the love of God was," he said.

Passing it on

David's involvement with the hospital continued in the years to come. Because patients sometimes needed a place to stay near the hospital after having surgery or when they were wearing plaster casts to help heal their ulcers, it was decided to open a house in a village near the hospital. David and his wife were involved with ministering to those at the house. In addition to being a place of convalescence for leprosy patients, the center was also used for church meetings and conferences for other churches in the area. By the early 1980s, a congregation of approximately 100 believers met on a regular basis and there seemed to be increasing interest in the gospel message.

Later, when both the leprosy clinic and the house were closed, David bought a house in a community where it was difficult to be known as a follower of Christ.[2] David and his youngest child Lydia professed belief, but none of the older three children were deeply committed. His oldest son and daughter went to live elsewhere in the country. Another son died when he was still a young man, leaving behind a small child.

Lydia, however, followed in her father's footsteps. Known for her outgoing and cheerful personality, she became involved in a youth group that grew out of the hospital's leprosy work. Many of the youth were children of leprosy patients who had come to believe in Christ. The group met occasionally for fellowship at the nearby beach or waterfalls.

Lydia married a leprosy patient, Matthew, who had first been treated when he was a small boy. His parents were not cooperative in administering his medication, however, and so his leprosy became more severe. Years later, he returned for treatment. After more than five years of medication and therapy, he made a good recovery and did not have any deformity. Matthew and Lydia were not able to have children, but they have cared for some of David's grandchildren. Lydia also became a valuable co-worker in literature work and recordings.

Lydia still encourages the family through readings and times of prayer. Her warm personality and caring nature draws others to confide in her, giving her opportunities to offer wise counsel and nurture faith. David died in the 1990s, but Lydia is fulfilling her father's wishes in quiet, yet persistent ways. She continues to "water the acorns" of faith planted by Minka Hanskamp and other believers who sacrificed much to share the good news of God's love in this area of Thailand.

---

[2]   The closures were due to a variety of factors: the progress made in eradicating leprosy in the area, new government restrictions regarding medical visas, lack of personnel and the expiring lease on the hospital property.

13. The Power of Touch

> CIM had a long history of treating both spiritual and physical needs through evangelism and healing, modeled from the start by James Hudson Taylor. In 1952, OMF continued to engage in medical work, establishing hospitals and clinics where the need was greatest. Manorom Hospital in Central Thailand opened in 1956 in a region where no other medical facilities existed at the time. Leprosy was widespread, and Manorom Hospital developed great expertise in treating sufferers, with both medication and reconstructive surgery. Drs. John and Anne Townsend served at the hospital from 1963 to 1979. Below is the story of one leprosy patient they met.

Mr. Boonrawt's face was lumpy and flushed. Partial paralysis in his eyelids prevented him from closing them completely. The conjunctiva above his lower lids was red with inflammation, the outer edges holding beads of pus. Leprosy had taken his eyebrows and the bridge of his nose. His thumbs could no longer move, but the leprosy had not quite reduced his fingers to stumps. There was still time to help him.

It was a pity that nothing had been done sooner. Boonrawt and his family had spent years believing that misfortunes like leprosy could not be changed. Buddhism, with its teachings of good behavior, compassion and kindness to all living things, had also taught him that his condition was the result of evil behavior in a previous incarnation. All he could do now was to live the best life possible, reaching out to help others and giving alms for good causes in order to make merit. If he made enough merit, he might improve his status in the next life enough to be born again without leprosy.

He could still remember being a young boy before his illness was discovered and the love that his parents, brothers and sisters showered on him. He still had clear memories of his mother hugging him. That all changed after his leprosy was found. After that, he spent each day in a tiny hut built by his parents 100 yards from the family home. He longed to be touched by someone, but as soon as the family knew, they were terrified of catching the disease. They would not touch him, and they left food for him twenty feet from the hut door. His favorite sister would sometimes call, "Little Brother Rawt, are you all right? Are you lonely?" Boonrawt would reply tearfully, "Yes!"

While the years passed and he grew into his teens, Boonrawt had a lot of time to think. He wondered how he could reach out to help other people and gain merit when everyone refused to come near, let alone touch him. Suppose he died without doing anything good. What then? Would he have leprosy again in his next incarnation? Or, much worse—would the anger, envy and greed in his heart weigh against him, leaving even less merit than last time? He might be reincarnated as a dog or crocodile.

John Townsend met Boonrawt during his and his wife Anne's first months at Manorom. Boonrawt was sitting by a bed in the leprosy wing. Kay Griffin, a missionary nurse with special experience in treating leprosy, introduced him to John.

Leprosy nurses arrived in Thailand in 1953. The government wanted them to help find and treat people with leprosy. They set up little clinics, which were just wooden platforms with thatched roofs near villages. Boonrawt came to them as a young man, sitting shyly at the back, working hard not to touch anyone or to let anyone touch him.

"Then I touched him," Kay recalled. "It was as though the world had stood still. With my very limited Thai language I asked him to look at me while I examined his eyes and face. My fingers gently felt his eyelids and then carefully took his hands to see how badly they had been damaged."

"Are you not afraid of me?" Boonrawt had asked.

"No, why?" Kay had replied.

"Because you have touched me and held my hands and you might catch my disease.

That touch was the beginning of many touches that led to healing for Boonrawt. Kay and her colleagues started him on a course of tablets that began to arrest the growth of his leprosy bacilli and then to kill them. His family had no objection; his situation could not be any worse. Perhaps these pale-skinned foreigners could help him. Maybe they used magic and had the power not to catch leprosy when they touched anyone with the disease.

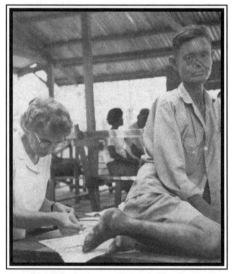

After three years Boonrawt had improved significantly. His parents could see his skin clearing, with better skin texture and color. They started to come with him to the clinics an d saw how the nurses dressed his foot ulcers, cleaned his eyes, held his hands to check finger movements and examined the skin where his eyebrows had been.

Caring for leprosy patients at Manorom

"But how can you touch him?" asked his mother.

"The medicines have stopped him from being infectious," a nurse said. "Look, I am using my fingers to feel his face. See how supple the skin is now. Would you like to touch your son again?"

She did—the first touch she had given him in seven years.

By this time Manorom Hospital was ready to open. One of the first wards to be occupied was in the leprosy wing. Boonrawt, with the backing of his family, became an inpatient. His foot had become ulcerated following his encounter with a rusty nail. Leprosy had destroyed pain sensation in his feet so that he damaged himself without being aware of the injuries.

Grace Warren, an internationally acclaimed leprosy surgeon, visited Manorom and advised that Boonrawt's infected foot be encased in a closed cast up to the knee. The plaster must be left intact for six weeks before being taken off. The idea shocked the Manorom doctors. "Leaving the plaster undisturbed is the only way his foot ulcers will heal," Grace said. "I've been running a leprosy colony on an island near Hong Kong for years and believe me, this method really works."

The doctors trusted her suggestion and, to their relief, the method worked. During her visit, Grace spent much time with June Morgan, the OMF doctor assigned to work as resident director of the leprosy program at Manorom. June had already had special training in leprosy treatment and her times with Grace were useful additional in-service trainings. June went on to become one of the world's leading leprosy reconstructive surgeons.

"Boonrawt is going to need tendon transplants to both his thumbs," Grace commented to June on a ward round. "And I think he would like some new eyebrows!" Boonrawt nodded vigorously as she touched the outline of where the eyebrows should be.

Boonrawt and his fellow leprosy patients experienced remarkable progress. Under the bright lights of the operating room, Grace and June worked together. Grace was a good teacher and June was delighted to add new operating techniques to her existing ones. Boonrawt received new eyebrows by the procedure of swinging a skin flap on each side from his hair-bearing scalp to his forehead above his eyes. The results blew him away: beautiful, bushy eyebrows that were so luxuriant that they had to be cut every week!

Grace eventually gave tendon transplants to Boonrawt and two women who also could not press their thumbs against their fingertips. A tendon from each forearm was transferred and attached to the thumb tendon. An OMF physiotherapist then taught them carefully, after the operation, how to adjust to the sensation of moving their thumbs across their palms.

Boonrawt and his fellow leprosy patients became good friends. They all had similar experiences of rejection and loneliness. In the clinics and at Manorom Hospital they had been welcomed by people who loved them and touched their smelly sores, gave them medicines that healed them and arranged surgery to reduce disfigurement and restore function. They began to feel like real people who mattered and were valued.

As the leprosy patients learned about Christ, who had come to touch, heal and save, and who was especially interested in marginalized people, they joined together to form a church. It was the very first church in Central Thailand. The church grew quickly, vibrant with new hope, joy and great singing. Gradually, another church whose members were physically healthy also developed, and thus they were known as the "well church." For years this group remained separate from the leprosy believers because they still feared any contact with the disease.

When John revisited Thailand 30 years later, the leprosy church and the "well church" had united. They rubbed shoulders together, shared communion together and reached out to each other and to people around them. The walls of division had come tumbling down. Many of the leaders in the united church were healed leprosy patients, won to Christ by the love shown to them by Christian doctors and nurses. People began recognizing the former leprosy sufferers as people who had known the transformational love of God.

Because someone chose to reach out to a leprosy patient as Christ reaches out to us, many lepers have come to recognize their true identities: people loved by God.

Christian leprosy patient

14. Light Shines in Mongolia

Kirk and Esther Matthews[3] have served for two decades in Mongolia with OMF. In a frigid climate where light and warmth are crucial to survival, more and more Mongolians are finding salvation in Jesus, the light of the world. The Mongolian church has grown from a handful of believers in the early 1990s to a thriving church of thousands of believers.

In the 1920s, China Inland Mission workers George Hunter and Percy Mather endured arduous journeys in what is today Xinjiang in China, as well as Khovd and Uvs provinces in Mongolia. They shared the gospel with Mongolians and Kazakhs. Mather was grateful to God for "the opportunities

George Hunter and Percy Mather

for preaching the Gospel to many who have not heard it before, and may never hear it again."[4] What would compel these men to uproot their lives, travel through desolate regions, and later suffer and die in China?

---

3   Names have been changed.
4   Mildred Cable and Francesca French, *The Making of a Pioneer* (New York: Frederick A. Stokes Co., 1935), 239.

Sun, light and warmth in Mongolia

The sun and a flame of fire are atop the national symbol on the Mongolian flag. Every *ger* (yurt, a round felt tent found in Central Asia) of this far northern country faces south so that the door opens toward the sun, toward the revered light. As temperatures in Mongolia plunge to minus 40 degrees in winter, heat is essential for life. Fire, giving both heat and light, is revered as well. Traditionally, trash should not be put in the fire at home.

A few years ago, Kirk and Esther Matthews, along with some Mongolian Bible college students,[5] sat in a Mongolian ger. They were in the Altai Mountains, sharing the gospel with nomadic herdsmen who had never heard the good news before. The nomadic family in this ger was about to ride horseback through a steep valley in order to get to a high mountain for an auspicious occasion. It would be 49 days since their 10-year-old son died, and they planned a special ceremony so that their boy would have a favorable reincarnation. Before the team traveled together with this grieving family, they noticed a picture of the boy at the back of the ger, with a candle before him. The little light was supposed to help the boy's spirit find his way home.

People understand something about light pointing the way, but they do not know the Way, Jesus. If only the family had known the one who said, "I am the light of the world."

"I will save you"

Delgermaa and her husband, nomadic herdsmen, fared well after Mongolia's Democratic Revolution in 1990. Under the Communist system, livestock had belonged to the state. Now that their livestock were privatized, belonging to them, they

---

[5]   From Union Bible Theological College (UBTC) in Ulaanbaatar, Mongolia.

worked harder and became wealthy. Life seemed good. But then Delgermaa's husband found another woman and left her. Delgermaa's world was falling apart. Distraught, she took a walk out on the lonesome steppe. Suddenly a voice said, "I will save you." She turned around, but nobody was there. "I'm going crazy," thought Delgermaa. Sometime later, she visited her friend in town. This friend invited her to an "assembly," yet Delgermaa did not understand what this "assembly" was about. Delgermaa was at what she later realized was a church, where she heard the gospel of Christ. She made the connection between the voice that said, "I will save you" and the message she heard at the church. That day, Delgermaa was saved.

A messenger of the cross

The sun rising over the vast land ocean of the Gobi Desert is awe-inspiring. Enkhbold, a Gobi camel herder, lived far from any town. He was grieving over the death of his wife, which left him to raise their children. He traveled a long distance to visit some relatives. In their home was a little book he had never seen before. He picked it up and read about a strange god who he had never heard of, about a man dying on a "cross." What did this mean? Enkhbold prayed, "If you are there, if you are a real god, then send somebody to me to explain about you better."

Shortly after that, an unfamiliar jeep pulled up to his *ger*. It was getting late, and driving over dirt tracks at night was difficult. Enkhbold, in typical rural Mongolian manner, offered warm hospitality. Out of his meager resources he served the best dinner he could—camel meat with homemade wheat noodles. After dinner, he invited the guests to stay with his family in his *ger*, which of course was just one room. The next morning the visitors told Enkhbold about the God who made the world, and how this world had gone wrong. He heard about God's son, a man dying for our sins on something called a "cross." After a long discussion, Enkhbold prayed to receive Jesus. He was overcome with such a sense of peace that his guests noticed how his countenance changed. That day, the little team of Kirk, Esther and Mongolian Christians left the *ger* rejoicing.

A multiplying seed

There was a narrow valley that quickly became dark when the sun went down. Altangerel, an elderly nomadic herder, lived there by herself. There were no other *ger* for miles around because others believed that this particular valley was haunted.

A team of Christians hiked nine miles through this valley to visit Altangerel. A Mongolian Christian asked her, "Aren't you afraid to live here alone in this valley?" Apart from any evil spirits, wolves are common, and one herder had seen a snow leopard.

"No," she laughed. "I trust in Jesus." This old woman trusts in Jesus and lives unafraid, dwelling in his light, knowing this light is brighter than any evil darkness. She added that since others were afraid to live in that valley, "my livestock have plenty of grass to eat."

One reason why Altangerel trusts the Lord is because of how her late husband Jargalsaikhan passed away. How was it that a fortune teller came to die in peace? Years before, Kirk had led a team of Mongolian Christians to this mountainous county. With the Bible in hand, they had shared the gospel with Jargalsaikhan and challenged him to depend on God alone. He would have to give up fortune telling. Jargalsaikhan quickly repented and turned to Christ, giving up his lucrative fortune-telling practice in the process. From that point on,

Jargalsaikhan was content to earn his living from his livestock, praying to Jesus to help look after his flock.

Years later, Kirk visited the region where Jargalsaikhan and Altangerel lived and was asked to visit the couple, as Jargalsaikhan did not have long to live. Years of heavy vodka drinking before his conversion had taken their toll on his liver. Kirk did not know what to expect, but as he entered the *ger*, old Jargalsaikhan was laying on his bed listening to an audio cassette of a Mongolian pastor preaching a sermon. The sick man was weakly crying out, "Amen, amen." Jargalsaikhan was at peace as the visitor shared some scripture with him and prayed. Before passing away, his family asked Jargalsaikhan if he wanted a *mullah* (folk Muslim leader) or a *lama* (Tibetan Buddhist monk) to perform the funeral ceremony. Jargalsaikhan refused, saying that he wanted Kirk to conduct his funeral. Jargalsaikhan urged his whole family to believe in Jesus.

Kirk and a Mongolian church elder conducted the funeral, probably the first Christian funeral in the area in modern times.[6] During the burial, each son suddenly reached into the fold of his *deel* (traditional Mongolian garment) and pulled out some barley seeds. They threw the seeds onto the body wrapped in homemade felt. In the solemnity of the moment, Kirk was not about to stop the proceedings and ask what this meant. But he prayed and the Lord helped him speak a verse, John 12:24: "I tell you the truth, unless a kernel of wheat falls to the ground and dies, it remains only a single seed. But if it dies, it produces many seeds."

All of the sons became "seeds" of Christ. One of them was named Zorig. Later, Zorig and other family members, with their livestock, moved 40 days and hundreds of miles east to

---

[6] A few ancient Syriac Christian/Nestorian graves have been found in Mongolia.

a new province. He invited Kirk to come and visit. Surprised that Zorig had moved so far away from home, he asked, "Why did you move?" Zorig replied, "Because we learned from you." Kirk was stunned. He had never suggested that they move. In fact, he had been hoping that they would remain in their province, where Christians were far fewer. "You see," explained Zorig, "you taught us not to be afraid. Because of Jesus, there is no need to be afraid of anything!" Casting aside the old fear of mountain passes, crossing rivers and angering local spirits, Zorig and his family decided to move to a new province with better grass, better weather and better access to markets to sell wool, cashmere, milk and meat.

What good news!

Some live in dim light and need somebody to witness to the light of Christ. A mustached Turkish-looking nomadic herder name Baatar lamented, "I'm an old man, and I won't have many more years left." In the course of conversation with Kirk, Esther and a group of Mongolian believers in Christ, Baatar sighed that he had to pay a large amount of money to a *mullah* to sacrifice a sheep on the mountain top in an annual ritual so that his family would not have to go to the "eternal fire."

Esther asked, "How do you know the eternal fire is there?"

"I don't know. That is what the *mullahs* say," Bataar replied.

Esther took out a Mongolian Bible and showed from Revelation that the eternal fire was there. Baatar exclaimed "Yes, that's it!" He marveled at the Bible, having never seen one before. She went on to explain how Jesus was the Lamb of God who took away the sins of the world and how he was sacrificed for our sins. Then she showed from the Book of Hebrews how Jesus was the final sacrifice.

"What good news! What good news!" Baatar was almost jumping up and down. "Why haven't I heard this before? Why hasn't anybody told me before?" Soon Baatar and his wife Sarangerel prayed to receive Christ. They beamed with joy, and the missionaries also rejoiced.

Guided by the light

Another nomad, Mishig, received Christ after listening to the gospel explained to him by a team of Christians as everybody drank goat milk tea with roasted barley powder. Mishig gladly received a book new to him, the Bible. The team had to leave for another province the next day. They explained what the Bible was about and the difference between the Old and New Testaments. (It would have been terrible to return and find Mishig performing Old Testament-style animal sacrifice!) The visitors could not say, "Go to church," for there was no church. They urged the new Christian to read a chapter of the Bible daily, starting with the Gospel of Matthew.

Two weeks later the team returned to follow up with Mishig and the other new believers. Mishig smiled, "There is a prayer that I pray every day."

"Really? What prayer do you pray?"

He opened his Bible to Matthew 6. "Here. Jesus said this is how to pray: 'Our Father, who is in Heaven ... '" Mishig already had the Lord's Prayer memorized! This Bible did not have any chapter titles or footnotes, nothing to indicate that this was a special and well-known prayer. Surely the light of Christ was helping teach this new believer to understand and follow the Bible.

A trail of light

Some respond suddenly to the light of Christ, while others respond slowly. Some find glimmers of light in unexpected places. Tuya, a Mongolian student, was studying to be a seamstress at a trade school in the Soviet Union. After the Soviet Union collapsed, the Siberian city where Tuya studied soon lacked groceries. She and other students had very little to eat, and she was hungry. A fellow student, a Russian friend invited her to a Russian Orthodox church. Her stomach and soul empty, Tuya marveled at the ethereal beauty. "What a beautiful God," she mused. She wanted to know this God better, but did not understand how to believe.

Later, Tuya returned to Mongolia. A friend invited her to see a movie at the local cinema. She watched an interesting film called *Jesus* with rapt attention. At the end of the *Jesus* film, it dawned on her: this is the same God that I wanted to know in Russia; now I know how to believe in this God. Tuya put her trust in Christ. Today, she is married to Boyo. Boyo and Tuya lead a ministry called "Soul of the Steppe,"[7] where street men have a place to live and learn construction skills. They also find freedom from alcohol as they turn to the light and warmth of Christ.

A different kind of joy

Many men and women go to an early grave in Mongolia due to vodka. Erdene was one of these who wallowed in the dark madness of alcoholism. His long-suffering wife and others who knew him called him an "eternal alcoholic." Then, a friend who had become a Christian invited him to attend a meeting at

---

[7] "Soul of the Steppe" partners with JCS International, an intra-agency consortium including OMF, Interserve, Mennonite Mission Network, SIM, YWAM and others.

a Mongolian church. Celebrate Recovery,[8] a project of Joint Christian Services International (JCS), was implemented by a Korean woman, a member of JCS and Youth with a Mission (YWAM). At the meeting, Erdene saw a special kind of joy in people, a joy not from vodka, but a joy of the Holy Spirit. There was warm fellowship where people could talk about their problems. He, like many others, turned from the numbness of alcohol to the comfort and forgiveness of Christ. Today, Erdene pastors a church, loves to share his testimony and seeks to evangelize and disciple nomads.

Hope through the cross

Like Erdene, Bolor also needed the warmth of Christian companionship. Bolor was a secondary school English teacher in a provincial town. She enjoyed her job and her English improved as she took English and educational methodology seminars from Kirk, who later moved to Ulaanbaatar,[9] the capital of Mongolia. She had bright career prospects, but then her school received a foreign English teacher who taught for free. Bolor lost her job. Like many others, her husband Dorj was also unemployed, so the young couple migrated to Ulaanbaatar in search of work.

In Ulaanbaatar, Bolor remembered her former English teacher and his wife, and found them. Kirk and Esther warmly welcomed her to their home. On the coffee table Bolor noticed a scrawled piece of children's art with a man and intersecting lines. "What is that symbol? I have seen it before."

---

[8] Celebrate Recovery began at Saddleback Church in the United States. In Mongolia, Celebrate Recovery developed out of the Alcohol Abuse Reduction Project (AARP) begun by JCS International. AARP was first run by JCS/OMF member Bill Fearnehough. Today, Celebrate Recovery is a Mongolian organization, with a national director and board.

[9] Also known as "Ulan Bator."

"A cross."

"What is a cross?" she asked.

Esther explained about the cross. In the course of conversation, Bolor revealed some of the problems in her life, including the pain of miscarriages and giving birth to a stillborn child. "I don't know where my babies are," Bolor sighed. That day Bolor received Christ, and she had the hope of seeing her babies again. It was Good Friday. (Each Good Friday since, Bolor contacts Esther to thank her for leading her to Christ).

Bolor and her husband, also now professing faith, had a baby. Two months later, the baby died. In the tradition of Tibetan Buddhism, the relatives wanted the baby to be "sky buried."[10] The young couple refused, wanting a Christian burial (even though their church had never done a burial before). Their relatives were angry, even blaming the death of the baby on the couple's belief in Jesus.

The Mongolian church and another OMF couple conducted the funeral and showered the grieving couple with love. Relatives, however, refused to attend. Bolor's mother was astonished by the lack of love shown by the other members of the family, and also impressed by the love and care of the Mongolian Christians and foreigners. She started attending the church, believed in Jesus and eventually led many others to Christ. One time, Bolor's mother asked, "Why has it taken foreigners so long to come and tell about Jesus?"

The way of light

Those who have carried the gospel to Mongolia have seen miraculous church growth in recent decades. In 1990 there

---

[10] Dead bodies are left out in the open, especially in high places, with the hope that birds or wolves consume the body, for a faster and better reincarnation.

were fewer than 10 known Christians in the country. Today there are more than 50,000. God's light continues to shine in Mongolia.

15. From Tragedy to Faith

December 26, 2004 is a date that will live forever in the memories of many Southeast Asians. A major earthquake under the ocean was followed by a terrible tsunami that affected numerous countries and led to an enormous loss of life, homes and livelihoods. OMF workers in several countries were able to assist both in the immediate aftermath and in the long journey towards rebuilding communities. Many national Christians also played a big role in caring for the injured, bereaved and homeless.

For Oruma, the busy day meant welcoming new guests, checking them in, showing them to their rooms and addressing a constant stream of inquiries. Each guest was greeted with typical Thai courtesy.

Oruma worked as the front desk assistant at a resort in Khao Lak, about 31 miles north of the popular tourist destination of Phuket. Khao Lak was popular, too, and at this time of the year was buzzing with vacationing tourists—as many as they could accommodate. Oruma looked out the big window in front of her desk to the crowded beach nearby. Some people lazily read books under large striped sun umbrellas. Some swam in the warm blue sea. Some busily lathered themselves with sunscreen, already looking pinker than they should. Children ran and chased each other across the beach, kicking balls and playing with the sand. The sound of their excited shouts and laughter floated through the welcome area to where Oruma sat.

For a while, Oruma focused on her computer screen and the task of identifying who would be checking out the next day; she needed to prepare their accounts. Soon, however, she felt that something was different. As she raised her head to look out of the window, she noticed that some of the children had stopped playing and simply stood there, staring in the direction of the ocean. Not just the children, she soon saw, but everyone seemed to have stopped their activities and stared curiously at the sea. Was there a shark or stingray in the water, she wondered?

The wave

She slipped outside to get a better look. At once, she knew. The beach was bare, and the water pulled back into the ocean as if draining out of a bathtub after someone yanked the plug. The tide receded further and further into the sea. A few boats sat stranded on the sand, though buoyant in the sea just minutes earlier. An eerie silence filled the air, almost as if the whole world suddenly stood still.

A moment later the wind changed and blew a strong gust across the shore. Trees swayed forcefully, and birds squawked in alarm. Oruma detected a faint line across the horizon—a high wall of water moving toward the shore, rapidly.

A sharp jab of terror struck Oruma. A huge wave, larger than anything she had ever seen before, raced toward them. Just as this realization dawned, she heard screams of panic as people all around her grabbed children and belongings and ran as fast as they could away from the beach. Tourists and resort staff no longer stared in disbelief or puzzlement—they ran for their lives. Oruma knew she must run, too, and get to higher ground. As she ran, the deep, thundering roar got closer. She did not dare look back but she knew the wave was gaining ground. Lungs stinging and chest heaving, she ran faster than she had ever run in her life.

The thundering roar advanced quickly. The mighty wall of water tore through surrounding structures, destroying everything in its path. Trees toppled in an instant. Beach umbrellas, chairs, tables and cleaning carts all disappeared into the churning water. Before Oruma could run any further or scream any louder, the wave swept her into its powerful current. She spun fiercely under the brown foamy water, head over feet, over and over, slamming into hard objects she could not see.

Would this Jesus save her?

It felt like an eternity under the water, but eventually Oruma struggled to the surface and took a huge gulp of air. Coughing and gasping for more as the strong currents tossed her around, she grabbed hold of a floating piece of wood to steady herself. A moment later, the force of the water took the wood from her grasp and once more the frothy, murky water pulled her under. "I am going to die," Oruma told herself. Then an image flashed across her mind.

A few days ago she had read something from a book she had seen advertised on TV. It was free, so why not order it? The book talked about God and his son Jesus and explained everything about the Christian faith. She remembered one page in particular that said Jesus' sacrifice on the cross meant that all who believed in him would be saved. *Saved*—would this Jesus save her now?

The strong current pulled her further and further down. She spun uncontrollably, painfully smashing into all kinds of loose debris. In absolute desperation as she began to lose consciousness, she prayed: "God, if you are there, please save me from this deadly water. Please, God, save me!"

Within seconds of that prayer, the currents pushed her to the surface and she grabbed hold of a rope that had caught on a tree. Again she gasped for air, coughing and choking, but holding tightly to the rope. Her mind raced and sticky blood dripped down her face. With every limb aching and battered, she could only think of one thing: "There is a God, and he saved me!"

News spreads

That same day, just an hour earlier, Matthias Holighaus, his wife Raphaela and their two young sons joyfully sang Christmas songs at their church service in Bangkok, Thailand. The small congregation was celebrating the birth of the Lord Jesus, their Savior.

Matthias and Raphaela were from Germany and had been serving with OMF in Thailand for six years. Now fluent in Thai, they served with a ministry called Baan Nok Kamin, which was established by an OMF colleague and cared for orphans and former street children. In addition, Matthias and Raphaela shared their own home with a group of troubled or otherwise homeless teenagers.

"We found this ministry very rewarding," said Matthias. "It was quite hard at times, but it was a very meaningful time for us. We were able to invest in young people who had very deep wounds from their past and little experience of love. It was great to spend time with them and simply to love them in Jesus' name."

Just as the service was ending that December 26 day (a Sunday), a Thai church member suddenly ran to the front. "She was one of our staff members from Baan Nok Kamin," recalled Matthias, "and she was pale and shocked. 'A huge wave has swept right over the island of Ko Phi Phi,' she stammered. Horrified, we rushed home and turned on the TV. Immediately we learned that there had been a huge earthquake under the Indian Ocean, measuring 9.1 on the Richter scale, and causing an enormous tsunami. It seemed thousands of tourists and local people may have been killed or injured."

Later it was estimated that some 230,000 people from 14 different countries lost their lives, but in the immediate aftermath the scale was beyond measurable. However, as news began to trickle through, Matthias wondered whether he might be able to offer some help. "I thought at least I could help translate," he said. "We knew how difficult it could be to cope with disaster as a foreigner. There are big language barriers. I could speak Thai and German and English, and could be a bridge between many of the tourists and the Thai. As Christians, we wanted to help anyway."

Urgent help needed

Initially, Matthias went to the university grounds in Bangkok. The university served as a temporary shelter for people being flown out of the tsunami-affected areas and waiting to travel home. The people were shocked and often injured, and Matthias was able to help, but as more and more aid workers arrived he felt he could be of greater usefulness in one of the tsunami-affected areas of South Thailand.

Within hours, Matthias hitched a ride on a Thai Air Force plane that had been mobilized for a mercy mission to Phuket. Traveling with him was Dam, one of the Thai teenagers living with the Holighaus family at the time. The scene that met them was horrifying and chaotic. Hundreds of people ran round in a desperate panic, trying to locate missing relatives or simply trying to get away. There were so many badly injured people that one of the airport hangers had been converted into a medical center, but that, too, was overflowing with people covered in blood and crying out in great pain.

Dam studying

Great as the need was there, an official at the airport told Matthias that the area of Khao Lak was probably in the worst shape, but had not received much help because it did not have as many tourists. The overwhelming needs in so many areas made it difficult to commit to just one location. The tsunami had hit only two days ago.

Matthias and Dam finally found a ride that took them to Khao Lak, a two-hour drive beyond Phuket. During that journey, they saw firsthand the total destruction caused by the tsunami. "There were buses upside down in the middle of the road, debris everywhere. We were over a mile from the coast, but there were boats washed up and a whole big ship sitting on a hill," Matthias recalled. "Everything—houses, trees, bigger buildings—had been destroyed. It was freezing cold as we rode that night on the back of the truck, but the smell of rotting corpses lying in the mangrove swamps was overpowering—the result of two days out in the blazing daytime sun."

Someone directed Matthias and Dam to the Buddhist temple in Khao Lak, the place where relief work for the area was being organized. The temple also served as the collection place for recovered bodies. Over a thousand decomposing bodies lay there, with no body bags available as of yet. "It was unbelievably awful," Matthias said.

All the same, Matthias and Dam had no other place to stay but at the temple; everywhere else was covered with stinking mud and debris. Lying awake that night, Matthias prayed that somehow he might bring a little of God's light into the darkness and despair.

For two days, Matthias and Dam did all they could, identifying bodies, helping desperate relatives search for missing loved ones, translating and helping some more. They eventually had to return to Bangkok.

For Matthias, however, it was the start of repeated trips to Khao Lak—16 visits in one year. Long after all the surviving tourists left, the local survivors still had acute needs. Matthias built relationships with them and helped organize the distribution of food, water and clothing. After a while, the Thai government built temporary shelters, but most people were too traumatized to do more than sit in despair. Soon, relief organizations from all over the world arrived with resources and skills to help rebuild. Matthias was able to help them, both as a Thai speaker and because of the relationships he had started to develop. Many psychological wounds are still raw, even today. Rebuilding lives and communities takes many years.

God rescues his people

During one of these many visits to Khao Lak, Matthias met Oruma and heard her story. He checked into a small hotel to stay during one of his visits and found Oruma working there. As they chatted, Matthias was astounded to hear Oruma attributing her survival to God. "It was amazing to hear how

God had prepared her for the disaster," he said. "That book she read about Jesus and Christianity reached her only a week before the tsunami. She had read it carefully, trying to understand."

She said that although she had attended the temple regularly, she always left feeling empty and unsatisfied. She went there to make merit and to make sacrifices to the gods and spirits, but she never achieved peace. When she saw the advertisement on TV, she wanted to hear about the Christian faith: could it answer her deep needs and questions? She called the number to have the book mailed to her, and when it arrived she read it eagerly. Even though this was the first time she had heard about Christianity, she thought that maybe this was what she had been looking for and what she had been missing when she went to the temple. She even highlighted the passages that really struck her. It was those words that flashed into her mind as she struggled under the violent water.

OMF came alongside several other Christian agencies in South Thailand to help with the cleanup and rebuilding. As Christians served the local people and spent time with them, some people came to faith and started new churches. Matthias put Oruma in touch with one of these new groups of believers near her home.

Before the tsunami, the area around Khao Lak was one of the least reached in Thailand, with very few known Christians. Through the persistent compassion and help of Christians long after others had left,

Matthias H, fisherman and new boat

people saw villages rebuilt and fishermen acquired new boats. These efforts completely changed the status of Christianity and the openness to the gospel in the area. "It was the Christians who helped us," people say. It is reported that hundreds have come to trust in the Lord Jesus.

Out of spiritual darkness, and out of the trauma of the tsunami, God in his grace has brought the miracle of light.

16. Seek the Truth from Facts

In recent years, an increasing number of Chinese intellectuals are finding in Christ the purpose and meaning they have long sought in vain from other sources.

At the entrance to a prominent university in China sits a large rock on which is painted a slogan in bright red Chinese characters: "实事求是" (Seek Truth from Facts). This Chinese saying vividly reflects the worldview of many Chinese atheists and intellectuals. Below is the story of a man named Carl,[11] in his own words:

> "I have decided to follow Jesus, willing to be led by our Lord. What an incredible thing it is when compared to the old me before I was converted. To me, this is truly a miracle. I recall my experience with a happy and grateful heart. I want to share with you the change it has brought to my mind and spirit.

I grew up in the 1970s, at a time when China was still isolated from the world and we accepted an ideology of communism

---

[11] Name has been changed.

and revolutionary heroism. At school, I was always an outstanding student. Consequently, I had more opportunities to attend social activities and represent my school. This helped me develop a special sense of responsibility. I grew up during a period of great change in China in which social transformation opened the door to the outside world. In the 1980s, after I entered university, I had to face a tidal wave of various new ideas from the West. The previous idealism lost its glamor, and we woke up to reality. I personally experienced a certain kind of ideological crisis. After a period of confusion, I gradually became a realist.

After college graduation, I entered the working world and my spiritual life became a low priority. Although I had woken up from my previous idealism, I was still unwilling to let the feeling completely pass. After I acquired a house and a car, I became eager to have more. I found myself sinking into a funnel of material desire.

I often worried about the benefits of success and failure, and became weary of the struggle. I was soaring in wealth, but sinking in spirit. I could not get rid of feelings of loneliness, emptiness and helplessness. Friends and relatives could not help. Reading celebrity biographies did not work. Sometimes, I felt like a wanderer who had lost his way in the wilderness. I wondered if this is how my life would end.

I tried to go to church several times, but the topics did not seem relevant to me and there was no one to talk to. I previously had read some Bible stories, but I treated it as literature. In the midst of loneliness, my soul continued to wander.

My sister-in-law's family lived in America. They became Christians many years ago and had given us a Bible, but it had sat unopened on the bookshelf for several years. One time, I went to the United States for a business trip and visited them. It happened to be Easter, and they took me to church. We worshiped, sang and talked together. I was very impressed by the atmosphere. It seemed like a big family. My sister-in-law and her husband are devout Christians. They were optimistic, enthusiastic and happy to help others. Their world was attractive to me, but it did not belong to me. I could only enjoy it as an observer.

Three years ago, my wife took our son to America to visit our relatives. A year later, they came back as Christians. Their personal character had obviously changed. My wife was gentle and my son had become sensible. Their changes touched my heart.

My wife wanted our son to maintain his English fluency, so she took him to an English class every Saturday. One day, she called and said there was a free Bible study class at the same place, and asked if I would like to join. I decided to go and try to learn.

Our English Bible teacher's name was Janice. It was already winter then. I recall she came to class very early on the chilly mornings, and had prepared the teaching materials in advance. She taught from the New Testament. This was the first time I studied the Bible systematically. Janice not only taught the Bible, but also answered various kinds of questions. Once I asked her a question about evolution, and at the next class she brought me a book about the topic.

She taught the Bible with such feeling. When she was on the topic of Jesus' suffering on the cross, I could see her devotion and determination as I looked into her eyes. I was deeply moved. She also shared with us her own story of personal transformation—how she became a Christian and how she gave up everything to come to China.

In almost every class, there were newcomers, and they would always ask the same questions. These repeated and simple questions were boring to me, but Janice always patiently answered, as if this was the first time she had answered such questions. Her great patience also impressed me.

Janice not only taught the class, but would also meet with us afterwards for lunch. I could feel a change taking place in my heart. The world which I previously could only admire from a distance was now becoming my own. Several weeks later, Janice invited me to join a Thanksgiving's Day party. This was the first time I attended a house church fellowship. Everyone was friendly. We worshiped, gave thanks and shared our experiences together. This atmosphere led me to feel that I was already in the world that I had been seeking and previously could not find. I was like a traveler who had come home after a long journey. That evening, as I shared my experience, I was so moved that for a moment I was unable to speak.

Yes, at every Bible class, every fellowship and every worship meeting, I felt more and more that I was entering a new world. But I was still not certain if I was ready to be a Christian, or if I needed to take some kind of "test." On Christmas Eve 2008, Janice invited me to dinner at a restaurant with several friends. We had a very pleasant discussion. When a choir started to sing the beautiful Christmas songs, I felt my heart yearning for something, and I saw the expectation in Janice's eyes. I asked her, "How would I know I was ready to be a Christian?" She said I needed only to believe and accept Jesus as my Savior.

I felt like I was in a dream as Janice led me through the prayer of decision. It felt like someone taking my hand and leading me through an open door. All of my friends prayed and wrote words of blessing for me. I was so grateful, even though my heart felt a little uncertain because I still did not understand fully what that night meant for me.

After the dinner and saying goodbye, I took a taxi back home. I got out of the car and walked toward my apartment complex. It was midnight. The air was cold but fresh. I raised my head and looked at the sky. I immediately stopped in my tracks. I saw a vision I had never seen before. The sky was a dark blue, clear and deep, and there were several bright stars in the sky. One of the stars looked like a diamond. It was twinkling, and seemed as if it was staring at me and talking to me. Its brilliance went into my eyes and to my heart, like a warm current pouring into my body. "God!" I cried out from my heart. The last bit of the icy gate around my heart disappeared. It was not opened by an intellectual key, but melted by faith and the warm love of believers. There was no longer any uncertainty in my heart. I knew what had really happened that night—my soul had found a perfect and wonderful home.

Like many seekers of truth, I had tried to believe our Lord by seeking proof, but finally I realized accepting our Lord is based on faith. I have come to know the meaning of Jesus as my Savior, and with the protection of the Lord, I no longer feel lonely, empty or helpless. I now know why we should be optimistic, thankful and forgiving. When we get into trouble, or face pain and misfortune, the Lord will give us strength, confidence, courage and wisdom. When we achieve success, the Lord will teach us how to be humble, grateful, generous and dedicated.

My life has improved since I believed in Jesus. There are still challenges and difficulties in my work, family and physical body. I am still busy trying to work in a material world, but my life is filled with meaning in the kingdom of our Lord.

Becoming a Christian is just entering the door to the kingdom of God. It is only the beginning. The Lord's kingdom is so vast, profound and treasure-filled. I know I need to keep studying, open my heart to pray and confess to the Lord. I need to be grateful, devout and keep growing up in this wonderful new life. Only in the kingdom of God can we find a home for our soul, a fountain for our spirit and the meaning of life."

Carl shared this testimony in 2010. It has not been easy for Carl to balance the demands of his work and the pull of the material world with his spiritual life. Also, because he is a Communist Party member, he struggled with making his faith public and with regularly being part of a church fellowship. In 2013, at Christmas time—exactly five years since Carl made his decision of faith—Janice received some delightful news from him:

> "Janice, I want to share with you some good news. I was baptized today and became a 'real Christian.' We had a wonderful Christmas worship party this morning, with nearly 300 attendees. I joined the choir of the home church. We sang 'Silent Night' and other famous songs. Twelve people were baptized. It's a good day. Thank you for praying and for your patience. Thank you, God!"

Carl now regularly attends Bible study groups and has a deep hunger to grow in his walk with Jesus. His testimony illustrates the stories of many Chinese atheists and intellectuals who share a deep sense that there must be something more to life, a great truth to be discovered. As in the case of Carl, it often takes time to break through the barriers and fully surrender to Jesus as Lord and Master, but God is faithful.

17. The Pearl Family Garden

> Tera van Twillert joined OMF from the Netherlands in 1988
> and went to Taiwan. Following language study and student
> ministry, Tera worked with the homeless and destitute of
> inner Taipei. When local believers took over responsibility
> for the ministry in 2005, Tera became drawn to outreach
> among women engaged in prostitution.

Wanhua, the name of the old city center of Taipei, means
"10,000 glories." Today that name is a sad mockery of the city's
reality. Wanhua is a place of spiritual darkness. Temples and
idol shops rub shoulders on crowded streets. Gangs permeate
the city, fighting and intimidating passersby. Prostitutes carry
on their business. The homeless sleep wherever they can find a
few feet of sidewalk, an alleyway or a hidden corner.

It would be easy to turn away in horror and condemnation.
Yet, the heart of God yearns for every person, however degraded
their lives may seem, and the Lord Jesus came into the world to
save sinners. Who would be willing to enter the dark world of
Wanhua for the Lord's sake and to share the message of his love?
Around 1990, the Holy Spirit convinced two OMF workers,
Chris Hartley from the U.K. and Debbie Glick from the U.S.,
that God wanted them to be a light in the darkness there. The
workers set out in obedience and faith.

Along a little lane, surrounded by teashops and brothels,
Chris and Debbie opened The Spring of Living Water, called
The Spring for short. Rieko Kinoshita from Japan and Tera
van Twillert joined the team soon after that and continued the
ministry after Chris and Debbie left Taiwan. The teashops in
Wanhua are not like Starbucks™; they are places where men
expect to solicit women for sex, or as escorts or drinking
partners. Despite the great need for ministry to these women,

the team ministered almost exclusively to the homeless. Occasionally prostitutes would wander in to The Spring from a neighboring teashop, but there was neither time nor energy to focus on them at the time. As the team spent time listening to the homeless, praying for them and offering acts of kindness, the homeless came to trust them and began to frequent The Spring.

Satisfying and valuable though that ministry was, Tera could not forget the burden God had given her for the prostitutes, many of them women in their 40s and older. How urgently they needed to hear the gospel! Yet the years slipped by, filled with caring for an equally needy group of people. She ministered to them with compassionate love, practical help and the message of hope. After 12 years of waiting and praying, and with Rieko having to return to Japan to care for her parents, Tera and Rieko handed over the leadership of The Spring to two Taiwanese co-workers, knowing that the ministry to the homeless was in safe and gifted hands. Now Tera could turn her attention to the prostitutes.

Tera's OMF leaders in Taiwan gave her permission to attempt this new ministry, provided she could find one or two people to work with her. They did not want her starting this initiative alone. At first, Tera drew a blank; none of her colleagues wanted to join her.

One day, as she shared her vision with a local church, two women came to her and volunteered to join Tera in visiting and making contact with the prostitutes. Every week for a year, starting from December 2005, they faithfully visited and began to win the trust of these needy women.

Soon another local volunteer, Sophia, joined Tera and her friends. Sophia went on to become the first paid staff person, but volunteers were still desperately needed. A local church became involved, first helping provide a Christmas party for the women and then monthly tea parties. With the help of a gift from a church in the U.K., Tera and her staff opened a center called The Pearl Family Garden. Step by step, they established the ministry.

Many of the women to whom the center ministered had been involved in the sex trade for 20 years or more, and some were as old as 70. Many were single mothers, widowed or divorced. Almost none chose this way of life, but it was often the only way they knew to support their children or dependent parents, to pay off debts to the loan sharks or sometimes to feed a drug addiction. The Pearl Family Garden provided a clean place with a free meal and caring people to listen to their stories of pain, loss and longing. In short, women accustomed to being regarded as sex objects, shunned by society, found themselves treated as valued people, known by name, with dignity restored.

Gradually it became possible to include some singing and Christian teaching after the meals, to offer health advice and to pray with those who were open to it. One Christmas, some local Christians took over a grimy teashop and transformed it into a dazzling beauty parlor. They offered free neck massages, manicures and beauty treatments for four Wednesday nights in a row. For many of the women, this was an extraordinary experience of being treated with care and respect: a gift beyond price.

In 2012, with the Pearl Family Garden firmly established with experienced staff, OMF leaders asked Tera to think about starting a new work in another city, Keelung, which also had a large red-light district. As Tera prayed once more for two local volunteers to confirm that this was God's calling, he surprised

Tera with his answer: not two volunteers, but two churches each offering a small team of volunteers! A year later, Tera received a large estate gift from a prayer partner who had recently died in Holland, with the money specifically designated for the ministry. With this confirmation from God, Tera started Promised Land in Keelung in 2013. Once again, the ministry extended unconditional love to women with histories of abuse and rejection.

Tera van Twillert and local church friends

Prostitution involves a complicated chain of factors and is a difficult cycle to break. Most women caught up in prostitution have no home or community to go to if they leave the streets and the teashops. They may have no other means of paying off their debts. They may be illiterate and unable to find employment anywhere else. Their families usually reject them. Occasionally a woman will put her trust in the Lord Jesus, but she will probably remain in the sex trade. Even more rarely, a woman comes to faith *and* is able to build a new life elsewhere. The chains have many links, and the darkness often seems very dark indeed. Just as the causes of involvement in the sex trade can be very complex, so solutions are equally very complex. Neither The Pearl Family Garden nor Promised Land can provide all the solutions. All the same, Tera and her teams can tell and show the love of God to the women and some come to experience his love for themselves.

Autumn's story

As a small girl, Autumn was taken to church by a friend. She loved it. Her mother did not approve, but did not stop her either. With eight more girls in the family to care for she had more than enough to do. Church made a deep impression on Autumn. Whenever she felt misunderstood or mistreated she would go to her room, close the door, kneel at her bed and pray to God.

Tera and her team met Autumn when her life had taken many turns for the worse. As a young girl she was introduced to the wrong places to earn easy money. The life appeared glamorous to her as a young girl and brought in lots of income. She sent some money home, which silenced her parents' questions. What they did not know was that Autumn had started using drugs and eventually became addicted, which she confided to Tera one day. When Tera and her team got to know her, Autumn was already 48. She was willing to receive help for her addiction, but before Tera could arrange for her to go to a Christian rehab center Autumn was sentenced to prison. It was her fifth prison sentence for drug abuse.

"We encouraged Autumn to check herself in to jail rather than wait to be caught," Tera recalled, "which would increase her punishment. She turned herself in for the first time in her life. Later she told us that at the same time we encouraged her to check herself in, the Evil One came with another suggestion. Her drug dealer suggested that she should start selling drugs, that way she would not have to work so hard and could provide for her own habit at the same time. Praise the Lord he helped her to refuse that path, otherwise her prison term would have been much longer."

The team sent Autumn off, gave her a Bible and some money and visited her regularly while she was in prison. When the end of her term came near, they realized that she had no place to go and that going back to her old life was the only option left for her. However, she had become a Christian. Tera offered for Autumn to come and live with her for a while so that she could find her footing and start a new life. She promised Tera she would come. Tera had in mind that she could stay for two or three months while she prepared to reenter society. Autumn's fellow prisoners laughed at her when she said that this time she would succeed and stay out of trouble. "See you again in prison," they mocked.

When Autumn found Tera and her team after being released from prison she had already spent some of her money buying drugs for a friend in need. Her promise to come and stay with Tera kept her from buying drugs for herself. When Autumn arrived, all her belongings—a few sets of clothing— were contained in one plastic bag. Tera quickly realized that two or three months would not be enough time for Autumn to prepare to face the outside world and survive.

"She is learning many things," Tera said, "like living in the daylight rather than at night. When we read Genesis 1 she learned that God created night and day, and that we are meant to work during the day and sleep at night. It was a great eye-opener for her to realize that her whole life she had been living

Tera van Twillert and Autumn

against God's natural law. It has also been a great eye-opener for me to have Autumn living with me. If we hope for the ladies to leave the old life, we need to provide an environment for them where they can experience healing and recovery and grow strong in the Lord before facing the challenge of finding a normal job and living a normal life."

Autumn eventually reunited with her family and reconciled with them. She was baptized, and started to serve God. Just two years after she came to know the Lord, she died. Now this broken woman has been made fully new by the grace of God.

Lily's story

It wasn't until she suffered a stroke did the chains of prostitution break. When Tera and her colleagues first knew her, Lily seemed wistful to leave the streets and to live a different life, but could not break away. She read the magazines Tera gave her and listened to the gospel, but would not believe. Following her stroke, Tera and others visited Lily in the hospital regularly and found her heart, as well as her body, changed. Lily prayed to accept the Lord Jesus as her Savior. When she was able to go back to her tiny one-room home that she shared with her son, she loved having the team visit for Bible study and to sing and pray with her.

Lily's story also illustrates how difficult it can be for women who have been engaged in prostitution to rebuild their lives. One Chinese New Year, after she became a Christian, Lily longed to be reconciled with her parents, whom she had not seen for 30 years. She had married against their wishes and her husband had turned out to be the gangster they had predicted. Lily's husband was long dead and her married daughter wanted nothing to do with her. Now, Lily only had the son who shared her small room and upon whom she was utterly dependent since her stroke. After having a change of heart, she badly wanted to see her elderly parents again, to thank them for caring for her as she grew up, to ask for their forgiveness and to express the filial piety so important in her culture.

Lily's son, Chongde, called his grandparents and asked for permission to drop by. Together with Tera and a colleague, they made the visit. Lily felt that having Tera as a foreigner along might give her some "face"—some social standing and dignity—and convince her parents to listen to what she wanted to say. However, Lily did not get her happy ending. Her mother made it clear that she had no place for Lily in her life anymore, and Lily's father said almost nothing. They acted as if Lily had been erased from of their minds. Rejection was final.

Lily had been rejected by her parents, but not by her heavenly Father. A few years after the heartbreaking meeting, Tera wrote about God's great love and care for Lily, demonstrated through the Christian director and programs at her nursing home, as well as weekly visits from Lily's son. At one point, the director explained baptism to Lily and asked if she would like to be baptized. Lily said she would. The director happily made plans and expressed a desire for all residents to attend the ceremony.

"I am so encouraged by God's amazing care. He has brought her out of the darkness of Wanhua into this Christian home. Yes, it has been a long journey, but God has been watching over Lily and prepared her heart, so we are preparing for Lily's baptism!"

God's Faithfulness to Provide

When James Hudson Taylor founded the China Inland Mission in 1865, it was in every way a huge step of faith and obedience. He had almost no money in the bank. He knew of nobody else except his beloved wife Maria who was willing to go with him to the unknowns of inland China. His heart's burden was for a vast area with very few support systems. In addition, he was adamant that funds and resources should not be diverted from other ministries; he would not make competing appeals. Humanly speaking, the whole enterprise seemed to be sheer madness.

But this was no crazy plan dreamed up by a delusional man. Hudson Taylor had struggled, fasted, prayed and wept as he sought God's guidance. Ultimately, he was convinced that this venture was birthed in the heart and will of God himself; to turn away would be disobedience. Moreover, Hudson Taylor had already learned well the lesson that if God called him to do something, he would supply the resources with which to do it. He had learned that instead of appealing to other people, his appeal should be directly to God by prayer, that if what was asked for was truly within God's will, provision would come. Had not the Lord Jesus himself told his disciples in relation to everyday needs, "Seek first his kingdom and his righteousness, and all these things will be given to you as well" Matthew 6: 33? Dependence for "daily bread" was to be on God. Those who came with him, said Hudson Taylor, must be willing to step out in the same faith.

Hudson Taylor often referred to two Old Testament terms that he adopted as mottos of the China Inland Mission: "Ebenezer" and "Jehovah Jireh." The first comes from the story of Samuel in 1 Samuel 7:12 when the Lord had enabled him to defeat the Philistines, and means "Thus far has the Lord helped us." The second comes from the story of Abraham—another man of God called to set out in faith to a distant destination.

In Genesis 22:14 Abraham faced a terrible crisis: in obedience he must offer a sacrifice, but unless the Lord intervened, Abraham had no sacrifice to offer but the life of his beloved son Isaac. When the Lord miraculously provided a ram to sacrifice, Abraham worshiped God in awe: "The Lord will provide," he said. The impossible had become possible.

Later Hudson Taylor had Ebenezer and Jehovah Jireh carved on the stone gateposts leading in to the China Inland Mission center in London. They appeared for many years in every edition of the CIM's journal, *China's Millions,* and in every book published by the CIM. The words were a constant reminder to members and supporters alike that first and foremost we look to God to provide every resource needed (both personally and as an organization), with gratitude for all that he has done in the past.

Much has changed in the past 150 years, since Hudson Taylor prayed for the provision of workers and funds to reach inland China. However, embedded in the ethos and DNA of OMF, Ebenezer and Jehovah Jireh remain as central as ever. Indeed, "thus far has the Lord helped us."

18. More than All We Ask or Imagine

Travel in China today is full of speedy possibilities, such as planes, bullet trains and subways. In the days of the China Inland Mission, however, it was quite different. Travel was especially difficult in periods of social or political upheaval. In 1948, veteran American missionary Ray Frame experienced God's unique and timely provision as he coordinated the whirlwind move of a language school and dozens of missionaries.

"I don't think we can stay here much longer," Ray Frame said anxiously to his wife, Helen. "I think we need to move everybody down to Shanghai."

It was 1948. China was in the midst of a civil war between Communist and Nationalist forces. Ray and Helen were in Anqing, overseeing a group of young male CIM missionaries part way through their language studies. The CIM put a premium on good language training and the men needed more time devoted to full-time study before they could be sent to places of service.

Ray knew that there were 40 more new recruits waiting down in Shanghai, eager to get started on the task of learning the Chinese language. For the moment, though, the Mission had decided to keep them there because of the growing turmoil in the country. Normally, new workers would have been on their way to Anqing soon after arriving in China, but in 1948 travel was disrupted and often dangerous. What should be done? The prospect of moving the school and language students from Anqing some 300-plus miles east to Shanghai was quite unsettling.

Furthermore, the war had disrupted communications and Ray felt isolated. No word was coming from the CIM headquarters in Shanghai, nor was money arriving safely. Perhaps it had been a mistake to relocate three years before to Anqing, thought Ray sadly. It had seemed right at the time. Shanghai was so cosmopolitan that it was tempting for new arrivals to get by without immersing themselves in the Chinese language. Anqing forced language learners to concentrate on their studies. Shanghai also had a distinctive dialect and pronunciation, whereas people in Anqing spoke in a way that was closer to that heard in most of China. Although there had been good reasons for moving to Anqing a few years prior, it now seemed increasingly unwise to stay.

Eventually, the decision was made: Ray decided that they must move to Shanghai as soon as possible. It is one thing to make a decision, however, but quite another to know how to implement it. How could he and Helen move not only 10 people, but also furniture and valuable equipment? It would have to be by boat, but most local boats were small and unreliable. If he hired one boat, he reckoned it would take four trips to ferry everybody and all their belongings. That would be wildly expensive. "Lord, you'll just have to take care of this," he prayed.

The group started packing. Many things were given away, but some things simply had to be taken. They needed to make arrangements to hand over the school building to the local church, and that involved setting up a trust and getting legal documents prepared and signed. The school's employees had to be notified and given enough money to live on until they could find other work. The tasks mounted.

Packing had hardly begun when someone brought the Frames an exciting message: a massive freight ship was arriving in Anqing that night. Could the ship take them on its return journey as far as Shanghai? Such ships rarely arrived these days and none had been seen for a long time. Someone rushed to the docks to the office of the shipping company. "They can take all ten people and all the belongings," he shouted in excitement when he returned, waving 10 precious tickets. "The only problem is that it will dock and turn around very quickly. We must be ready to board at midnight tonight!"

News of the ship's arrival seemed to be both a wonderful answer to desperate prayer and also an impossible challenge in order to be ready. "You have never seen packing go so fast in all your life," one of the group later said. Ray was especially troubled that it would not be possible for an orderly handover of the building to the church, which might make it prone to being seized illegally, but they could only do so much in so few hours. They had to trust God to take care of what was left undone. Cramming shut their last bundles, they somehow managed to get themselves to the harbor at the stated time.

Then the Lord intervened again. A message came about the ship's arrival in Anqing: "We regret to inform you that there has been a delay, and the ship will not arrive until a day and half after schedule. Please accept our apologies." No apologies were needed: this precious extra time would be just enough to do all that was needed. A few more loads were gathered, but even more importantly, there was time to sort out the legal deeds and to say a sad farewell to local believers. With scarcely a moment to spare, they were back at the ship just when it was ready for them to load their belongings and themselves. How they thanked God!

That was not the end of it. Once on board, they discovered that contrary to their expectations they could buy whatever food they needed. The crew was friendly and curious. The weather was unusually calm and sunny so that the sometimes-choppy waters were smooth as they traveled. It almost felt like a holiday.

As they approached Shanghai, Ray's last concern was how to transfer passengers and belongings from the freight ship to the harbor. Normally, such ships would be required to anchor some distance away, and the little boats that scurried to and fro between them and the shore made the most of it by charging exorbitant fees for carrying passengers that vital last lap. Imagine Ray's surprise when the captain cheerfully said to him, "For the first time ever I've been invited to dock at the wharf. You're in luck!" Not luck, thought Ray, but the sovereign hand of a loving Heavenly Father.

Soon, the CIM truck collected the thankful group and their luggage and they were quickly delivered to the CIM compound. What stories they had to tell of God's loving provision! Almost at once suitable buildings were found to rent for the language school to begin once more. "The Lord truly guided us to make the right decision at just the right time," said Ray thankfully. "This is surely God giving us so much more than we dared ask or imagine!"

19. A Bible College for North Thailand

By 1965 it was becoming clear that the growing tribal churches of North Thailand needed a place where intensive Bible training could be given to present and future leaders. Such a provision had been talked about for several years, but the need was growing increasingly urgent if the young churches were to be established deeply and led by their own people. This was confirmed at the time when OMF leadership in North Thailand asked Thai pastor Thongkam Pantupong how the organization could help the Thai church grow. His answer was to start a Bible school.

Where would be a good location? It needed to be near a town but not in it, in the region where most tribal people lived, with a clean water supply and with space to grow some food. Yet another issue was that there were no funds available to buy land, although a modest rent could be paid. OMF member John Davis from the United Kingdom was assigned the task of finding a site.

Filling up my little Honda, I set off down the dusty road towards Phayao. I knew there was a nice lake there. Would it be a suitable location? I thought I would drive around the whole lake to see what it was like, but as I traveled along the oxcart trail that was the only "road," my heart sank. It would be impossible to navigate in the rainy season. As it was, it took an hour to drive around on the track.

Greatly discouraged after completing the journey around the lake, I stopped at the small town of Phayao for a bowl of noodles before setting off for home again. Just a couple of kilometers (1.25 miles) along the road towards Chiengrai, I passed a hillside. The lake was on my left, the hill on my right. There was a small trail going up the hill. I drove past. Then, strangely, I felt compelled to go back and follow the trail. I drove the protesting Honda up the hill and then looked back at the view. It was more beautiful than anything I had ever seen, except in Switzerland. The view was spectacular. On the shining lake below, fishermen in hollowed-out wooden tree trunk canoes glided along the surface and threw out their nets. Beyond the lake was a range of mountains and a tumbling waterfall between two ridges.

I stood there in awe, and excitedly cried out to the Lord, "Please, Lord! Nowhere else please, Lord! Surely this is the place for the Bible School!" I almost burned the old Honda engine out as I rushed back home to share my discovery with Muriel, my wife.

Phayao Bible College, 1968

I had no idea who owned the land, which was so overgrown that it looked almost like jungle. A huge ditch surrounded the property, showing the boundaries, and in one corner a miniature house for the demons. My mind filled with questions: Who owned the land? Why was it left neglected? Would it be possible to rent it long-term? Who was putting fresh offerings for the demons?

The local fishermen told me that the owner, Boonsing Boonkham, was a former lawyer and education officer for the province, a prestigious position. He lived in Chiengrai, a few minutes away from where Muriel and I lived. He had been given the land by a client who could not pay his bill for a court case in cash. Now retired, he regularly drank whiskey, allegedly as medicine for an old injury. Later, the whiskey played a part in the story.

When I went to see him, he agreed to rent the site and drew up a rental agreement. I had to get clearance from the OMF superintendent before signing, but next time I went back it was evening time and Mr. Boonsing had already drank several glasses of whiskey and was slightly drunk. Chuckling and a bit uninhibited, he let out that he could take the land back after 10 years instead of the 20 that I had asked for and that he had given me to believe would be part of the contract. It really was not long enough to justify the work and cost of clearing the site and building on it. He had been planning to deceive me. I was completely dismayed and left without signing.

I took advice from a Christian lawyer in Chiang Mai, who confirmed that the contract as it stood could be interpreted in such a way that Mr. Boonsing could claim repossession after 10 years. Muriel and I decided that the only solution was to appeal to OMF's team in Singapore to suggest purchasing the land outright. The chances were slim, as there was no budget for such a purchase, and the organization never goes into debt. Imagine our shock when our letter crossed with one from Singapore saying that they had unexpectedly received a sum of money from England, specifically designated for establishing a Bible school in Asia. God was already providing.

I rushed to see Mr. Boonsing to ask if he would sell outright and if so at what price. At first, after two whiskeys, he demanded a totally unreasonable price, but I was able to show him that this was double the cost of land in the area. "Do you really want me—or worse yourself—to be accused of arranging a corrupt price for our own greedy gain?" I asked him. That would be shameful and in Thai culture to be publically shamed is a dreadful thing. He drank another whiskey. No, he could not sell at the lower price. I walked away.

Five days later, a young boy brought a note from Mr. Boonsing. Yes, he would sell the land at the market price. Muriel and I jumped for joy. God had answered our prayers beyond our imaginations.

I still had to get permission from the local authorities to build the Bible school. My first stop was the mayor of Phayao. How do you explain to a devoted Buddhist that you want permission to build a Christian Bible school in the area for which he is responsible? This grumpy man claimed he could not grant permission; we needed the approval of the education officer for the district since this would be an educational establishment. As the mayor called him, I waited nervously.

Shortly after, a man stepped into the room where we waited and burst out in excellent English, "John, my friend, how lovely to see you! How are you? How many years is it since we played badminton together in Chiengrai?" I was as flabbergasted as the mayor. Here was Mr. Sanoh, to whom I had taught English eight years' before. Now he was the education officer for the very area where we needed clearance to build the Bible school. "If you know him and trust him I have nothing else to say," the mayor finally managed to say, dismissing us.

Within a few minutes I clutched in my hand the most precious document (still in the Phayao Bible College archives)—a hand written letter of approval to establish the center we planned. Once more, God had graciously provided just what we needed. It was the Holy Spirit who led John Davis all those years ago to turn around in his little old Honda and go up a simple ox-cart trail to the top of a hill. In 2015, as OMF celebrates its 150th anniversary, Phayao Bible Seminary celebrates its 50th.

20. Enduring Power of Print

Since the early days of the CIM, Christian literature has been a strategic way to inform those who pray, inspire people to be involved with God's purposes in East Asia, instruct believers in biblical truths and introduce people to the gospel. Members of the CIM and OMF have engaged in Bible translation work where needed, as well as the production of Christian literature and other discipleship materials. Presenting material in people's native language is crucial to effective outreach. In the 1960s, God did a transformative work in Hasolan Oppusunggu's life and used him and others to increase the impact of Christian literature work in Indonesia.

Hasoloan Oppusunggu was in the middle of his final exams in his senior year of high school in North Sumatra when all his teachers left to join the rebels fighting against the Javanese head of the government in Jakarta. No one could get a job without a high school diploma, so all of the young men in Hasoloan's class joined their teachers in the fight against the Javanese rulers.

When the rebel leaders surrendered, however, Hasoloan and a few others decided not to because they knew how badly prisoners were treated. They began living out a real-life version of "Robin Hood," stealing from the wealthy to help the poor. They were eventually caught and imprisoned for 18 months. Part of the charges against Hasolan included writing anti-government newspaper articles.

OMF missionary Jack Largent, working in South Sumatra at the time, taught a weekly Bible class to about 100 men at the prison where Hasoloan was being held. Hasoloan attended every class. When he completed his prison sentence and was released, he went directly to Jack's home, since Jack was the only person he knew in that area.

Hasoloan was from the Batak people group, many of whom are Christians, so Jack asked Hasoloan if he was a Christian. His immediate reply was yes, he was born a Christian, was baptized as a child and had been a member of the church ever since then. On Jack's wall hung a "Human Heart" poster with pictures explaining the sinful condition of people's hearts and God's way of salvation through faith in the Lord Jesus Christ. Jack showed Hasoloan these pictures and asked him whether he had ever invited Jesus into his heart. He said no, but he would like to do so.

Following that time, there was a dramatic change in Hasoloan's life. He joined Jack in evangelism, Sunday school teaching, youth work and prison ministry. But he had a problem. After having a certain job for a time, his employer would discover that he had been in jail and would fire him immediately. This went on for several months and Hasolan became very discouraged, to the point that he decided to move to Jakarta and perhaps work on a ship that was going to America, where he might "get lost" after arriving.

Jack knew Hasoloan had previously published articles in local newspapers and that the OMF offices in Jakarta were looking for a young Indonesian with writing skills to hire as their editor. So when Hasoloan told Jack he was going to Jakarta, Jack wrote a letter to Nancy Deischer, an OMF worker who had recently been brought to Jakarta to help train Indonesian writers and editors. Via the letter, Jack introduced Hasoloan as a possible person to become the editor they were looking for and urging her to do all in her power to keep Hasoloan in Jakarta. He gave his letter to Hasoloan, asking him to give it to Nancy when he passed through Jakarta.

Hasoloan agreed to deliver the letter, but he did not want to meet Nancy; so he tried to think of a time when she would not be home so that he could just leave the letter at her door and leave. There are times when what seems to be a chance meeting is seen later to be part of God's loving design. Nancy taught at a Christian publishing house (Badan Penerbit Kristen, or, BPK) that sponsored her; but her office, due to a shortage of space at the publishing house, was actually in her home. Thus, when Hasoloan arrived at Nancy's home, she was there. Nancy opened the door and invited him to sit down and have a drink while she read Jack's letter urging her to do her best to keep Hasoloan there and give him a job as an editor. The only problem was that both the leaders who could hire him were out of town. She phoned the publishing house office and asked for one of the editors to come and meet Hasoloan.

Nainggolan, one of BPK's top editors, came. It turned out that he was a Batak from the very same area as Hasoloan. The two of them talked for about an hour and a half in their local language. When they finished, Nainggolan told Nancy he wanted to hire Hasoloan, but they dare not hire an ex-prisoner who had fought with the rebels. Then he urged Nancy, "He'll be an excellent editor. You hire him. You're a foreigner so people won't blame you ... you wouldn't know any better. "

Nancy asked how much Hasolan would want and Nainggolan told her, "He's tired and hungry; he has no money and needs a place to stay. Give him a job. But you must do it now. If he leaves you'll never see him again." So Nancy overstepped all protocol, gave Hasolan enough money to rent a room in a local student hostel, told him to report for work at eight the next morning and gave him a good meal from her own kitchen to take with him. It was a miracle that her leaders, when they returned, allowed him to stay, but they did.

Hasoloan learned fast and became the kind of editor OMF needed. At first he did routine work such as typing and proofreading, but soon he was writing fresh material and his role at the press expanded. The Christian publishing house was working hard to provide the kind of books needed by church leaders and theological schools, but the director of BPK also wanted to provide books for children, young people, and lay Christian adults.

Thus, when American publisher, David C. Cook, who was giving aid to publishers in developing countries, offered BPK a series of picture-strip Bible stories that covered the Bible in 36 books, the project was gladly accepted and Hasolan was asked to be the editor. Hasolan and the OMF literature team were excited. Such a book would be especially helpful for those who had difficulty reading. Also, cartoon-style comics similar to the format of the proposed books were very popular in Indonesia. The series was an immediate success, and brought Bible stories to a wide readership, among both children and adults.

Later, in the 1970s, the OMF literature team began translating a much-needed one-volume Bible commentary, choosing their Indonesian friends to do the translating. Hasolan saw at once that it was a poor translation. The leaders at the press, however, would not let him check it because he did not have any theological training, and so Hasolan resigned.

At that point, Dennis Lane, an OMF leader in Singapore who had recognized Hasolan's gifts, intervened. "What are you doing?" he asked the leadership at the publishing house. "Give that man whatever he wants, but keep him!" When asked what he wanted, Hasoloan said he would stay if he could be the director.

In fact, it was time for OMF's literature work to be indigenized, and so in 1978 Hasoloan became the director of a new, Indonesian-led Christian publishing house which he named Yayasan Komunikasih Bina Kasih (YKBK), known in English as Bina Kasih Press. The first thing Hasoloan did was to discard the poor Bible commentary translation and invite top church leaders who had both good theological training and good language skills to help with a revision. They came to Bina Kasih from all over Indonesia to help.

Hasoloan's Spirit-led role in Indonesian Christian publishing has been a crucial part of producing a growing body of books that have helped spiritually nourish Indonesian churches. In addition to writing and editing, Hasoloan oversaw the production and distribution of a steadily increasing range of volumes.

A Christian curriculum

One of the first people Hasolan had met who was involved with Christian literature work in Indonesia was OMF missionary Leatha Humes from the United States. Leatha had first arrived in Indonesia in August 1957 to teach English at a newly established teacher-training school in Central Java (now known as Universitas Kristen Satya Wacana, or True to the Word Christian University). Later, in 1961, she was invited by BPK director Alfred Simanjuntak to join his staff at the large Christian publishing house in Jakarta.

In 1963, Muslim government leaders in Indonesia—in order to counteract the threat of Communism in Indonesia—mandated that every Indonesian student from kindergarten up through university receive two religious instruction classes each week. Students could choose between five religions: Islam, Protestant Christianity, Catholicism, Hinduism and Buddhism. Students had to pass that class each year before they could advance to the next grade.

The curriculum for teaching each religion was to be produced by the leaders of their respective religions. Alfred Simanjuntak, director of BPK, was already preparing a Sunday school curriculum and was asked by the Department of Religion to prepare the Protestant Christian curriculum for teaching religious instruction classes in the schools.

Leatha did not know about either of these initiatives, but she strongly sensed the need for a Sunday school curriculum to be published in Indonesian. Thus, she went one day to talk about it with Alfred. Unlike his usual responses when she went to him with suggestions, that day he just gazed out the window and said nothing. Leatha left his office feeling completely frustrated.

Two days later, she received an official letter inviting her to join a team of 25 pastors and school teachers chosen to write the required religious instruction curriculum. A problem soon appeared: the pastors did not have a clue how to teach children and teenagers. Also, the teachers only told Bible stories in their classes; they had no training for writing a Christian curriculum. Leatha had both complete training in the Bible and extensive experience teaching in schools. She was given the brunt of responsibility of writing the 12-year curriculum for the Indonesian schools.

It was not a solo project, however. Five others shared the responsibility: Nainggolan perfected the language; Situmorang, a retired school inspector, made sure the lessons were suited to each grade level; Pastor Solaiman carefully checked the teaching in every lesson; Demak, a Christian teacher, checked each lesson to make sure the lessons were written properly for the teachers to understand; and Alfred Simanjuntak made final edits to each lesson.

This assignment jumpstarted another vital publishing project for Indonesia. Leatha liked to include hymns in teaching her lessons and added translations already available. But Alfred, who was gifted in music and often commissioned to write songs for official occasions, threw out the hymns every time, saying, "We can't use bad translations for lessons in schools!" When she asked his help to get good translations, he put her in touch with a team that was working on developing Indonesian hymnology and improving hymn translation.

Finally, in 1975 a collection of 115 songs was published to go with the Christian religious instruction curriculum. Immediately a new problem surfaced: if the children sang good translations in school and then sang poor translations of the same songs at church, it might lower their opinion of church. All of the churches that had published hymnbooks were invited to a conference in June 1975 to decide what should be done about it. Thirty-one delegates came and they decided to work together to make good translations they could all use together. In 1984 a new congregational hymnbook named *Kidung Jemaat* that all churches could use was published. It included 478 hymns and responses, a third of which were written by Indonesians. Increasingly Indonesians wrote original material rather than using translated material.

As early as 1963, OMF had been training local writers. American OMF worker Mary Jane Faircloth was conducting workshops and writing courses and later developed Indonesia's first Master's program in Christian Mass Communication at Tyrannus Bible Institute in Bandung. The M.A. program addressed other media besides print media, but has certainly contributed to the flow of good Christian literature produced by Indonesians and published by Bina Kasih and other Christian publishers in the country.

Today, there are Christian publishing houses in most Southeast Asian countries. The publishers feed the spiritual hearts and minds of many and contribute significantly to the life of local churches as well as to the wider community. God lovingly wove together many threads along the way, providing just the right people at the right time.

21. Foxes Have Holes, Birds Have their Nests

Ten house moves in 10 years is not everybody's idea of God's kindness. But for New Zealanders Alan and Averil Bennett and their four children, the moves confirmed to each one of them their Heavenly Father's personal care and salvation purposes as they served him—together.

After 10 years in one home in Central Thailand, in 1983 the Bennetts unexpectedly were relocated to Chiang Mai for Alan to serve as Interim Director of the Voice of Peace recording studio. In Chiang Mai, God's provision was a one bedroom flat in a classic teak northern Thai home owned by a well-to-do couple. The family quickly realized that God was using their home as an integral part of their ministry. They became close friends with the owners. The wife, Mrs. S, had led the Christian group at her school as a teenager, growing slowly towards Christ. Then a zealous new missionary teacher thought that she was not yet "born again" and made her resign the role. The hurt drove her away from the Lord for years.

Two events drew her closer to God again. At that time, the Lisu Bible manuscript had finally been finished and was ready to be published. However, OMF worker Andy Thomson could not download the script from his computer. Alan offered to take the machine on the overnight express bus to the Thailand Bible Society, where the issue could be fixed. As Averil took Alan to the bus station, a massive explosion erupted in front of them. That Sunday morning they had read Psalm 46:1-3: "God is our refuge and strength … Therefore we will not fear … though the mountains fall …" It now seemed as if the mountains were crashing. A building lurched above the car. Airborne bodies blew across mingled with debris. A bomb had been set off after a drug feud involving a powerful drug warlord in the area.

"Drive to the corner!" Alan urged a shaking Averil. He had to get the precious Lisu Bible manuscript out of the danger zone. "The army will block the area off for sure. I'll come back if the place really goes up in flames," he said. Nearly 60 homes and a Christian school nearby were damaged by the blast. Next door to the drug warlord's fortress, four houses—including the one that housed the manuscript—burned down. Later, however, they found mattresses had fallen through the burning floor and sagged over the downstairs filing cabinet. The Bible manuscript was safe. Mrs. S, however, was badly shaken; her inner idol room was demolished. Averil prayed with her, then with other neighbors who were too scared to re-enter their homes, before going to help guard the trashed school.

Not long after this, Mrs. S's first grandchild was born with a hole in his heart. The child was given a 50-50 chance of survival if the family took him to either Texas in the United States or to Auckland, New Zealand. As the family matriarch, Mrs. S made the decision: Auckland. For three months, the anxious family stayed with some prayer partners of the Bennetts in New Zealand. The precious little grandson was healed and Mrs. S offered her deep thanks to God and turned again to him.

After several months in Chiang Mai, the Bennett family moved to the capital of Uthaithani province in Central Thailand where they had been invited by Pastor Prawat to go after their home assignment. Though there were many churches in the countryside, no one from the capital city had believed. After Chiang Mai, the family was cured of their need for conventional housing and were happy for God's leading to a vacant shop on a main street. Within three weeks, a businessman turned to Christ. Overflow queues from the ice cream parlor on the right and the noodle restaurant on the left snaked around their display boards and reading racks filled with Christian literature. The Bennetts' young daughter Kristina serenely played with her Lego on the footpath.

It was an ideal public base for the family to continue ministry after Alan was called urgently to Bangkok to direct the Far East Broadcasting Company's (FEBC) Thailand operation. Since Alan could only return home once a month, it was a good setup for Averil. Youth, women's and lay training groups flourished beyond the 12-foot wide front door and in full view of the street.

In Bangkok, Alan became increasingly uneasy that FEBC had to spend so much money on rent. On New Year's Day 1986, he checked the ministry's savings account: 500 Thai baht (about 18 US dollars at the time). Almost nothing. Still, Alan sensed the Lord saying, "Great! Let's get started!" A flyer tucked under their truck's windshield wiper alerted him to a development in an excellent location in Bangkok. If the Bennetts lived onsite that would help with finances, travel and hospitality in such a gridlocked city.

Earnest prayer work began, followed soon afterwards by construction. At the beginning of each month there was insufficient cash in hand to pay the builders; then each month just enough trickled in to do so. In September 1986 the four-storey building opened free of debt with the Bennett family at home on the fourth floor along with two chickens, two doves and a stream of Uthaithani teens looking for work in the city. During that time, Alan also had to deputize for the OMF Area Director in Thailand. Fortunately, the new FEBC site was just a 20-minute walk away.

In January 1988, the Bennetts began their home assignment in New Zealand. Alan's widower father had the same familiar home ready in Wellington, New Zealand, right down to flowers in vases and teddy bears on beds. It would be such an easy transition that Alan decided to stay behind in Thailand for three months, and at the other end of home assignment Averil would return three months ahead of him. In that way, the children could enjoy a full academic year without upheaval and the work of Thai leadership training would not languish, either. However, soon after the family's arrival Alan's father died from a massive heart attack. Averil had to quickly prepare the home to be sold.

From Thailand, Alan used his amateur ham radio to contact friends in New Zealand. Did anyone want a mother and four children—with the pastor to follow in three months? A Southland church replied that the family would be welcome. Just three days before school began, the Bennett family moved into the manse in Mataura. They were still in a state of shock, but the relocation proved to be God's perfect provision for the family. Each person—including the children—found a mentor who has journeyed with them in friendship and prayer support through university, marriage and family to the present time.

After a year in New Zealand, the family returned to set up a lay training center as originally planned by Pastor Prawat years before. He had died in a motorcycle accident in Uthaithani in 1984. By the late 1980s, it was clear that a lay training center would best be established in Nakhon Sawan, the largest city between Bangkok and Chiang Mai. A Christian rickshaw driver alerted them to a large building and it was quickly acquired. Within a day of moving in and naming it the L.I.F.E. Center (Leadership, Instruction in God's Word, Fellowship, Evangelism), the next door neighbor entered the center. Could Averil translate the horoscope for her to teach her high school English class?

"Sure," said Averil. "I'm pretty good at writing them, too. I write them from God's point of view, using his manual!"

Ten years before, a woman serving with OMF had met and introduced this teacher to Christ, but there had been little growth. Now God had given this teacher another opportunity to become alive in Christ. She took it and a flourishing working friendship began between the two teachers, Sally and Averil.

Sally was the only Christian high school teacher in a Central Thailand population of six million people. She knew to stand publicly for Christ would be costly. She was right. Over the next five years, it cost her a promotion, her marriage and her popularity. She desperately needed Averil's friendship as much as Averil needed hers. Together, they developed creative ideas to reach the education community. Sally's stand for Christ was spiritually contested, too. She was reluctant to remove the idol shelf from her home since the images were not her personal property. The absentee owner procrastinated about removing them. Averil pulled at the shelf. "It's very firmly fixed," she thought. "It will need some tools to remove it." A few days later, she went to visit again, but she discovered that Sally was in the hospital, suffering from concussion. The idol shelf had fallen on her head. Once home from the hospital, she called the owner: "Collect them immediately or I'm throwing them in the river." Such events made a deep impression on Sally's mother who eventually believed, as did Sally's children.

In 1989, the Bennetts' daughter, AnnaMarie, wrote to her Southland friends urging them to visit them in Thailand. She forgot to mention this to her parents. Just before Christmas, Alan and Averil had the surprise excitement, long known to AnnaMarie, that the then mayor of Gore and Mataura (in the Southland region of New Zealand) together with his wife and their four children were about to arrive at Bangkok airport. Sally arranged for both families to be on stage at the school on Christmas morning. Almost 4,000 students from the largest high school between Bangkok and Chiang Mai gathered to listen. The hastily rehearsed concert about the true meaning of Christmas was a resounding success.

The Gore (New Zealand) mayor and the Nakhon Sawan (Thailand) mayor were both owners of transport companies; they got to know one another, with far-reaching results for the gospel. An idea was born. Why not have teenagers from New Zealand come to share the good news of Christmas in the area's high schools? The idea then spurred other possibilities. Why not have English camps? Such camps were part of the state curriculum, but few teachers, even those who could speak English, had the ability to run the camps in such a way that students would register unless they were compelled under threat of failing their English exam. And so Sally and Averil developed the annual OMF GO teams composed of New Zealand Christian high school students aged 15 to 18 years old, to come for three weeks before Christmas.

The first GO Team camps and school assemblies were such a success that state schools and technical colleges booked the teams two years in advance. Inland Thai schools in the 1990s had neither Christian students nor teachers. At most, there might be one lonely Christian in a school and he or she often feared discrimination such that they would not admit to being a believer. There was no such thing as a youth group for Thai Christian teenagers. The arrival of high school teams from New Zealand changed all that as they modeled what Christian peer support looked like. Soon, reciprocal trips were made to New Zealand, with Thai students staying in the homes of GO team families and giving cultural concerts in their churches. Such interaction helped break down suspicion towards Christians among the Thai business community so that parents became willing for their young people to believe in Christ and be baptized. It also led to the formation of the Thai Christian Teachers Fellowship.

Sally longed to have a home built without spirit involvement and dedicated to the glory of God. A few years later, as her new home was built, it was apparent to the superstitious neighbors that no spirit ceremony had been arranged and no special incantations made around the central pillar. Disaster would strike for sure. When the GO team from New Zealand arrived in December, they divided into groups and stood on every floor of the new four-storey home. In unison they all read a formal prayer written by their leader, then the prayer was framed and hung up by the lintel. God has blessed the home and made it a place of amazing hospitality for Christian students and workers for over 20 years.

While the mayor's family from New Zealand was staying with the Bennetts that Christmas 1989, an eviction notice arrived without warning asking the family to leave immediately. It was December 31. In between evangelistic parties and celebrations, Alan and Averil scouted the city. On January 2, 1990, 11 utility vehicles driven by friends arrived to help the family move into a ramshackle and lopsided vacant building. The whole move was accomplished in a day as they all worked together. Meanwhile, the previously planned seasonal functions sailed on without a hitch. The L.I.F.E Center sign went up at the new location and the Bennetts' ministry resumed without missing a beat, at an even more convenient place for residential lay training (lasting from one weekend to two weeks) than the previous home.

Averil, as a previous lecturer, was given permission to hold extension classes from Bangkok Bible College to help pastors upgrade their training and credentials. At last, the Bennetts thought they could settle down into a long-term work.

Then a letter arrived from New Zealand. OMF's New Zealand Council had decided unanimously that Alan should become the next National Director there. Alan and Averil were unsure how to respond. It seemed counterproductive and premature for them to break off from what they were doing.

They were in the middle of a residential lay leaders retreat when they received the letter. That evening, the group discussed John 14-17. The Thai asked why foot washing was no longer practiced. Alan suggested they wash one another's feet right then and there. It was an emotionally intense time as a man who had never had leprosy knelt to bathe the deformed feet of one who had.

Halfway through the service, the door burst open and an angry woman came in. Averil calmed her down and led her to a seat. She was from a neighboring province and had driven 50 kilometers (30 miles) to complain to the Bennetts about her Christian husband's shortcomings. As she watched the foot washing, she began to weep. Eventually, she returned home committed to a difficult relationship for the sake of the Lord Jesus Christ who would also enable her to have peace and joy.

Somehow, that evening became a parable in action for Alan and Averil. They could submit to the New Zealand Council's decision even though it was bewildering to them. God would make a way for them and for the Thai believers. The Bennetts were able to hand the lay training program over to German colleague Ulrike Schnurle, who facilitated the construction of a permanent L.I.F.E. Center building. Though they did not know it at the time, the Bennetts would later return to this ministry for another 10 years.

However, before they could head to New Zealand, Alan and Averil were asked to delay for two years and go to Bangkok as Acting Area Director again. Making yet another sudden house move, the family squeezed into a small townhouse in Thailand's capital. It should have been only 20 minutes' drive from the OMF office, but it frequently took well over an hour due to the horrendous traffic and regular flooding. Sometimes, there were sudden changes in political power or political protests that made travel precarious. Some days Averil, going to lecture at Bangkok Bible College, or Alan when he was going to the OMF office or FEBC, spent hours traveling. The local newspaper claimed that Bangkok residents spent half their day traveling to and from work. It was easy to believe. The Bennett children noted their parents' frustration. "If this is so difficult, what are you going to do about it?" they asked.

Alan and Averil decided they must trust God for a way of escape, which meant finding a property close to the OMF office. Very few places were available. Nearby, there was only a private park and a complex that housed a nightclub, a brothel and a men's hostel. Not exactly a promising proposition for a family home.

Is anything too hard for the Lord? The answer to that rhetorical question had to be "No." At midnight on July 11, 1991 Averil drove along the lane beyond the OMF office. A couple of nightclub bellhops were nailing up a board that read, "For Rent." She paused and asked for details. The nightclub and accommodation were closing due to the AIDS scare at the time. The idea of living in such a place made Averil shiver.

At their wedding, Alan and Averil had been given a copy of *Daily Light,* a small book with a selection of Bible verses for each day of the year. The Bennetts had often used it to jot down dates when they had laid before the Lord a particular prayer request and to chart the answers. As Averil turned to *Daily Light* that July day, she read: "Have I not commanded you? Be strong and courageous" (Joshua 1:9). The nightclub property was such an awful prospect that she dared not even tell Alan about it. After years of the Thai church growing mainly among the outcasts of Thai society (such as leprosy sufferers), the church was finally becoming respectable in Thailand. A seedy nightclub did not seem to fit the desired profile for a productive ministry.

Even so, Averil went to meet the landowner, who was stunned at her interest in the property. His reaction was to make an insulting offer in order to get rid of her. *Daily Light* again: "We made our prayer unto God, and set a watch against them" (Nehemiah 4:9).

Averil enlisted prayer groups in New Zealand and consulted the four Bennett children. The two at university in New Zealand were excited. "We've been praying in the Christian Union for a brothel in Taiwan to burn down," they said. "How much more sensible to live in one instead!" The youngest child, at Faith Academy in the Philippines, wrote: "Go for it, Mum. We never were respectable, were we?"

Averil took a Thai staff member from the OMF office in Bangkok to look. He paled at the very thought and urged her to forget all about it. *Daily Light* once more encouraged her: "He staggered not at the promises of God through unbelief" (Romans 4:20). Is anything too hard for the Lord?

It was time for Averil to tell Alan about the possibility. Thankfully, he was delighted at the common sense of it all.

They went together to see the landowner. Over the next month, they bargained him down from 38,000 Thai baht (1,520 US dollars) to 8,000 (320 US dollars) baht rent per month. The nightclub reopened and the men's hostel was still busy, but by September 1 the Bennetts were living in the former brothel. They prayed their way around the rooms, plugged the peepholes between a bedroom and the hostel, removed all curtains from the sitting room to snuff out any ugly rumors about what they were doing and tackled the problem of the super-sized rats that even their intrepid Siamese cat slunk away from. They enjoyed plenty of humor as staff from other mission groups found their van doors briskly opened by the nightclub bellhops who then ushered them in to the Bennetts' home with professional aplomb. The bellhops also made sure that the Bennett girls were safe as they came and went; it was probably the safest they had ever felt in Thailand.

Early evenings were noisy as the men returned to the hostel above and beside the bedrooms. The thin plywood walls shook, and doorknobs on bolted doors were regularly tested. The Bennetts responded with the weapons of music and praise songs. Soon, regular tenants were calling Averil "Happy Mother."

One evening as they sat at dinner, first feet, then legs, then whole people appeared in their window, scaling down the metal grills outside. "Excuse us, but could you help us with our English homework from night school?" they asked. One young man looked familiar. Could it be Denchart? The girls stared. So did he. It was indeed Denchart. Years before, an old woman, Auntie Sword, almost destitute and disfigured by leprosy, had found a baby thrown out to die on a rubbish heap. She took him home and raised him for the Lord.

Denchart eventually turned his back on Auntie Sword, however. It so happened that at that time the Bennetts, who knew the family, went for a picnic in the temple grounds. They had long ago discovered that such places were good for meeting people, even for conducting a well-attended Sunday school class. On that day, they saw Denchart and were able to help him get to engineering school in Bangkok. He kept in touch for a while, even sending small sums of money back to Auntie Sword. Then he disappeared from sight.

Now, Denchart was standing in the Bennetts' dining room. The enormity of God keeping track of him in a city of 10 million really hit home. He stared in disbelief, then found himself wrapped in Alan's arms in a huge hug. English homework was forgotten as reunion became a party. Denchart shared for the first time with his friends from the hostel that he really did trust and love God—the Christian God. He started sending money again to Auntie Sword. Alan was able to help him get back on track. Today Denchart is a Christian lay leader with a true pastor's heart. The Bennetts' decision to dare to live in a former brothel was worth it.

All too soon, it was February 1993 and time for the family's eleventh relocation, this time back in New Zealand. Brydon and Carey Lois, at university in New Zealand, found a strategically placed rambling old villa. The owner had gone bankrupt in the building slump at the time, and was anxious to leave. By then, Alan and Averil fully trusted their children's judgment when it came to housing. After all, the family had proved they could live almost anywhere. It was time for another adventure for the advancement of the gospel. The whole family was ready for the challenge. Together.

22. A Misunderstanding—and God's Answer

Chang-Nam Son and his wife Sylvia, Koreans serving in Indonesia, started a small English club in 1992. Over time, it became a large student ministry named JOY Fellowship. In 1996, the Sons hoped to take a small group of Indonesian students to Korea to participate in Mission Korea, a large student mission conference.

One day in June 1996, Sarah, a Gajah Mada University student, said she had something urgent to talk to me about and came to the JOY office. I had no clue what she wanted to discuss.

Song Chang-Nam, Indonesia

After arriving, she began telling me about her father's concerns over her trip.

"Pak Son ("Pak" is an honorific term in Indonesian equivalent to "sir" or "Mr." in English), yesterday I discussed my plan to go to Korea with my father," Sarah said. "He asked me how I could finish my graduation thesis if I were to go to Korea during the summer. I realized that if I go, I will certainly lose time that I could use to write it. I think I have to give up going there this summer."

Sarah was one of three JOY students selected to participate in Mission Korea that August. When she first mentioned her difficulties, I thought it was ridiculous to give up such an opportunity. Gradually, I came to understand her position. I asked her who she thought should take her place. Immediately, Sarah recommended Opin.

Opin wanted to go to Korea more than anyone else. Not only that, but she was actually qualified to be selected. The students had organized a selection process to choose the three students who went to Korea. Opin had been ranked third out of five students. Sarah had been ranked second. However, in order to have a male student among the three, Wiwit, who had been ranked fourth, was chosen. Opin was disappointed.

While Sarah was still with me, I phoned Opin and told her that Sarah would not be able to go to Korea because of her thesis. Would Opin like to go instead? Opin responded enthusiastically: "Oh, yes!" she replied at once. After Sarah left the office, I thought the issue had been resolved. Actually, it was just the beginning.

Later, after a JOY leaders' meeting, I returned home and went to bed. As I was about to go to sleep, the phone rang. It was one of the JOY leaders calling. I knew he must have some urgent problem because it was so late, but I was puzzled because we had had plenty of time to discuss all the relevant issues during the leadership meeting just a short time before.

He sounded as if he must have something important to talk about, but he just kept talking about minor matters that were not pressing at all. After some time, when he had still not come to the point, I asked him directly why he called so late. Only then did he tell me the real reason: "Pak Son, Sarah actually does want to go to Korea."

I felt slightly confused. I told him about the discussion Sarah and I had that morning. "I know that only yesterday Sarah was wanting to go to Korea, but we met this morning, and now Opin will go instead," I told him. "You don't need to worry about Sarah. It's already quite late, so let us go to sleep and we can meet tomorrow."

I hung up the phone.

I was once again almost asleep when the phone rang once more. This time it was Dito, the president of JOY at the time. He wanted to discuss the same issue.

"Sarah actually does want to go to Korea," he insisted.

I explained again to him what Sarah and I had discussed. "There's been a miscommunication," he said several times before hanging up. By then, I was thoroughly confused. My first reaction was to think these two students should mind their own business.

I went back in my mind over the process of choosing who would go to Korea. It was the Indonesian students, not myself, who had decided. If I was the one to decide, I could be blamed for being too subjective or showing favoritism; so I told them to make the decision themselves. At the time, there was enough money to send three students, but I asked the students to pick five in case some additional donations came in. They would not be in a position to raise the money themselves. Private university tuition fees at the time were about 100 US dollars per semester, while the cost of going to Korea would be about 1,000 US dollars for each person. No student would turn down such an opportunity.

The students demonstrated a lot of maturity in establishing the criteria for selecting the five best candidates and ranking them one to five. Choosing the students to go was quite a challenge from among about 70 active members, any one of who would like such a scholarship. The only suggestion I made to them was that both male and female students should be represented.

The students chose three female students, who were all outstanding, and two male students. They were all able to work relatively well in English and they also had great leadership skills. So that both male and female students could be represented on the trip, Opin had to make way for a young man, Wiwit. I told the three students chosen to prepare their passports as soon as possible; there was not much time to spare to send the passports to the Korean Embassy in Jakarta and apply for visas to Korea.

All this had happened openly and by agreement. Consequently, the two late night phone calls were very perplexing. Then, suddenly, it came to me: maybe Sarah had said she could not go to Korea, not because of her thesis, but because she was upset and embarrassed by Opin's disappointment. If this were the case, then I had failed to understand what Sarah was saying in the context of Indonesian culture. In Indonesian culture there is something called *basa-basi*, which is a way of interacting with others such that people tend to be polite at the cost of being direct.

As I replayed the conversation between myself and Sarah in light of that cultural pattern, the pieces of the puzzle began falling into place. If Sarah had been talking in a *basa-basi* way when she came to see me, it just meant that she was extremely disturbed by Opin's misfortune. Opin, with higher scores, was not selected because there needed to be a male in the group, which was why Wiwit (with slightly lower scores) had been chosen. Opin must have shared her disappointment with her cell group. Thus, Sarah would find it difficult to be happy while Opin was so sad.

I realized that Sarah had come to me for some kind of confirmation. She talked about her father's concern, but that was not really what she wanted me to hear. She had hoped that

I would respond differently and say something like this: "What are you talking about? They voted for you, didn't they? As for the thesis, go to Korea, and if you work hard you can finish it when you come back."

The trouble was that I was an oblivious foreigner who was too foolish to read between the lines. I had not taken cultural differences into consideration. I merely took Sarah's words at face value, had quickly dropped Sarah and took Opin in her place. It must have hurt Sarah's feelings badly. When her friends heard about it, they had gathered up their courage and called me to explain Sarah's real intentions.

Finally, I realized why they had phoned so late at night and not waited to speak to me face to face. It was easier for them to indicate that I had erred this way. However, now I had a problem. It was too late to retract my decision and put Sarah back on the team. I could not break my word to Opin, but there were only funds enough for three places. Even if funds came in to take Sarah as a fourth member of the group, that would then make it difficult not to take the fifth, Martin, a young man who had scored close behind Wiwit.

What a muddle! Where would the funds for two more students come from? The more I thought about it, the more I despaired. I was quite tired and longed for some good sleep. I hoped in vain. I spent the rest of the night tossing and turning.

The next morning I opened my Bible to meditate on God's word. The verses for the day were Matthew 7:7-8: "Ask and it will be given to you; seek and you will find; knock and the door will be opened to you. For everyone who asks receives; he who seeks finds; and to him who knocks, the door will be opened." These verses gave me much encouragement. If God provided a sponsor, then I would be able to make up for my mistakes.

While I was praying, Professor Shin, who took over the Christian Club I attended at the National Tax College (NTC) in Korea, came to mind. In the past, he had been the person that God had sent to help me during my time of need at the NTC. I remembered that when I had met him during my home assignment in Korea, he had said if there was anything he could do to help my ministry in Indonesia to please call him.

Before I called him, I prayed to the Lord. "Lord, I am going to call Professor Shin. I won't tell him that I need this money. Please talk to him on my behalf so that he offers from his own initiative to sponsor Sarah and Martin so that they can go to Korea this summer."

After praying, I phoned Professor Shin. He was delighted to hear my voice.

"Mr. Son, where are you calling from?" he asked.

"From Indonesia. I am going to Korea in August,"
    I replied.

"For what?" he inquired.

"To participate in Mission Korea with some Indonesian
    students," I explained.

"I see," he said. "How much does it cost for one student
    to come to Korea?"

"It costs about 1,000 US dollars," I answered.

"Well then, I would like to donate 2,000 US dollars for
    two students," he said.

"Ah! Thank you so much!" I said.

After I hung up the phone, I shouted "Hallelujah!" The Lord had answered my prayer and provided for the students. The students went to the conference and returned with a greater awareness of global mission and a greater heart for student ministry. It was a happy ending, but also an important lesson in Indonesian culture for me.

Sarah later served as a full-time staff member for the JOY Fellowship after returning from Korea. Opin now teaches at a university, where Wiwit also works. Martin returned to his hometown to work.

23. A Huge Gift in Japan

Acquiring property and facilities can be a faith-building experience for any ministry. Such was the case when OMF's Japan Field offices sought to relocate to Tokyo in the 1990s. But the Lord was already at work preparing for a unique and joyful provision of space through a Japanese believer. The story behind the gift reveals God's power and loving care.

"We need to be completely unanimous that the Lord is leading us to move our offices to Tokyo," declared Bill Fearnehough at OMF 's Japan Field Conference, "or we should not attempt it. It is far too big a step to take otherwise. It could cause real tensions among us if we are not totally agreed, and then willing, for the huge challenges that will follow."

It was 1990, nearly 40 years after former China Inland Mission members, no longer able to work in China, had begun pioneering mission work in Japan. Administrative offices initially were established in northern Japan, close to where church-planting efforts were then focused. Now, however, four decades later, there was an increasing need to be based in Tokyo, Japan's capital city some 550 miles further south.

Obstacles to such a move were many. Land and suitable property in Tokyo were extremely expensive, well beyond the total field budget for several years combined. Registration rules to develop a site were very complex, and building regulations to meet standards to withstand earthquake and fire were also difficult and expensive to satisfy.

After much prayer and discussion, everybody was invited to close their eyes. Those who were against a move should raise their hands. Bill Fearnehough fully expected several hands to go up. None did. The decision was made.

Early searches for property in Tokyo and the surrounding area proved fruitless. Property was either too far out, requiring long journeys to reach the city center and the travel hubs, or astronomically expensive. At that time, OMF already had one small property in Tokyo, but selling it would only raise a fraction of what would be needed.

Had the team mistaken God's guidance? It was a faith-stretching time. Friends around the world prayed.

Then one day came some exciting and unexpected news. A woman in Ichikawa, Mrs. Ukiya, was offering a large plot of land to OMF. Ichikawa is a satellite city of Tokyo, on its eastern side. From there, subway connections to central Tokyo take only 20 minutes and it is conveniently located between the international and domestic airports. The site was valued at approximately 7 million US dollars. Moreover, there was already a church meeting on one part of the site, although it did not yet have official registration. Mrs. Ukiya was especially keen for OMF to take over the pastoral care of the church and ensure its future.

Behind this gift lay a remarkable story. Mrs. Ukiya had twice in earlier life encountered the Christian faith. As a young child, she had heard stories of Jesus from an English missionary. Years later, as a young mother, she started attending church and was baptized in 1946. However, she later said, she had no understanding of salvation through the Lord Jesus. Her husband's family was horrified that she had been baptized as a Christian. Under strong pressure from them, she was won over to embrace the traditional religion the family had followed for generations.

In 1965, her only son, Tojiro, already at age 23 a famous racing driver, was killed in an accident while trying to avoid two people who had wandered on to the track. Mrs. Ukiya's grief led to her being overwhelmed by feelings of guilt and to a collapse in her health. Ten years later, in 1975, Mrs. Ukiya's husband died. Shortly afterwards, her house burned down. In absolute despair as she watched the flames consuming her home, she first called out to the whole pantheon of gods she could think of, and then to the Christian God. Alongside her was her daughter, Asae, who had been baptized as a Christian some years before while an overseas student in New York. As Asae prayed, Mrs. Ukiya called out to the God she did not really know. Mrs. Ukiya heard a voice that she knew at once to be the voice of the Lord Jesus. He reassured her that her prayers were answered, that nobody would be hurt and that he was bringing her forgiveness and new life.

Next to the burned down house were two of Tojiro's racing cars. He had already become a racing legend before his death; afterwards people came to see his cars and trophies. Amazingly, the cars and trophies were unharmed by the fire. Soon after, Mrs. Ukiya built a new home and a complete display room for the precious cars, with a hall above it for Christian worship. Just after the fire, Asae had written along the fence at the front of their property a Bible text: "Come unto me all you who are weary and burdened, and I will give you rest" (Matthew 11:28). As people came to see Tojiro's cars or inquire about the verse, Mrs. Ukiya and her daughter shared the gospel tirelessly with them all, often insisting that if anyone wanted to see the cars they must first attend a service. Before long, the cars were moved to another building and the former display area, along with the hall above it, were devoted to Christian worship, evangelism and training.

Neither Mrs. Ukiya nor Asae knew anything about running a church, but a number of gifted and experienced preachers visited regularly, and so the Chapel of Adoration congregation became firmly established. Among those coming to faith were members of "Toji's Club," which had been set up initially at the request of several car magazines. Over the years, some of the club members' conversions led to the transformation of complete families in different parts of Japan and produced several pastors. However, there was a problem. The Ukiyas had not been able to gain religious registration with the government. They were anxious to ensure the long-term future of the church, but that would be difficult if the church were not registered. In particular, without religious registration, the church and the land on which it stood would be heavily taxed when Mrs. Ukiya died.

One Sunday in late 1991, Warren Payne, a New Zealand member of OMF, officiated at a wedding, standing in for a Japanese Christian leader who found himself double-booked that day. Subsequently, Warren was invited to preach at the church some weeks later. In the congregation that Sunday was Koichi Ohtawa, the East Asian Regional Secretary of the International Fellowship of Evangelical Students, and a member of the OMF Japan Home Council. He was also, amazingly, a childhood friend of Tojiro, and thus, in the tender providence of God, this relationship led to Mrs. Ukiya's encounter with

OMF leaders and to her offering her land to meet OMF's need. OMF was in a position to facilitate the registration of the chapel and appoint a pastor, thus relieving the burden on Mrs. Ukiya's heart. How beautifully the Lord had answered the prayers of so many!

So, in 1992 the long and complicated process of transferring the site into OMF's hands began. The Ukiyas retained one portion of the land for their own new home. The church and the museum with Tojiri's cars were also left on the site. In order to meet various legal requirements, development could not begin for several more years.

By the time everything was in place to start building, Japan was in a recession. Consequently, the construction company did the work at a lower cost than would have been the case earlier. As the main structure reached completion, teams of volunteers came from nine different countries to work on interior. The teams' work saved much money; it also often significantly changed the lives of team members themselves and was a wonderful opportunity for witness as local tradesmen and people who interpreted for the visitors, observed the way the Christians worked so well together.

At long last, on September 27, 1999, a triumphant dedication and thanksgiving celebration marked the formal opening of two new three-storey buildings. One building houses OMF's Field and Home Council offices and an auditorium. The other has four apartments for permanent staff, guest rooms and other facilities. God had provided "more than all we ask or imagine" (Ephesians 3:20).

Mrs. Ukiya did not live to see the completion of the building, though she saw its beginning. She died in February 1999, content that so much that was dear to her, including the

Chapel of Adoration and Tojiri's museum, were secured for the future. She also died content that her gift of land was being put to such good use in the Lord's service. Most of all, she died trusting in the Lord Jesus.

The Chapel of Adoration has grown steadily, with men and women coming to faith and growing in the Lord. Attendees of the Field Conference in 1990 had prayed for the Lord to provide an office building. The Lord had not only answered that prayer—but had thrown in a vibrant church for good measure.

OMF Office, Tokyo, Japan

24. Loved into the Kingdom

> Sin Ee Teo, from Singapore, serves in Taiwan. Most Asian
> cultures expect a high level of family loyalty. Children, even
> as adults, might be expected to support their parents and
> take into account their parents' wishes for how they should
> live. Such demonstrations of loyalty can contribute to social
> stability, but also present some challenges, especially when
> the parents of a Christian are not yet believers.

Sin Ee Teo grew up as an only child in a Mandarin-speaking
family in Singapore. Like many Asian parents, hers had a fixed
idea of how she should live her life: study hard, go to university,
get a good job and live a comfortable life. They had Sin Ee's
interests at heart, but they also made it difficult for her to make
her own choices. When Sin Ee accepted a scholarship to study
economics at Cambridge University in England, she thought,
"Finally I'm free from my parents' control! They can't tell me
what to do or not do anymore!"

Increasingly, Sin Ee felt that she and her parents had little
in common. For example, she was more comfortable speaking
English, while her parents spoke Mandarin in the home. It
was difficult to have a deep conversation with them due to the
language, culture and generation gaps. Despite living at home
again after completing her studies, she felt distant from them.

The problem was made worse during Sin Ee's second year
at university when she came to know Jesus personally. Philip
Yancey's book, *The Jesus I Never Knew*, opened her eyes to
the radical nature of Jesus and the gospel. Although this was
not Sin Ee's first encounter with Christian teaching, it had
never especially interested her before. Her parents had no
religious convictions, although when she was a small child

they had enrolled her at a kindergarten run by Zion Bible Presbyterian Church because it was a good school. What would they say now?

Her mother had always assured her, "Once you are 21, you can choose your own religion. Just don't become a fanatic." Consequently, Sin Ee thought they would have no problems when she told them she had decided to follow Jesus. However, to her great surprise her father reacted strongly, starting to cry. It was the first time she had ever seen him shed tears. Perhaps he thought he was losing his only child to God and the church.

After university, Sin Ee enjoyed two well-paid jobs in succession. The first was at a venture capital firm; then she worked for a telecommunications company. Initially, she was content with a safe, comfortable and secure life. Soon, though, she felt God calling her in a different direction: she felt that she should attend Singapore Bible College. Her mother was surprisingly relaxed about it, but her father objected strongly. "We're not a rich family," he said. "How would you support yourself? Why can't you do this when you have made more money?" To Sin Ee, it felt like another guilt trip.

After finishing Bible college, Sin Ee decided to spend a year in Taiwan as a missionary. Her father had expected her to return to her old job because, although she had taken unpaid leave, she had continued to receive bonuses and some income from the telecommunications firm (probably thanks to a godly supervisor). By the grace of God, Sin Ee's parents allowed her to make such a drastic career change. This change in posture (especially her father's) was all the more surprising because in her home culture even adult children may expect to need parental approval of significant decisions. The answer can often be "No."

Sin Ee went to Taiwan as an Associate with OMF for one year. At the orientation course about a month before she was to leave, Sin Ee was moved to tears as she listened to OMF General Director Patrick Fung's testimony. Patrick's father, like Sin Ee's, was unhappy when Patrick and Jennie left well-paid medical jobs to become missionaries; he feared they would not have enough money. However, Patrick testified to the way the Lord had provided faithfully for them as a family ever since. Sin Ee was challenged to trust that God would be faithful to her family, too, even though her parents were not believers.

The day before she left, Daniel Wong, the National Director of OMF Singapore, visited the home. Sin Ee's father poured out all his fears, for Sin Ee and for himself and her mother. It was the second time she ever saw him cry. Years later, her mother explained why her father was so upset. Sin Ee had the privilege of receiving a scholarship to study at the prestigious Cambridge University and then a well-paid job, but she seemed to be throwing it all away. By contrast, her father had grown up in a poor family. His father died when he was still very young, and there was no money for him to go to university. He had always lived frugally and knew too well the pain of being poor. How could he then accept that Sin Ee was going to depend on God's provision, with no secure income?

Arriving in Taiwan, Sin Ee was assigned to a church-planting team in Hengchun, a sleepy seaside town of 30,000. She joined teammates Christine Dillon and Randy and Janet Adams. Christine encouraged Sin Ee to be sure to write to her parents every week, but because "my Chinese script was terrible, Dad would send each letter back with corrections marked in red ink." Sin Ee tried to explain to her colleagues that this was his way of expressing love, wanting her to improve her skill and be the best at what she did.

After her year in Taiwan, Sin Ee returned to Singapore convinced that God wanted her to serve in Taiwan long term, but she struggled with how this could fit with her duties to her parents. Even her pastor said, "What about your parents? You are an only child and they are not believers. Is this the best witness to them?" Sin Ee cried out to God: "I don't know what will happen but I trust your sovereignty. I know that you love my parents more than I do. You are a faithful God and you will provide for them. Help me to take this step of faith".

God answered that prayer in wonderful ways. First, OMF Singapore allows missionaries to designate a portion of their budget for parents; it is not a large sum, but it indicates cultural sensitivity. Then, OMF Singapore staff members visit overseas workers' parents and families twice each year at festivals when it is customary for families to gather together. If there are special needs, they visit more often, taking on, as it were, the responsibilities of the absent child. Once a year, all parents are invited to a Family Appreciation Lunch. Sin Ee's father even received a card from the General Director, wishing him well, while he was in the hospital. The OMF family showed care and Sin Ee's parents were touched.

Sin Ee also had some good friends, Sin Cheng and his wife Shireen, who visited Sin Ee's parents regularly. Mr. Teo grew fond of them and their young children. Sin Cheng tried to encourage the Teos to attend church, but they resisted. Then Sin Cheng had the idea of asking his own mother to invite them to some special events held in Mandarin. It would be harder for the Teos to decline an invitation from someone of their own age.

Soon after, Sin Ee's father faced major surgery that was expected to last five hours or more. He was anxious and fearful.

Sin Cheng brought an oncologist from the church to visit Mr. Teo. Dr. Wong not only gave medical advice and reassurance, but also gently shared the gospel with him: "Please put your trust in the Lord!" he implored. "He loves you and can give you peace of heart. He is longing to bring you forgiveness and a new life!" As the Holy Spirit used those words, Mr. Teo responded to Christ, asking for forgiveness for being such a proud and self-sufficient man.

Sin Ee was able to fly home for two weeks when her father had his surgery in November 2010. Friends from church and from OMF Singapore visited him in the hospital and encouraged him in his new-found faith. As Sin Ee left Singapore to return to Taiwan, she realized that the Lord had done something special in her, too. "Waving goodbye to Dad, I realized that the unfamiliar feeling in my chest was the first time I felt sad rather than guilty at leaving my loved ones behind," she recalled. "Perhaps this is the most difficult or painful part of the missionary journey when our parents start to age and fall sick. After all, we are the ones who enjoy the many blessings of serving God, even though others may see it as a sacrifice; but our parents, through no fault or choice of their own, have to pay the price of our absence."

Mr. Teo recovered well and soon both he and his wife attended church regularly. Sin Ee's mother joined a Bible study group and a seekers' group "because she wanted to know 'what exactly it is that my daughter believes,'" said Sin Ee. Her father also joined a Bible study group, to the surprise of her mother. "Your Dad is so diligent," Sin Ee's mom told her one day. "He's reading the Bible and praying every day."

A year later, Sin Ee flew home again, this time for her parents' baptism. Mr. Teo testified at the service, saying "I am so grateful that God pardoned my sins. He had mercy on me. I want to thank the brothers and sisters in church who visited me in hospital," He clutched a hand to his chest as tears ran down his face. "I'm so touched by their care and concern," he sobbed.

Now Sin Ee's parents attend a monthly prayer meeting for OMF Taiwan and are eager to use their remaining years to serve the Lord. Sin Ee believes God took her to Taiwan so that her parents would be reached for Christ. "First I learned to share the gospel in Mandarin. Second, working with the elderly helped me understand better the traditional Chinese worldview. Third I had access to many good books and other resources in Mandarin, which I was able to send home for my parents. God used these to narrow the gap between my parents and myself. Lastly, through my leaving home, many people at church and in OMF prayed for my parents and demonstrated constant love and care."

"I know my parents were loved into the kingdom!"

25. Typhoon Blessing

Sometimes our cries to the Lord for his provision are not related to big things like land or large sums of money, but for something as basic as friends in an unfamiliar place. For Wendy Marshall from Australia, a broken-down van and a typhoon compounded her feelings of loneliness—until God provided. Wendy shares her story here.

My hands were full of wet towels. Water dripped into the buckets under the windows. A typhoon raged outside and my kitchen window had water running down the inside. "How will I get my son to kindergarten tomorrow?" I began to panic. I would have quit right there if I knew what the next few days would bring.

We were new to Tokyo. Just four weeks earlier, we had moved back to Japan from Australia with our three young sons. This sprawling metropolis has more people in it than our entire home country. We came so my husband could begin his new job at the international school, the Christian Academy in Japan. The phrase "lonely in a crowd" described us perfectly. We were pressed on all sides by millions of people but knew almost none of them.

Every morning, as my husband left for work, the reality of the sole care of two lively boys and a baby who smacked me in the face. I had no friends or family nearby to help in the task. My heart's desperate cry to the Lord was for friends. I longed to walk through the streets and see someone familiar. I yearned to say, "Hey! Great to see you again! What have you been doing?" During the day I felt completely cut off. I worried about what would happen if something went wrong. Whom could I call for help?

I knew making Japanese friends was not going to be easy. We previously lived on Japan's northern island of Hokkaido. Through this, we learned that Japanese are often quite reserved. It can take many months to get past basic greetings. They seem especially shy of foreigners. At least I could speak some Japanese.

We enrolled our son at the local kindergarten for several reasons. One factor was that I wanted to make friends. Our new home was another factor. The yard was "smaller than a cat's forehead," as the Japanese would say. Most mornings our energetic six-year-old began to bounce off the walls by 9:30. I could not send him out to play in our yard, however, and our local parks were very small. In contrast, the kindergarten had a large playground, trees to climb and lots of playground equipment: plenty of room to run off all that excess energy bottled up inside him. It seemed like a good idea … until the van broke down and it started raining.

We had not had time to go shopping for a car, but someone loaned us an old van until we could get our own wheels; I was so thankful. Three young children seriously inhibited our mobility on foot or bikes, and the train station was not close enough to be of any help. The van was our escape route.

The van unexpectedly refused to start just two days before our son's first day of kindergarten. We called the roadside service. After the mechanic examined it, he gave a report that would threaten my sanity in the days that followed: "Your car could blow up at any moment. Actually, it is too old to fix. You need to throw it away and get a new one." He drove away. What had been our lifeline for transporting our three boys suddenly became a lump of junk in our driveway.

The next evening the typhoon hit, and our house leaked. Hence all the wet towels and buckets. I called the only family we knew in our local area, the family who had loaned the van.

"Is there any way you can help me? I need to get to kindergarten tomorrow."

"We are so sorry," came the reply, "but there really is not anything we can do. We're sorry about the van we lent you. We'll get it towed away as soon as we can. Good luck for tomorrow."

I went to bed that night with no idea how I would get us all to kindergarten and back the next morning. I hoped desperately the rain would stop. It did not.

Monday morning dawned all too soon. The rain was still pouring down and the wind blowing strongly. After the frantic preparation common to young families getting everybody ready in the morning, the boys and I struggled out the front door. The umbrella barely covered the hefty three-month old on my back. The other two boys shared the only other umbrella we owned. Our elderly neighbors across the road spotted us as we trundled along the road. Out of pity they gave us a large one of theirs, freeing the older boys to walk separately. The wind whipped our legs as we struggled on. Douglas, our two-year-old, enjoyed the first 10 minutes of our walk and then the whining began.

"Don't go so fast, Mommy!"

"Why can't I splash in that puddle?"

"I want to stop!"

"Why can't we sit down?"

If the weather did not get me down, the relentless verbal onslaught was going to. He soon tired of the umbrella and did not appreciate my constant urging him onwards. He wanted to stop and watch the rivers of water dashing across our path and ponder the drops cascading off the rooftops. These sights were far more inviting to him than the sanctuary of home. I struggled just to stay upright with my precious but increasingly heavy bundle on my back. Between kindergarten and home the elevated awning of a car salesroom offered temporary shelter. Ignoring the curious stares of onlookers, we paused there out of the relentless wetness.

However, my baby needed to nurse, so we could not rest there long. Douglas abandoned the struggle to keep his umbrella upright. It was not much help anyway. The rain slanted in under the umbrellas as if they were not there. My baby, though heavy, was not quite big enough for my hard-framed carrier. He slipped sideways and began to cry. We must have made a pitiful sight. Soaked, whining and crying, we plodded along the last stretch of our walk. By the time we staggered up our driveway past the useless van into our house, we were exhausted, hungry and sopping wet. We stripped off just inside the front door and everything went straight in the wash. I tipped half a cup of water out of Douglas' rain boots before we raided the kitchen.

It seemed no time at all before we had to pull our wet shoes back on and trudge back again to pick up our oldest son for lunch. We walked nearly two and a half miles that day, but the rain was not over yet. It was only just beginning.

The next morning we woke again to the relentless and increasingly familiar sound of rain drumming on our windows. Yesterday's saga was about to be repeated. Thankfully, my husband had been able to buy me a raincoat and a baby-carriage cover. This time it was a big relief not to have to control an umbrella or carry the baby on my back. This made my task less physically exhausting. Now the biggest obstacle to overcome was Douglas' reluctance to cooperate in this crazy scheme.

This continued all week. By Thursday lunchtime the typhoon had intensified and the winds were even stronger. Thoughts of escape from this ordeal had fled: in their place was just an intense focus on simply making it through the next trip. As I began to gather the damp raincoats and rain boots together yet again to collect our son, the phone rang.

"Moshi, moshi," (the traditional Japanese greeting) I said.

"Hello, this is Mrs. Tarukado," said the woman on the other end of the line. "My son is in your son's kindergarten class. Isn't the weather terrible?"

"I can't disagree with that," I thought.

"We live very close to you. Would you be interested in a lift in my car to kindergarten to pick them up?"

"Would I be interested?!"

During that short trip to kindergarten and back I lost count of how many times I said "Arigato," or, "Thank you," to my new friend. I also praised my loving Heavenly Father as I watched with joy another of his amazing plans unfold.

Never could I have imagined that the story would pan out like this. The Lord used a broken-down old van and a typhoon to bring me my first new friend in Tokyo.

God's Faithfulness Through the Fire

The Lord Jesus Christ frequently taught his disciples that following him would bring suffering as well as great blessing. He, of course, led the way, suffering the agony of death by crucifixion as he bore the sins of humanity. Yet that death was not a waste: it opened the gates of heaven to all who trust in him. The faithfulness of our Savior, God the Son, flows from the very nature of the Triune God. Because God is faithful and strong, he is able to redeem and transform suffering into something beautiful, something that leads to eternal gain.

Ever since Pentecost, the story of the church has been one of both blessing and suffering. Some suffering is simply part of the fallen human condition. Other suffering, however, comes as a result of being a follower of Christ.

Over the years, workers with CIM and OMF experienced this truth many times. In the early years especially, many missionaries died prematurely (in the world's eyes) from ailments such as typhus, tuberculosis, septic wounds or cholera, to name a few. Many women died in childbirth, often far from even the most rudimentary medical help. Hundreds of babies and small children were buried. Yet, even as many of these people died, their dying testimony was marked by peace in the will of God, steadfast love for the people to whom they had gone in order to share the gospel, thankfulness that they had gone to this land, and longing for the day when there would be a great harvest of souls for the glory of God.

William S. Fleming, first CIM martyr

The first martyr among the CIM membership was William Fleming, who was killed along with local Chinese Christian Pan Xiushan in Guizhou Province in 1898.

Since then, there have been others who have lost their lives specifically because of hostility to the gospel where CIM and then OMF members have served. Others have died at the hands of robbers, or through accidents. Some have suffered life-changing illnesses that they might not have contracted in their own homeland.

Has this been a reckless and irresponsible waste of life or health? No! Most people who leave homes and families for the sake of the gospel and in obedience to Christ find it costly. Sometimes their service leads them through experiences they never could have expected and certainly would not have chosen. Yet, throughout East Asia today there are communities of God's people whose life in Christ is the fruit of that costly service. God has been faithful to create new spiritual life from the suffering and sacrifice of his people.

The stories that follow tell of some of those who have experienced great trials, yet still trusted in the wisdom and faithfulness of the Lord.

26. The Boxer Rebellion of 1900

Church history reminds us that from just after Pentecost until the present there have always been some followers of Jesus who have been called to lay down their lives in martyrdom. Sometimes, persecution has led to the death of many Christians at the same time. The year 1900 was such a period for the church in China. During a few blood-soaked months, it is estimated that nearly 50,000 (both

Boxer Rebellion martyrs' plaque

Martyrs' graves

Protestant and Roman Catholic) Christians were killed for their faith. An unknown number of Roman Catholic priests, nuns and lay religious people died. Alongside them, 188 Protestant missionaries and missionary children were also murdered. Among them were 58 adults and 21 children of the China Inland Mission.

Far away in Switzerland Hudson Taylor and his beloved second wife, Jennie, were convalescing in a quiet and beautiful mountain village. After 35 years of leading the CIM, Hudson Taylor had recently suffered a complete physical and mental breakdown while on a lengthy speaking tour of Australia and the United States. He had struggled with serious illness for several years, but this was the worst of all. Jennie had brought him back to London initially, but fearful that there he would try to immerse himself once more in constant correspondence and decision-making, she took him to Switzerland where once before his health had been restored.

It was early June 1900. For several years, conditions in China had become increasingly unsettled. Following China's defeat in the First Sino-Japanese War (1894-1895), both Korea (China's most important tribute-sending nation) and Taiwan (Chinese territory) had been annexed by Japan. In addition, Western powers were becoming increasingly assertive within China's borders.

In Shandong Province, Germany controlled many of the railways, factories and coalmines. In building railways they were often insensitive to Chinese protests and destroyed anything that stood in the way, including ancestral graveyards. Other European powers were equally exploitative, becoming rich while most Chinese languished in poverty. It is not surprising that a sense of collective humiliation and grievance steadily built up among China's populace. To growing numbers of Chinese, it seemed obvious that foreigners were the cause of almost all of their troubles.

At the same time, the reigning Qing Dynasty (1644-1912) was mired in corruption. Within the imperial family, the power-hungry Dowager Empress Cixi had pushed her emperor son aside and was the de facto ruler of China. Cruel and unpredictable, the dowager had little concern for most of her subjects, except as the source of her own wealth and position. She was ruthless with anyone who stood in her way, and increasingly paranoid about plots to overthrow her.

Many of those plots originated from a secret society that Westerners came to call the Boxers, due to their reputed martial arts ability. The Boxers were fanatically nationalistic, and vowed to destroy or expel every "foreign devil" from Chinese soil. In addition, they hated Chinese Christians, seeing them as under the influence of Westerners and no longer loyal Chinese.

In recent years, China had suffered an ongoing drought, which caused widespread famine and death. The Boxers blamed the Christians, saying that they had angered the traditional gods and disrupted ancient Confucian social patterns and customs, including proper respect for the ancestors. The drought was the gods' way of showing their anger. Desperately needed rain would not come until the Christians were destroyed. To the many Chinese who were illiterate, superstitious and suffering at the time, the Boxers' explanation sounded plausible.

It was a volatile mix. There were sporadic attacks on foreigners for several years, with property destroyed or people beaten, but in 1900 the situation exploded. In Beijing, Boxers assassinated the German ambassador as he complained to the authorities about the growing number of attacks on Europeans.

Hundreds of Europeans and also of Chinese Christians took refuge in the British legation. The siege lasted for 55 days as the Boxers continued to whip the public into a frenzy. The Western powers' response was to send in troops. A Western coalition force of more than 2,000 soldiers was sent to quell the rebellion and deal harshly with its perpetrators.

The Boxers were already emboldened and hunting down foreigners and Christians to kill or harm, but when news came that foreign troops were on the way, they went to the Dowager Empress and demanded that she defend Chinese sovereignty. Thinking that appeasing the Boxers would protect herself, the Dowager Empress signed a decree on June 18, 1900 that all foreigners should be killed and all property seized. She ordered that this decree should be conveyed by telegraph to every part of China.

Horrified at this instruction, one brave official changed the wording of the decree that went to many parts of the Empire from "kill all foreigners" to "protect all foreigners." He paid with his life when he was found out. His act, however, probably saved the lives of many foreigners who were able to escape to the coast before the message was corrected.

The Boxers wasted little time. They now claimed imperial authority and insisted that all local officials and administrators obey the edict on pain of death. Their terror was most deeply felt in China's three northern provinces. Many Chinese had already been won over by the Boxers' propaganda there. Over the next three months, not only larger numbers of national Christians and missionaries, but also other foreigners (for whom no reliable statistics were gathered) lost their lives. China's pent-up anger and resentment exploded into dreadful violence.

As news began to trickle across the world, Jennie Taylor at first tried to shield her husband from it. In his fragile state, how could he bear it? But as the telegrams started pouring in, with news of one atrocity after another, of one dearly loved colleague after another tortured and killed, of Chinese brothers and sisters in Christ being martyred because they stood firm in their faith, Jennie could hide it from him no longer. The pain of so much suffering in his beloved China was devastating. How could he be so far away when he was so needed among his people? Yet the Lord had removed him from the scene, and all he could do was absorb one blow after another. "I cannot read; I cannot think; I cannot even pray; but I can trust," he told Jennie.

By the time the worst of the news came to them in August, Hudson Taylor was so weak that he could only walk across the room with Jennie's help. He longed to be back in China, but his daughter-in-law Geraldine, who had joined Hudson and Jennie to help care for him, gently insisted that it would not be possible for him to return. This letting go was yet another deep bereavement for him, and he struggled with it. Finally, with acceptance came the realization that back in China the CIM urgently needed a new General Director. Hudson sent a telegram to Shanghai appointing Dixon Hoste as Acting General Director. Hudson had done that most difficult of things for a pioneer: hand over the baton of leadership to another. The CIM was no longer his personal responsibility. It had always been God's, first and foremost, but Hudson Taylor had driven himself relentlessly for 35 years, almost as if the Mission could not survive without him. Now his own total weakness and the terrible events in China meant that he must learn to sit on the sidelines and simply trust God in a way different than ever before.

Back in China, the international army reached Peking on August 14 and lifted the siege. The Dowager Empress and her court fled, and the Emperor was reinstated. He was more open to Western influence, which he saw as important for China's modernization. Gradually, the tide turned. The rabid hatred of foreigners slowly subsided, and the Boxers lost their influence. By the end of the year, there were no more killings, but it took far longer for wounds to heal.

The CIM headquarters in Shanghai had gathered information throughout the crisis, passing on news by cable to all the home offices. As the eyewitness accounts piled up, together with last deeply moving letters from missionaries aware that the Boxers were at hand and intending to execute them, the courage and faith of those who died became increasingly clear. Many of the letters spoke of the joy that would soon be theirs as they saw their Savior face to face. Many expressed the privilege it had been to be in China, and their joy at being "counted worthy" of laying down their lives for Christ's sake. Accounts also recorded the courage of many Chinese believers, some of whom gave their lives trying to protect their missionary friends. The stories of the CIM missionaries who died inspired many men and women to take their place in taking the gospel to China. In the years that followed, there were also many Chinese who professed faith who said they had first been drawn to Christ while watching how Christians died so bravely in that dreadful summer of 1900. The Lord brought something precious out of trauma and costly sacrifice.

There were many foreigners, including many CIM personnel, who survived; but only after great suffering along the way. For example, Archibald and Flora Glover, together with their two small children and a single female missionary, endured two months of almost unbelievable hardship before reaching the safety of Shanghai. They were beaten, stripped, threatened with death repeatedly, robbed, betrayed and starved.

Flora arrived in Shanghai only to die within weeks as a direct result of their experiences. Many others had similar stories of intense suffering and yet the Lord's merciful deliverance on many occasions. Some had narrowly escaped death by leaving their places of ministry for some last-minute reason, while those who remained were executed. It took huge courage for survivors to go back to their stations as soon as the rebellion had spent itself. Their testimonies were that God had spared them for that purpose, and that the people still needed to hear about the Lord.

The Western powers demanded massive financial reparations from the Chinese government, in recognition of so many people killed or wounded, and of so many buildings and so much property having been destroyed. What should the CIM do? Would this be the means by which churches, schools and homes could be rebuilt?

Back in Switzerland, as Hudson Taylor and Jennie received news of that demand, they knew that the CIM had suffered as much as any foreign organization in terms of loss of lives and property. Yet as they prayed, they knew that it was not right for them to exact such crippling sums. What had happened had occurred within the sovereign purposes of God. He was still sovereign over the affairs of his world. If the Lord Jesus had died for us, and the Father exacted no revenge, then the Mission would follow the same sacrificial path. No payments, to the Mission or to CIM individuals, would be accepted. Later this policy was to bear extraordinary fruit as Chinese were confronted with love that could forgive, and the deliberate refusal to exact revenge. It became a powerful sign of the gospel.

Hudson Taylor did not expect to go back to China ever again, much as he longed to do so. He and Jennie would make a permanent home in Switzerland. However, after a few short but serene years together, Jennie died in 1904 from cancer. The following year, frail but better than he had been for several years, Hudson Taylor's wish to return to China was granted. His son Howard and daughter-in-law Geraldine took him back, tenderly caring for him all along the way. For several wonderful weeks he revisited places especially dear to him, including the place where Maria, his first wife, and four of their children lay buried. At the end of one particularly precious day of glad reunions, he went to rest for a while. Instead, he gently went into his Lord's presence. His earthly journey was complete. Fittingly, this servant of God whose heart was in China could be buried there.

27. For Love of Children

Children have always been especially vulnerable to illness. Even today there are places in the world where child and infant mortality rates are distressingly high. In the nineteenth century, both Chinese children and missionary children died in large numbers, victims to many diseases that are readily curable today.

Jeanie Lawson stood by yet another small grave and wept. It was late 1899. Over the previous eight years, she had borne five children, all of whom had died in infancy. Was this the price she must pay for obeying God's call and going to China?

It was not that Jeanie was unfamiliar with infant deaths. Back home in the burgeoning, dirty cities of Great Britain, the mortality rate was also high. China was neither better nor worse in that respect. Yet Jeanie yearned for a living child. Was it too much to ask the Lord to grant her just one? She thought of Hannah in the Old Testament, who had also cried to the Lord for a child; God gave her Samuel. Jeanie was not barren, as Hannah had been, but still she had no child to hold in her arms.

Jeanie's husband Dugald was also sad, but did not share the depths of Jeanie's grief. For him, the thing that mattered above all else was reaching Chinese with the gospel. He was convinced that the Lord's return was imminent and that not a moment could be spared from pleading with people to trust in Christ. Jeanie was also committed to sharing the gospel wherever she could and to teaching women and children who came to faith. Yet the hole in her heart would not heal and by the time she buried her fifth child, her grief overshadowed everything.

A few months later, Jeanie could no longer cope. A letter from Shanghai suggested that she go there for medical help. The CIM headquarters there could provide a safe place for her to stay and there were good doctors who might be able to bring healing to her, both body and mind. In May 1900, she went.

Dugald stayed behind, feeling he could not leave his post just then, but would follow when he could. Suddenly, one June day he sensed the Lord's prompting that he must leave at once, sooner than planned. The prompting was confirmed by a telegram urging him to join Jeanie immediately. He set off for Shanghai, with part of his journey by train. It proved to be the last train along that track. The next day, the Boxer rebels destroyed that stretch of railway line. Had Dugald set off a single day later he would have been unable to reach Shanghai. He would almost certainly have been murdered. Those colleagues who were still in the town where the Lawsons had been working were among those who lost their lives at the hands of the Boxers. Jeanie's illness and grief had become the means by which God spared their lives.

They returned to Scotland for a brief period of recuperation. It had been there, in 1886, that they separately had responded to the CIM's call for 100 new workers during the following year. At that time the CIM membership was entirely British. Had it been faith or madness to expect the Lord to provide so many in so short a time from so small a country? Yet, having identified at least 50 more places where the Mission longed to start work, and on the principle of a minimum of two people for each place, it was truly a prayer of faith. Dugald and Jeanie were among those who answered the call. By the end of 1887, the prayer of faith had been transformed into a prayer of glad thanksgiving: 100 men and women had responded to the call for more workers.

Both Dugald and Jeanie grew up in poor families living along the banks of the Clyde River near Glasgow. At that time, Glasgow was one of the major ship building centers of the world, and nurtured a great awareness of the many countries to which those ships traveled. Growing up, Dugald and Jeanie had watched the proud sailing ships, and then the early steamships, moving back and forth along the river. They were fascinated by the tea clippers racing in and out of the city, bound for China to gather the first tea harvests each season, then racing to be the first to return to Britain with their expensive cargo. The ships were a dramatic sight: sleek, multi-masted and with many sails blowing in the strong winds from the nearby Atlantic Ocean. It was Jeanie and Dugald's first encounter with the exotic world of the East, and sowed the seeds of their growing interest in China in particular. They each became shop assistants in grocery stores. They also came to faith in Christ and were deeply involved in a lively local church, whose pastor was himself a man with keen interest in reaching the whole world with the gospel. God was shaping these two young people.

Now, in 1901, after only months back in Scotland, Dugald was impatient to return to China. He wrote, "Now again the call has come, in obedience to which I gladly go forward, whether for service, suffering or death, as God shall appoint. As a Mission, God has permitted us to pass through deep waters, beloved workers have been martyred, native Christians massacred, Mission stations destroyed, and the work apparently upset and disorganized, and others who 'escaped the edge of the sword' have suffered in ways too awful to describe. But God has answered our prayer in again opening up the country to preaching of the gospel … "

Jeanie remained in Scotland a while longer until her health was restored, then headed back to China to rejoin Dugald. Over the next few years they experienced both famine and devastating hailstorms that destroyed precious crops, yet Dugald could write, "I have been much among the distressed people during the last few days, and it is indeed painful to listen to their sorrow and cry for help. They are more ready now to listen to the word preached, and we sincerely trust that the Lord may, by this tragedy, bring many to himself." The church was growing steadily, with a steady stream of baptisms. On one short journey in the surrounding area, Dugald and a colleague saw 78 converts baptized. Jeanie traveled less, but taught two classes a day at home and spent much time with women and children, rejoicing in each one who came to faith.

Trouble was never far away, and in 1911 once again many CIM missionaries were withdrawn to the coast, Dugald and Jeanie among them. After another short leave, they returned once again to China. Soon, though, the First World War created yet more turmoil, even far away in China. Dugald, always rather headstrong, fell out with his CIM leaders. By the end of the war, he and Jeanie left China and returned to Scotland, where Dugald died in April 1930.

That was not the end of the story for Jeanie, however. Her heart was still in China, and she longed to be nearer to those five little graves. Like her children, she, too, wanted to die in China. She also wanted to be back with the people she had come to love so dearly and whom she thought of as her true friends. By now, though, she was in her 70s. If she were to go back to China it would have to be independently, without any help from the CIM or anybody else. So she gathered together a handful of possessions, a pitifully small sum of money left after paying for Dugald's burial, and set out for China.

As her strength waned, but opportunities abounded to teach the Christian message, Jeanie prayed for a young woman to come and join her. Far away, a London housemaid named Gladys Aylward heard, through a friend, of Jeanie's need. Gladys herself wanted to go to China, but had been rejected by CIM. Hearing about Jeanie, she immediately saw herself to be the answer to Jeanie's prayer, and Jeanie to be the answer to her own prayer. Before long, and after an adventurous journey, Gladys reached Jeanie, discovering a still active, though rather frail, old lady with an unpredictable temper and big ideas. They turned their courtyard home into an inn for some of the muleteers who passed their door on their long journeys. What an opportunity to spread the gospel!

Their partnership did not last long, however. Following a fall, Jeanie died and was buried as she had wished in Chinese soil, just like her precious children. But in that short time Jeanie had passed on to Gladys a deep love for children. In subsequent years, Gladys spent most of her time looking after them. She helped at a missionary school where more than 100 boys and girls were cared for, and taught them about the Lord Jesus. In 1940, it was these children that Gladys took on an epic journey lasting weeks, across the mountains and beyond to Xi'an to escape the approaching Japanese army.

Many people have heard of Gladys Aylward. Her fame came largely through a film made about her flight to safety with so many children, with trust in her faithful Lord to provide for them and deliver them from harm all along the way. The Lord protected them from danger many times over, and their story became a powerful testimony to the love and power of God, touching many people in many countries. Few, however, have heard of Jeanie Lawson. Yet in the sovereign kindness of God, Jeanie's loss of her babies later led to the lives spared of more than 100 Chinese children, and seeds of faith planted in many, both old and young. The fruit of Jeannie's life and sacrifice was great.

28. Wheelchair Evangelist

God delights in using the weak for his purposes. As seen in this story, physical disability is not a barrier to the advance of the gospel. On the contrary, God mightily used a wheelchair-bound missionary to reach patients at Manorom Christian Hospital in Thailand.

It began with a headache—not the "headache" of trying to get mind and tongue around a foreign language, nor even the headache that comes from being out in the sun for too long. It was a headache such as Jean Anderson had never experienced. As her temperature mounted and pain spread through her body, Jean and her colleagues knew she was in trouble. Then paralysis set in, along with the stark reality of her diagnosis: Jean had polio.

Jean had arrived in Thailand in 1953. Like a number of other Christians around the world, she had felt called during the last years of the 1940s to serve in China with the CIM. Initially she hoped to sail in the autumn of 1950. She completed her nursing training and spent two happy years at the CIM training center in London. As she neared the end of that time of preparation it became clear that neither she nor many others would be able to go to China following the Communist victory in October 1949. It was more than two additional years before Jean's destination became clear: Thailand. As she gladly testified, "God's way is perfect, and I will trust him!"

The team in Thailand was very new and still working out what to do and where. Jean began some language study in Bangkok and wrote home enthusiastically—and vividly—about all that she was seeing and hearing: the colors, the smells, the wooden houses along the riverside, the dirty waterways, and the Buddhist monks in their saffron robes. Even before she had any language other than a greeting or two, she and colleagues went out energetically distributing gospels and gospel tracts. Trips to the market, to temples to try to understand Thai Buddhism, or outings on the river boats, were all opportunities to hand out literature that explained all that she could not yet explain orally.

Soon, Jean joined a small team settling in the large city of Paknampho in Central Thailand. Work there was already proving fruitful. "Altogether 25 people have professed to accept Christ whereas two years ago there was not a single Christian," Jean wrote home in late 1953. "Our home, the usual Thai kind, is built of teak wood on high stilts. The large and rather wild garden makes an excellent meeting place for the Friday afternoon children's meeting. It also provides us with bananas, mangoes, papayas, coconuts and other tropical fruit—not to mention poisonous snakes such as cobras." Apart from the snakes, it sounded idyllic, though Jean was no mad romantic. There was much spiritual darkness, too.

There were growing openings and quietly growing responsiveness to the gospel, but it was still a struggle to teach in Thai. As the months flew past, Jean gained increasing fluency to say what she longed to say clearly about the Lord Jesus and his love, and about his power to forgive. Yet, more and more her heart was drawn to the needs of the many leprosy sufferers in the country. OMF medical colleagues were setting up a number of small clinics across Central Thailand specifically to treat leprosy. Jean knew that her nursing skills could be a good contribution to this work.

By 1956 Jean was writing home about the medical teams' findings. They were learning how best to help patients with advanced leprosy, which was highly visible and usually accompanied by major deformities and open sores, as well as those in whom the disease was still in its early stages. Most people were terrified of those who were already clearly affected, and feared to have contact with them. A life of isolation was the norm. Those in whom the disease was still beginning were concerned about their disease being discovered, so they tried to conceal it. Treatments were available that could arrest and even cure the dreaded disease, but it was essential to diagnose leprosy as early as possible. Those who came for treatment needed to receive it consistently for as long as necessary. The clinics, usually monthly in each place, meant that OMF medical personnel could administer treatment in different areas of the country on a regular basis. In between clinics, the medical missionaries visited patients in their homes.

Steadily the team built trust. These foreigners really cared. Moreover, they could treat a devastating disease successfully and restore people to their families. Patients learned that they needed to keep coming faithfully, and most did so. Jean was especially troubled that many children and young people were exposed to the disease; many would never know life without it. At the same time, she was moved by the patients' openness to the gospel. The medical teams' repeated visits to the clinics afforded opportunities to keep explaining the Good News to those who came. One by one, leprosy sufferers were coming to faith. Often it was the combination of hearing the gospel spoken and seeing the gospel demonstrated, as sores were lovingly dressed, that led to faith.

By early 1960, Jean was happily at home in Thailand. She felt she was exactly where the Lord wanted her to be, doing what he wanted her to be doing. By then she was living in Inburi, a rather remote small town in Central Thailand, and starting to see patients fully healed. Life was good.

Then the blow fell. It was not only leprosy that was widespread in the area. Polio, too, spread easily via contaminated food and polluted water. In fact, it was much more infectious than leprosy and international programs to counter it through vaccines were still in their infancy. Somehow Jean caught it.

Her colleagues were frantic with anxiety. How could they possibly get her to hospital in Bangkok, which at that time was the only place where emergency treatment was available? Polio can progress swiftly to complete paralysis and even to death. Every moment counts if treatment is going to be effective. As they prayed, God answered in a startling way. Somehow, a nearby American military base learned about Jean's illness and raced to her rescue. A helicopter landed in Inburi, collected her and delivered her an hour later to Bangkok Christian Hospital. The doctors and nurses quickly sprang into action, fighting to save Jean's life. Later, a Royal Air Force ambulance flight took her to a hospital in her Northern Ireland homeland.

Months later, Jean was still paralyzed from the hips down, unable even to sit up, and yet in faith she knew that God's way was still perfect and that she could trust him even though she could not understand what he was doing. She even believed that one day she would go back to Thailand. She was right. It took four years of intensive physiotherapy, constant prayer and sheer grit and faith. She learned to use a wheelchair, to walk a few steps at a time supported by leg calipers and to drive a specially adapted car. Would OMF be willing to let her return? Her heart was still in Thailand.

The answer came with a warm invitation to join the staff at Manorom Christian Hospital in Central Thailand. "I knew the layout of the hospital," said Jean. "It would be ideal for a wheelchair. As I thought and prayed about it, the Lord gave me two clear messages: Judges 6:14, 'Go in the strength you have …. am I not sending you?' and Psalm 71:16, 'I will come and proclaim your mighty acts, O Sovereign Lord.' Yes, I could go in the strength of the Lord!" Jean spent a few months at a hospital in Ireland gaining some experience in a hospital laboratory, since this was a job that could be done sitting down and would serve the hospital well. Then in March 1964, 11 years after her first arrival in Thailand, she packed for another adventure with God and set off for Manorom.

By now Manorom had a leprosy wing alongside the main hospital. This setup enabled the team to accept leprosy patients for longer-term treatment, and especially to undertake reconstructive surgery together with physiotherapy and occupational therapy. Such a process could lead to the successful rehabilitation of patients who would otherwise have had little chance of being accepted back into society. Even then, it was hard for them. Many hurdles remained before Thailand's young churches could one day show that leprosy sufferers and healthy believers could worship side by side.

Jean was in her element at Manorom. She could travel around the hospital in her wheelchair, or even go farther in her specially adapted car. She could spend hours with inpatients and their relatives. She could see each one over long periods. Jean was a passionate evangelist, and loved to speak about Jesus to everyone who came to the hospital, inpatient or outpatient. Again and again she found that her own disability and obvious problems broke down barriers. Here was someone

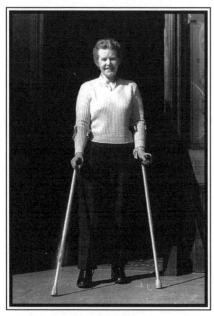

who understood what it is to struggle with a damaged body. Every day, she could be seen in her wheelchair alongside one bed and then another, gently talking about her Savior.

She had her own fairly private area in the laboratory, and many outpatients came to her there. "Some are just plain scared of the strange foreign woman sitting in a wheelchair," she wrote, "or of that nasty looking needle or scalpel. Others are much

Jean Anderson at Manorom   more afraid of the results of those tests. Would their dread of having leprosy be confirmed? Most who come to us already know they have leprosy but keep hoping that it may be something else. Reassuring such patients, explaining the necessity of regular and often prolonged treatment, and, above all, telling them of the One who cares for them, is a far more demanding task than just doing a few simple laboratory tests."

The busy medical staff were delighted at God's goodness in providing them with this faithful servant whose main job was to share the gospel with unbelievers and nurture the faith of those already believing. Most of the team, both missionaries and Thai Christian nurse aides, also loved to witness to patients, and indeed they did it powerfully through the care they gave. Often, however, there was too much to do to be able simply to sit with a patient or a group of relatives for any length of time. Jean, though, could spend all day and many a night listening to questions, hearing about patients' hopes and fears, comforting the dying and their relatives, and gently pointing to the Lord Jesus.

Jean finally retired in 1986, 33 years since she first arrived in Thailand, and 22 years after contracting polio. She maintained that God had kept all his promises to her, that his way has always been perfect. That terrible, polio-induced headache was not the end but a new beginning, not only for her but also for many who came to faith through her.

29. A Heart Prepared by God

> Since the beginning of OMF's ministry in Thailand in the 1950s, a number of members have laid down their lives through accidents, diseases or violent assaults. Roy Orpin from New Zealand was killed by robbers while still in his first term of service among the tribes of North Thailand. This is the story of Gillian, his wife, and his son Murray born just after Roy's death, as God led them through the fire and enabled them to trust him.

One May morning in 1962, Gillian Orpin sat reading her Bible. She was staying at Manorom Christian Hospital in Central Thailand, awaiting the birth of her first baby. The hospital was opened in 1956 by OMF missionaries. Since many workers lived in places where medical care was not available, expectant mothers were encouraged to come to the hospital a few weeks before their babies were due in order to have a safe delivery.

Gillian and her husband Roy lived high up in the mountains of North Thailand in a Hmong tribal village. They had gone there together as a newly married couple just over a year before. Now Gillian had come down the mountain to Manorom, while Roy stayed behind to organize the building of a new home in the village to which they expected to move as a family. The new home, in Bitter Bamboo village, would be near some tribal Christian families who were relocating there. With the building under way, Roy planned to join Gillian in time for the birth.

That morning, Gillian read Psalm 112. "I came to verses that suddenly stood out for me, and I knew that God was telling me something," said Gillian. "The psalm begins 'Blessed are those who fear the Lord, who find great delight in his commands.' Later it says, 'They will have no fear of bad news; their hearts are steadfast, trusting in the Lord.' I just knew God

Roy & Gillian Orpin 1962

was speaking to me, and the worst news I could think of was that something had happened to Roy. A little while later when I looked out the window and saw the hospital superintendent walking towards the house where I was staying, I knew that he brought the bad news that God had warned me about, and my heart was 'steadfast, trusting in the Lord.'"

Roy had been shot by robbers. He was still alive, but gravely ill. He had been carried to a small hospital at the foot of the mountains, at Phitsanuloke. Doctors operated on Roy and gave him several pints of blood, but he went to be with the Lord a couple of days later. With the help of Manorom colleagues, Gillian traveled to be with Roy for those last few precious hours. "Roy was just 26 years old when he died," recalled Gillian. "A lifetime of missionary service lay ahead, but that was not God's will for him. I know the lives of all God's children are in his hands, however long or short. The most important thing is for us to live our lives wholly for him. We are involved in a spiritual battle when we take the good news of the gospel of Christ into Satan's territory, and there are bound to be casualties."

Roy was neither the first, nor the last of those who would lay down their lives for the sake of the gospel in the often lawless tribal areas of North Thailand, but today there are established churches among many people groups in the area. God used the seed sown with tears and sacrifice, as he promised in his word, to reap a harvest. Roy did not live to see that, but his brief life and his death certainly contributed to it.

After Roy's death, Gillian returned to Manorom, where nearly three weeks later she gave birth to a son, Murray. Many people assumed that Gillian would return to the United Kingdom, her own home country, or to New Zealand where she had worked as a nurse several years before. Roy was a New Zealander, and it was at the Bible Training Institute in Auckland that he and Gillian had first met. Each separately had sensed the Lord's calling to service with OMF. In due time, the calling led to Roy and Gillian's assignment to work among the Hmong of North Thailand. Despite Roy's death, Gillian believed that the call remained, and that she should return with her son to the work. Again, the Lord spoke to Gillian clearly as she read scripture, assuring her that returning to the Hmong was the right decision.

So, bravely, Gillian returned with baby Murray to the mountains to live with two single ladies, Doe Jones and Doris Whitelock, in the Hmong village of Palm Leaf. Over the next few years, interrupted only by home leave in the U.K. and New Zealand, Gillian shared in the typical pioneering missionary tasks of translating scripture, teaching literacy, training leaders and sharing the gospel in the surrounding villages. Often, the women provided some basic medical care to the people around

Gillian Orpin & Hmong children

them as well. During those years, Gillian frequently experienced the loving faithfulness of God in protecting her precious young son through illnesses and accidents. Murray played with local Hmong children and was as at home in the Hmong language as in English. From the day's first light, when children came to the home for lessons before daily chores, through the daytime when it was often the women looking after babies who came, until the evenings when both older children and adults would come after work in the fields was finished, there was a constant flow of Hmong people visiting their little house.

When Murray was old enough to go to Chefoo School, the primary school for OMF children in Malaysia, Gillian and Doris moved to Laos. At that time, many Hmong young people were studying in Vientiane, the capital of Laos. Doris was steadily translating the New Testament into Hmong. Vientiane was not a suitable place for Murray during school breaks, however, so after a couple of years Gillian began a new ministry in Bangkok, caring for new workers at the Study House. This setting provided Murray with children to play with during school holidays and also brought Gillian closer to Chefoo.

When Murray was 10 years old, he began attending boarding school in the U.K. In those days, it was not possible for missionary children to fly back to Asia to rejoin their parents during most school breaks; separations could be for long periods, though not the years at a time experienced by earlier generations in China. OMF had a system in place of house parents who would look after children between terms and visit them at their schools during terms. Even so, Gillian described leaving Murray at school in the U.K. as one of the hardest things she ever had to do.

After another year back in Bangkok, it was again time for Gillian to go on home assignment. As her time in the U.K. drew to a close, she wondered what the Lord wanted her to do next. Should she go back to Laos and rejoin Doris, especially as political changes in the country suggested that it would not be long before work there would no longer be possible? Should she go back to North Thailand and work among the Hmong? Should she go elsewhere in Thailand? "Then I did something I had never done before: I asked God for a sign," recalled Gillian. "I wanted to be absolutely sure that I would make the right decision. So I prayed, and asked for this sign, that when I told Murray I expected to return to work in Laos his response would be God's guidance. I honestly believed that his response would probably be non-committal, or at least accepting the fact calmly." However, when she visited Murray, to her surprise, he spoke longingly of one day having a home of their own, of having his own pet dog, of his fears that she might be killed if she returned to Laos or catch leprosy if she went to help in a leprosy clinic in Thailand.

It was clearly time for Gillian to make a home in the U.K. However, "my mind was in turmoil as I went to London to see the Home Director," said Gillian. "God's answer to my prayer was as clear as it was unexpected. Yet I had no idea how God was going to work it out. My parents lived far away in Scotland, and I had been out of the country for 20 years, except for three home leaves. How could I possibly find a job and have a home for Murray where I could be with him, especially in the school holidays? I had no money and no prospects. But I did have God's clear sign that he wanted me to stay here and I could only trust him to work it out his way. The next morning, at a worship service, the speaker spoke from one of the Psalms. My eyes wandered across the page to the verse underlined in my Bible, which I had proved true over and over again since Roy died. It was Psalm 68:5: 'The father of the fatherless and the protector of widows is God in his holy habitation.' But this time, I especially noticed the following verse. It was as if I was reading it for the first time: 'God gives the desolate a home to dwell in.' I knew that this was his personal promise to me and Murray. I still did not know how he would do it, but I could trust God."

Shortly afterwards, Gillian was shocked one day to receive no less than three offers of work as a house matron at three different public (independent boarding) schools. The role involved caring for a group of boys during the school terms in their boarding home. A friend had mentioned Gillian's need for a job and a home at a gathering of school chaplains. As a result, Gillian found herself with a job and with a home that was available to her during school holidays as well as during the term. God in his tenderness had kept his promise, and provided for the widow and the fatherless. Soon Murray received a scholarship to a nearby school. He was even able to have his longed-for dog.

To add to the blessing, Gillian was able to find a church nearby where she quickly felt at home. Soon she was invited to preach there from time to time, and to help with other ministries through the church. Four years after starting the school job, Gillian was invited by this church to become a full-time member of the parish staff, with a curate's salary and a house rented for her. This proved to be a joyous home for herself and Murray. Eight years later, when the Church of England voted to ordain women as deacons, Gillian was among the first women to be ordained.

In 1992, 31 years after her marriage to Roy, and 19 years after leaving Bangkok, Gillian was able to take a sabbatical and return to Thailand for a few months. She joined Doris Whitelock, still faithfully translating scripture and study materials, and felt immediately at home as she daily typed up the work that Doris had written down that day. They made a good team. Should she take early retirement from the church back in England and return to Thailand to work with Doris? They could make such fast progress together. Refugee camps in the area included many Hmong who had fled from Laos. Often, they were receptive to the gospel. Was the Lord calling her back to the Hmong, the people for whom Roy had given his life and who she was called to all those years ago?

No. As Gillian prayed, she realized that the Lord was indeed stirring her up, not to return to Thailand but to go north to Scotland to care for her now widowed and nearly blind mother. It was another unexpected turn in the story, but clearly a word from the Lord. Murray by now had his own home and no longer needed to be with his mother. Soon Gillian left her many dear friends at the church in Deanshanger, near London, and went to Oban on the west coast of Scotland. There, she was soon invited to become Honorary Chaplain at Oban Cathedral. When the Episcopal Church of Scotland voted to ordain women as priests in 1994, Gillian was among the first to be ordained to that role. After her mother's death, God led Gillian south again, this time to be chaplain at a Christian conference and training center near London.

The young woman who went joyfully to Manorom Hospital to await the birth of her child, in full expectation of being joined shortly by her beloved husband, could never have imagined the paths the Lord would lead her along. She was tested by fire. Yet, 50 years later she could say with her whole heart: "God has wonderfully guided me, and shown himself to me as my loving heavenly Father, and Jesus as my Savior and Friend. Despite all my failures, in grace he has chosen to use me and to give me the inestimable privilege of serving him in Asia and in the U.K. I praise him also, for keeping Murray through his growing up years, bringing him to a firm faith in Jesus as Lord and Savior and giving him a lovely Christian wife, Jenny, and a son, Sam. 'To you alone, O Lord, to you alone, and not to us, must glory be given because of your constant love and faithfulness' (Psalm 115:1)."

30. From Killing Fields to the Love of God

In this moving testimony, Solina Chy tells of the terrible suffering she shared with her family and the great majority of Cambodians during the brutal Khmer Rouge regime under the infamous Pol Pot. After four years, she fled to a refugee camp in Thailand. She eventually emigrated to Canada in 1981. As a Canadian citizen, she joined OMF in 2002 for service in Cambodia. This is her story in her own words.

Daily we hear news of war and terror around the world. What is your reaction? Are you sensitive to the suffering of those involved? Do you say, "That's too bad, but it wouldn't happen to me?" Growing up, I had a similar response as I enjoyed the security and luxury of our middle-class home in Battambang, the second largest city of Cambodia. Yet, we do not know what tomorrow will bring, as we discovered.

It all happened in April 1975, during the hot season. The communist army known as the Khmer Rouge took over Cambodia, marking the end of the five-year-old Republic of Kampuchea. At first we hoped the Khmer Rouge would bring peace. Instead, chaos erupted. The Khmer Rouge ordered us to leave the cities immediately and go to the countryside for a period of three days. Before I left home, I went up to my room on the third floor and brought my favorite things such as photo albums down to the first floor where I thought they would be safe. There were rumors that the U.S. military was going to bomb the city.

Men, women, children and even hospital patients were ordered to leave at gunpoint. My mother, who had been in hospital for knee surgery, came with us. Three days passed, but we were not allowed to return home. Instead, the tragic news of killings began to threaten our lives. A month later, my mother died by the roadside as the result of an infection in her right knee. After a simple cremation we were forced to go on.

Step by step, the new regime took all our belongings: car, clothes, blankets, jewelry, medicine—everything. Then I was separated from my father and sister and was sent to the fields for hard labor. I worked day and night digging and planting with little food to eat. We were under constant surveillance. Many people were killed. Those who were known officials in the previous government, soldiers, merchants or educated people were killed without trial.

One morning I was walking by the foot of the mountain to water the plants. I started asking myself, "Where did I come from?" I thought about the answers my grandmother handed down to my mother, and my mother to me. Now I looked at the fields and asked, "Where did the crops come from?" The seed and the plant. But there must have been someone who created the very first crop!" Now I started to believe there must have been one God, who created the world and whose name I did not know. He is the first one, so no one needed to give him a name.

From then on, I started to pray every night without letting my friends know that I was interested in religion even though I had grown up in a Buddhist country. When I prayed, I prayed to my mother, Buddha, the spirits, to Jesus whom I thought was one among the gods of the white people, and lastly to God as the only one in the world and whose name I did not know.

In mid-1977, I was put in jail with my feet in the stocks. The Khmer Rouge had tried to force me to marry someone against my will. In prison I suffered from lice, mosquito bites, starvation and torture. They gave me electric shocks, put plastic bags over my face until I fainted and held bayonets to my head. Then they beat me all over my body, accusing me of being an agent for the CIA. I lay on the floor, unable to move because my body was so bruised and swollen. Tears began to fall. My heart stirred with hurt, hatred, bitterness, self-pity, anger and revenge.

I thought of my family, for no one knew what had happened to me or where I was. I thought more and more that there must be one God who is living and watching over me, seeing my tears. When they put me in the Buddhist temple known as the "killing place," I questioned whether Buddha could help me, for he had not been able to help himself: the idols had all been destroyed. I despaired of life. Few people survived this jail. Two years and three jails later, I emerged alive, even though I had been reported to be dead.

The end of 1979 brought the Vietnamese liberation of Cambodia. Vietnamese troops invaded Cambodia and the Khmer Rouge fled to the hills. In the new situation, it was possible to move more freely within the country. I managed to escape from the Khmer Rouge and after a few months was reunited with some of my family.

As a family, we decided to flee the extreme poverty and unrest of our homeland and escape to Thailand. We had long since been stripped of all our belongings, and our lives had been extremely difficult. We had only the clothes we wore. I had no bed but the hard ground, no roof but the sky and only hay to serve as a blanket. Even so, the physical suffering was nothing compared with the mental and emotional anguish. A deep hatred towards my own people and country had built up in me. When I reached Thailand, I vowed to never return to Cambodia. I also resolved that when I reached a third country, I would never again associate with my own countrymen.

We escaped safely at last to Thailand, after more suffering along the way. Our pain did not end there. We were placed in refugee camps with limited food, water and privacy. The living conditions were often appalling. In addition, there were the daily rumors that we would be sent back to Cambodia. We lived for different periods in seven different camps, one after another. Finally, we arrived at the Rangsit Transit Center Camp and my dream of reaching freedom seemed about to be fulfilled. However, at that point there was a miscommunication regarding my father's health and we were not allowed to leave yet. I was overwhelmed with self-pity, constantly crying as other people were able to move on to their third countries.

One afternoon in October 1980 I went to my friend's place and cried until I fell asleep, exhausted. Then my friend shook me awake and asked me to translate for her because a white woman had come to say goodbye. The woman was from Youth With a Mission (YWAM) and was being transferred to work in another camp. She had been teaching English to my friend's family. She listened to my story, and told me how sorry she was to be leaving, and not to be able to help me.

About a week later, another YWAM worker, Yvonne Dos Santos, came to Rangsit looking for me. She told me the gospel, beginning with the creation story ("In the beginning God created the world," Genesis 1:1) and continuing to Jesus' death on the cross, when he said, "Father, forgive them, for they do not know what they are doing" (Luke 23:34). Jesus' words touched my soul, and I was converted. Here was the God I had been searching for. His Son came to earth to show us what God is like. He died on the cross and forgave those who crucified him, even though he had done no wrong. He rose again from the dead. Jesus could forgive his enemies:

by his power I could forgive the Khmer Rouge. The miracle happened, and God changed my heart. In time, I realized that bitterness and hatred had been replaced with a deep love for my people and my country.

God provided me with others who taught me more about Jesus. I thank the Lord that he allowed me to know him first in the refugee camp. Otherwise I could easily have been swallowed up with the desire for material wealth after those terrible years of suffering and poverty. In March 1981 I was sent to Ottawa, Canada. It was a bewildering experience, but God looked after me. I prayed to find a good church, and by the second Sunday I was taken to the Metropolitan Bible Church. Here I discovered a small group of Cambodian believers, and I also met Evelyn Armstrong, who had served with OMF in Thailand. They helped me to adjust to the new country, and they helped me grow in my Christian faith.

A year after I reached Canada, I was able to go to a YWAM discipleship training camp for six months and also to go on a short-term mission trip to Guatemala. In 1984 I went to Prairie Bible Institute in Alberta. After graduating, I went on a short-term placement with OMF in Thailand, working with Alice Compain who had a beautiful ministry among Khmer refugees. That year I was also able to face members of the Khmer Rouge at the Third International Conference on Kampuchea, held in Bangkok. I knew that it was only because the Lord had made me a new creation, with the old things passed away, that I was given grace to forgive those who had caused my family and me so much suffering.

After five years working for a company in Canada, I went to Manila, Philippines to prepare and deliver broadcasts for Cambodia through the Far East Broadcasting Company (FEBC)

Solina Chy

in 1993. I was also able to help answer letters from listeners. I could understand the barriers that hindered Cambodians from trusting in the Lord Jesus, as well as the problems with which Cambodian believers struggled. I had also come to see the great possibilities of radio work, and we saw the Lord using it in the cause of the gospel. In 1996, FEBC sent me to Cambodia as they were opening a radio station there. I was also loaned to Trans World Radio for three years to launch their Women of Hope program. God had brought me back to my people.

In 2002 my work with FEBC came to a close. Back in Canada, I was invited to apply to OMF, initially as an Associate member, and then since 2005 as a full member. I have continued radio ministry at a local Christian radio station, and trained three others to edit scripts and record programs. In addition, I have translated helpful books and worked with women, including many deeply affected by the Khmer Rouge years. A young church meets on my property as they wait for their own building. God shaped my life for this ministry. My burden and vision is to reach Cambodia for Christ. I have learned that "the will of God will never lead you where the grace of God cannot keep you."

31. Suffering Can Open Doors

Losing a child can bring pain different from any other. Wilson and Irene McMahon from Ireland were looking forward with joy to the birth of their third child. It did not work out the way they anticipated. Through her grief, however, Irene found that their experience would bring a level of identification with people around them that perhaps could not have come any other way.

Words. The dictionary defines "words" as "a sound or combination of sounds that symbolizes and communicates a meaning." The truth is that you learn so much more than words when you learn a new language.

McMahons

I spoke very little Cebuano when we moved from Davao City to the mountains of Mindanao in the Philippines, but I needed to use the little I did know to learn the local Manobo dialect. So I threw pride to the wind and went out to try to get to know my new neighbors.

"Good morning!" I said, that being the only phrase I could use with confidence.

"What is your name?" I asked a little more hesitantly.

The response was giggles and embarrassed hands held up in front of their mouths to hide their blackened teeth. No names were given.

I was certain I had used the correct words, but I could not account for the unwillingness to answer such a harmless and unobtrusive question. I tried again.

"How many children do you have?"

The answers I got put an abrupt end to my desire for further language practice that day or the next.

"I have seven children but five are dead," replied the old woman with the wizened face. "I have six children but three are dead," added another. "I have five children and two are dead," said a very young-looking mother.

Every woman in my neighborhood had buried at least one child; most had buried more.

I was pregnant at the time with my third child. I was certain (and delighted) that it would be another little girl. I had chosen her name already: Rebekah-Joy. I could not wait.

Five months into the pregnancy I was done with the weariness of morning sickness and not yet feeling the heavy tiredness of the last trimester. After two safe previous pregnancies and with two healthy children, it did not occur to me that anything could go wrong.

But it did. I threatened to miscarry. After two months' bed rest and repeated trips to the hospital, I gave birth prematurely to a tiny baby girl. She weighed only one pound, six ounces, had a club foot and a shock of jet black hair. I still recall how afraid I was to hold this tiny child as she lay across my belly, knowing her chances of survival were slim. Yet I hoped against hope that she would live. She did not. After just 10 hours in an incubator, Rebekah-Joy died, and I was thrown into a world of grief and pain that was all too familiar to my Manobo neighbors.

For weeks after her death, we were showered with love and compassion from family, Filipino friends and OMF colleagues. We held a memorial service, were given two months' compassionate leave and went through all the rituals of "getting over" a bereavement.

Then came the time to pack up our boxes and get back to the mountains. I was consumed by anger. I was not angry at anyone in particular, not even at God, just angry at the injustice of death. I worked in my garden digging a set of steps going nowhere just to rid myself of this terrible force threatening to erupt into our previously tranquil lives and to keep away from anyone upon whom I might unleash my rage.

My neighbors came to visit. Experienced in dealing with grief and there being no area of life considered too personal for discussion, Inoy ni Toting (the mother of Toting) and Asawa ni Karlos (the wife of Carlos) sat down beside me and began to ask me questions.

"Was it painful to give birth?" they asked with all seriousness.

"Yes! Isn't it painful for you?" I retorted in disbelief.

"Oh yes … " Then they proceeded to give graphic illustrations of the pains of labor.

"Were you sick when you first got pregnant?" inquired Inoy ni Toting.

"Terribly. I could hardly get up in the morning I felt so nauseated," I replied as I recalled all too vividly the debilitating feelings of morning sickness.

"Why did your child die when you were in a hospital and doctors were nearby? Did you not have enough money?" asked Asawa ni Karlos.

"Oh, people still die even in the hospital, even if they have lots of money," I replied.

"But you're a missionary, bad things shouldn't happen to you. You have God's help," responded Asawa ni Karlos, puzzled.

Ah. So this was the key moment. "While we live in this world no one is exempt from pain and suffering," I said, experiencing once again the deep truth of what I was saying, "but God is still with us."

God does not always allow us to see the reason for our suffering or its meaning in life. However, after that conversation I realized that prior to Rebekah-Joy's birth and death these ladies had seen me as some extraterrestrial being, devoid of pain or suffering, protected from hurt, almost not human. It was only after this (and at the end of more language study) that these women began to open up to me, to treat me as an equal and to allow me to share intimately in their lives.

God is an incarnational God. In his book, *Five Smooth Stones for Pastoral Work,* Eugene Peterson writes that God has entered "into the life of suffering humanity, accepting and sharing suffering. The suffering is there and where the sufferer is, God is ... Nothing can provide more meaning to suffering than a resolute quiet faithfulness in taking the suffering seriously and offering companionship through the time of waiting for the morning." God calls us to live incarnational lives, to enter into the suffering of those around us, not to belittle their grief or trivialize their pain, but to acknowledge that to be human is to suffer grief.

It is in the depths of the darkest chapter of Lamentations, a book full of grief, that we find beautiful words spoken by someone in pain: "Yet this I call to mind and therefore I have hope: because of the Lord's great love we are not consumed for his compassions never fail. They are new every morning. Great is your faithfulness!" (Lamentations 3:22-23).

These are more than just words. This is a whole language of hope.

32. Life-changing Illness

Sickness can happen to anyone anywhere. However, living in a country far different from one's own can make a person more vulnerable to serious illness. Australian members Steve and Sarah had served In Indonesia for three years when Steve became desperately ill.

As the bus left the sprawling and polluted city and began the long climb into the cool hills, Steve noticed he was getting very hot. Being hot is part of life in Indonesia, but this was different. Steve's head was soon throbbing and his body burning, and he found himself unable to appreciate the beautiful gardens and panoramic views of the retreat center as they arrived. He, his wife Sarah and young son Daniel had come to join colleagues for a much-anticipated time of fellowship and conference. Instead, for Steve and Sarah it was the start of a long nightmare.

Within a short time of their arrival at the center, Steve's temperature shot up, he could neither walk nor stand, and his speech became incoherent. In the providence of God, two medical doctors were at the gathering. They worked hard to lower Steve's soaring temperature and diagnose what was wrong.

For Steve, it was as if his brain had gone into overdrive, with at least five thoughts in his head at once, all mixed up, and without the ability to put any of it into coherent speech. "I soon became convinced that I was going to die and meet Jesus there and then," recalls Steve. "Was I ready? This soon escalated into the thought that maybe Jesus was going to return that night. The thoughts became more and more intense until I was absolutely convinced of Jesus' imminent return."

Terrified of being alone when the doctor watching him left for a moment to get a book, and convinced that he must warn all of his friends that Jesus was about to come back, Steve somehow staggered to where the opening meeting was under way. As he spoke insistently into the microphone, it was clear that Steve was very ill. He was put back to bed, and under constant guard.

Just when it seemed that things could not get worse, young Daniel developed a high fever that Sarah struggled to get down. That night she wondered if both Steve and Daniel would die. Blood tests established that both of them had dengue fever. Dengue is a mosquito-borne illness that is endemic in some tropical countries. It produces very high temperatures, which can cause serious complications. Sufferers often feel that every bone in their body has been broken. There is no immunization, and in many places it is simply impossible to avoid mosquito bites.

Steve and Sarah's colleagues at the retreat lifted up the beleaguered family in prayer. Soon, praying friends in many other countries joined in as well. In God's mercy, Daniel recovered quickly, and in about 10 days was back to normal.

For Steve, however, it was a different story. The doctors were sure that he had dengue fever, too, but also thought that there was something else wrong as well.

After the retreat was over, Steve was taken to a clinic in the capital for some tests. "The clinic was full of people, some looking decidedly unhealthy," recalled Steve. "Despite this, there was a somewhat festive mood. What was going on? 'It seems rather busy today,' I said to a nearby woman. 'Oh yes,' she replied. 'Today is discount day. They have a discount day every week!'" This struck Steve as incredibly funny. "Sarah, there's a discount!" he exclaimed. "Two tests for the price of one! What else could we have done while we're here?"

It was hard for Sarah to be amused. Her baby son was still not fully well at that point, and her husband was unpredictable. Steve talked compulsively and often incoherently, had difficulty sleeping at night and jumped from one delusion to another.

After 10 days, it was decided that the family could return to their own home in another city. It proved a bad decision.

"On our first night back I could not sleep," remembered Steve. "My thoughts were racing once again and I became agitated and began to pray. I was unsure if God was speaking to me or not, but my racing thoughts soon led me to strange behavior. Numbers took on new and frightening significance and words had strange associations with others. Once again I was hypersensitive to the spiritual. Eventually, Sarah found me and realized that I needed help. By morning I had not improved, and with the help of friends I was loaded into a car and driven to the hospital."

"On the way I started using a man's leg as a calculator to process the numbers in my head—he was a visitor from Australia whom I had met almost for the first time. (I met him again recently and he described that car ride as a combination of hilarious and terrifying.) God faithfully surrounded me with people, knowing what I needed: the head of the hospital I was taken to was a friend; a doctor from the recent conference who happened to be in transit came to check up on me (and summoned another doctor from Singapore); colleagues watched me round the clock; doctors and nurses looked after me well."

It soon became clear that Steve faced a protracted recovery. It was recommended by OMF's International Medical Advisor, one of the two doctors who had treated Steve at the conference, that when he was well enough he and the family would return to Australia indefinitely.

Steve and Sarah's dreams were crushed by the pace of Steve's illness. They had to leave at four days' notice, only a few days after Steve first entered the hospital. The squeeze of time heightened the pain, but their teammates were a phenomenal source of support, staying by their sides each night and helping them to prepare for their departure.

This decision was particularly hard for Sarah. She and Steve had prepared for some years to minister in Indonesia, where they believed the Lord had called them. After their first three years they were just beginning to get established, with growing ease in the language and good friendships with local people forming. Leaving would be a form of bereavement. At the same time, Steve's illness was compounding her grief. Sometimes he didn't even recognize her or respond to her. Other times he was completely manic and rambling, with totally unpredictable behavior. She seemed to be losing her calling and her husband simultaneously. All the dreams she and Steve had shared seemed to be shattering.

For Steve, dengue fever had triggered acute mental illness. When he reflected back on the time, he described his mind as "the most frightening place I have ever visited." His condition was made all the worse by the distorted, confusing thoughts he had about God, heaven and hell and the devil. It was a time of terrifying darkness. Later he was to reflect, "I have learned that sanity should never be taken for granted. The journey to the other side is only a short one and much more terrifying than you could imagine. There is intense isolation, the gaping gulf of communication with the sane that cannot be crossed. You know that like a prisoner being visited you cannot express what you want to say. You can hear and see your visitor, and they you, but the clear cold screen between you scrambles all communication. You will never know closeness until you are back from the other side."

As soon as it was safe for Steve to fly, Steve and his family traveled to Singapore. He was grateful for the friends and colleagues who rallied round to help him, but recognized that it was God who would have to be his healer. "God calls us to give him all of our burdens," he says. "He will never collapse under the weight of our struggles. He is willing to hear the whole story." In Singapore, Steve began to regain strength, though the healing and recovery would take a long time, long after he was back home. Sarah's father, a doctor, joined the family in Singapore and escorted them back to Australia just before Christmas 2005.

Steve, Sarah and Daniel stayed for several months with Sarah's parents on their small farm. The quiet beauty of the countryside and the love of family made for the best possible environment for the family. Steve began the long journey of physical and mental healing.

For Sarah, however, the ordeal was far from over. She still grieved for Indonesia, and was at the same time dealing with her own trauma from the nightmarish period of the preceding months. She felt she had lost her husband and gained a second very difficult child, alongside one-year-old Daniel. Steve required constant supervision. His recovery was both slow and unpredictable, with days of progress followed by days of regression. A television program or book could plunge him into flashbacks or reactivate some distorted conviction about spiritual things.

Gradually and painfully, Steve began to recover. OMF Australia's leadership did all that they could to help, ensuring there was extended compassionate leave, with full financial support. They encouraged Steve to access the best specialist help available. Rest, a good diet, medication and a helpful psychiatrist all played a role. Family and friends prayed in faith.

It was a significant milestone when Steve was finally well enough to go on his own to share an evening meal with friends. "I was dropped off early and went for a walk along the local creek where years before I had spent many happy hours removing weeds and encouraging the native plants to grow," Steve says. "As I walked, my head a little drowsy from the medication, I remembered the seemingly simple life we had led before leaving for Indonesia. A wife, a dog, a job I liked and a passion for native plants and caring for the environment."

"Now I felt very different from how I had felt years before, but the familiar lifted my spirits and the exercise did me good. Soon I found myself knocking on our friends' door. It felt like a first date. I knew that I needed to make a good first impression on my hosts, for Sarah would surely receive a report. If it was not good, I might not get a second date—certainly not one without a chaperone! Thankfully, all went well, and I knew the Lord had enabled me to take a step forward."

Later Steve was able to say: "Although I can now laugh about how I was at my worst and my bizarre behavior, the scars are still obvious to me every day. Sometimes I am curious to see how much the wound has healed. Looking at it and poking is painful, but I want to make sure the wound does not become infected. This is hard when nobody else has seen what I have seen and I am unable to distance myself emotionally in order to give an objective assessment.

"When is it time to leave the past behind and to stop scratching through the ruins searching for something of value? There is always a danger after major trauma that your experience comes to define you, and you become a victim of it. Repeated self-analysis is no healthier than avoidance, and leaves little room to enjoy the new and current. The journey from trauma to the present begins with an acknowledgement that life can indeed improve and that there is hope. The focus must be on the progress made, not on the distance of the journey. I will never forget the trauma of my illness but I am intensely grateful to God for the progress I have made."

Steve and Sarah did not lose their love for Indonesia, but it was clear that returning was not an option, at least in the foreseeable future. Instead, little by little, they discovered that the Lord was opening up new opportunities for ministry in Australia. They could still serve the cause of the gospel in Indonesia as they mobilized people and prayer for that country. They could dream new dreams together: good dreams given by the Holy Spirit. After their difficult journey, they could testify with the psalmist: "Cast your cares on the Lord and he will sustain you; he will never let the righteous fall" (Psalm 55:22). They had been through the fire, but experienced the loving faithfulness of God.

God's Faithfulness to Teach and to Guide

The theme of God's loving care for his people expressed in teaching and guiding them runs like a golden thread throughout the Bible. From the very first creation of human beings, God's desire has been to communicate with us and to show us how to walk in his perfect ways. As the writer of Hebrews so vividly puts it: "In the past God spoke to our forefathers through the prophets at many times and in various ways, but in these last days he has spoken to us by his Son, whom he has appointed heir of all things, and through whom he made the universe" Hebrews 1:1-2.

The Bible captures for us God's heart, his character and his commands. It records God's dealings with people from the beginning. Scripture gives us portraits of Christ and shows us God in the flesh. It gives us songs to sing and wisdom to live by. It teaches us what the church should be and do. In every generation and in every place, the Holy Spirit loves to bring

God's word to life and draw out meaning for anyone who hears or reads it with a humble, prayerful heart and commitment to obey it. The promise of God flows to us through Proverbs 3:5-6: "Trust in the LORD with all your heart and lean not on your own understanding; in all your ways acknowledge him, and he will make your paths straight."

Of course, there are times when we are puzzled because we do not understand exactly what God is doing. Perhaps circumstances or events seem to put roadblocks in the way we thought God was leading us. Perhaps we are simply not clear as to what God wants us to do, and clear guidance does not seem to come. Perhaps the answers to our fervent prayers are delayed, or different from what we expected and hoped for. It is when we are most uncertain that we most need to hold on to God's faithfulness, and trust him even when we cannot see.

These stories tell us about God's loving guidance, sometimes at one particular moment, sometimes over a long period, and his gentle teaching and training as we put our trust in him. Walking by faith is a great adventure!

33. Joy, Suffering and the Awakening of the Kachin[1]

Witnessing the joy of Lisu believers in China, an old Kachin man requested that Francis and Jennie Fitzwilliam share the gospel among his people as well. Hardships, sickness and death followed. But so did the joy of the Lord among the Kachin.

Francis J. Fitzwilliam and Jennie Kingston arrived in China in October 1926. It was a tumultuous time in China. A few months prior, the First United Front between Chinese Nationalist and Communist forces had launched the Northern Expedition, a military campaign designed to wrest power from the hands of local and provincial warlords and unite China. In the midst of the chaos, missionaries and other foreigners were sometimes affected by the conflict.

In response to the volatile situation, more than two-thirds of CIM's ministry stations were temporarily closed in 1927. Most workers retreated to the coastal cities.[2] New male missionaries, including Francis Fitzwilliam, studying at the CIM's language school in Anqing withdrew to Shanghai. There he was reunited with Kingston, his classmate at Moody Bible Institute and also his fiancée. The two had become engaged shortly before leaving for China, but CIM policy at the time required new single workers to serve two years on the field before marriage. Under the circumstances, however, the CIM shortened the time and

---

[1] This story has been partially adapted from a chapter in Sik Pui Wong, *Sheming de ai: Zhongguo Neidihui xuanjiaoshi xiaozhuan* 捨命的愛：中國內地會宣教士小傳 (Sacrificial Love: Portraits of CIM Missionaries), CCM Publishers, 2006. English translation by Greta Y. Wong.

[2] It should also be noted that at this time of uncertainty the CIM issued its famous "Call for 200" new workers. Four years later, the call had been answered by 203 new workers going to China.

allowed Fitzwilliam and Kingston to marry after just one year in China, on October 18, 1927.

The following spring, James O. Fraser, superintendent of the CIM work in Yunnan Province and pioneer missionary among the Lisu people, escorted the Fitzwilliams to Yunnan. In the previous decade, 800 families in the region had accepted Jesus and nearly 2,000 people (mostly Lisu) were baptized, but there were still numerous unreached tribal people groups scattered among the mountain ranges.

"Why can't we have the gospel?"

While ministering among the Lisu, one of the highlights each year was the annual Harvest Festival held at Christmastime. Prior to the festival, each family in a village who wished to contribute to the church's work would report to the village leader how much they intended to give. Their contributions came in the form of corn, rice, buckwheat, pigs, cattle and money. Although the Lisu were extremely poor, their contributions often supported two or three evangelists, a schoolteacher and the building of their own chapel and school.

The day before the festival, Lisu believers arrived from places two or three days' journey away. When they arrived, each party entered the village through a bamboo archway decorated with orchids built for the occasion on "Reception Hill." The guests would wait outside the gate while a welcoming party sang them the "welcome song." The singing was punctuated by gunshots to help celebrate the event.

The evening before the festival was devoted to prayer and singing. On the first day of the festival, three services were held: one before breakfast, one (lasting about three hours) in the middle of the day and one in the evening. On Christmas Day, long before daylight, guns began to go off and carolers started making rounds in the village.

The noon service on Christmas Day was briefer, followed by a baptismal service. Afterwards, time was spent playing sports and games. Leaders arranged different kinds of contests and awarded prizes. In the evening, after a short service in the chapel, the believers sang around the campfire. Each village took turns singing Christmas hymns and other favorites.

During one of these festivals, an old man came to the festival with his family out of curiosity. He was a member of the Kachin people group inhabiting parts of Yunnan (in China), Myanmar and India. He was impressed with what he saw. The Lisu people were so happy and had joy he had never seen before. He approached Francis Fitzwilliam and asked, "Why don't you send teachers to us Kachin people? Why can't we have the gospel that make these Lisu people so happy?"

The Fitzwilliams immediately felt called to take the gospel to the Kachin, but the death of their senior missionary colleague Carl G. Gowman required them to stay with the Lisu for the time being. Before their first home assignment in 1934, however, Francis felt compelled to visit the Kachin and scope out the possibilities of future work among them. He set out on a three-day journey to what was known as "wild Kachin country" due to the Kachin's unsavory reputation. As Francis approached the first Kachin village he saw, he noticed a house with a cross on top, signifying the residence of the headman for that area. A young man came out of the house and rushed up to Francis, saying, "Well, thank God, I asked him to send you and here you are."

As a boy, the headman had run away from home due to threats from his father and fled to Myanmar, where he met a Baptist missionary, attended a Christian school and became a follower of Jesus. After his father died, his mother sent messengers asking him to come home since, as the son of the deceased headman, he would be now the headman in the area. He returned to China with the Lord Jesus in his heart and a desire to teach his people the gospel. After arriving at the village, he told them about all the things he had seen in Myanmar and that he no longer worshiped demons, but that he worshiped the living God. Initially, the villagers approved and were willing to do the same, but then they discovered the new headman would not drink, smoke, go with them on their thieving expeditions, or join in their fights. He tried to tell them that because he was a Christian, he did not do those things, but the villagers rejected his message. "That's not the Kachin way," they told him.

The man felt that if he could get a missionary to come, learn the language and devise a writing system, eventually his people would listen and believe. The problem was he did not know where to find a missionary. So he prayed for God to send one. And so it was that the very first trip that Francis took among the Kachin, in the very first village where he stopped and the very first man he talked to was the headman who had been praying for God to send him a missionary.

During the trip, Francis preached the gospel in the villages he visited, often drawing a large crowd. Some made decisions to follow Christ and burned their idols, but the next day became scared and were not sure if they would continue following Jesus or not. Francis—like the village headman he had met—thought that if a missionary were permanently based there, then many would turn to Christ. By staying long-term among the people, the missionary could disciple new believers so they would be less susceptible to giving in to fear.

In 1936, the Fitzwilliams returned to China after a one-year home assignment in the United States. The Christian headman in the first village Francis had visited had been killed by his villagers while Francis and Jennie were away, so the Fitzwilliams moved to a town near the China-Myanmar border in western Yunnan in order to reach out to the Kachin people. The Kachin were similar to the Lisu in some ways, but quite unlike them in others. There were several different branches of the Kachin tribe, but mainly they were divided into two chief branches: the Jingpo in Myanmar and the Atsi-Kachin in China. American Baptist missionaries had translated the Bible into Jingpo, but the Atsi-Kachin had no written language at the time. Therefore, the Fitzwilliams soon went to work preparing a catechism to teach basic Christian truths. In addition, a few hymns were produced for the Kachin in the Lisu script.

In God's sovereignty, one of the first families to convert was the Kachin headman of the district where the Fitzwilliams lived. His wife was a Christian Jingpo who was converted while attending an American Baptist Mission School in Myanmar. Through her influence, the headman turned to God. In reality, as a headman, he owned all the land in the district. Without his permission, the Fitzwilliams could not have lived there.

While the door was opened to ministry among the Kachin, the missionaries also felt the influence of satanic forces resisting the advance of the gospel. It seemed that whenever a Kachin became a Christian, sickness followed. Fraser shared with the Fitzwilliams about his similar experiences during the initial years of work among the Lisu. He encouraged them to not be disheartened.

Awakening among the Kachin

In 1937, while Francis visited the nearby Kachin villages, three families burned their idol shelves and became followers of Jesus. A few weeks prior, another family had done the same. Around the same time, a Kachin leader came to the Lisu Harvest Festival to see how Christians worshipped. He went away a changed man, saying he was going to become Christian, even if no other families did. Throughout the area, there seemed to be an awakening interest in the gospel.[3]

In the fall of 1937, Francis, accompanied by a Lisu Christian who spoke Atsi-Kachin, set out on a four-week journey among the Atsi-Kachin. They traversed the district west of Longchuan, visiting 24 villages and covering an area of 200 square miles. Preaching was done after the evening meal until midnight. Francis played a phonograph in order to gather the people. With the help of visual aids, they shared the gospel with about 500 people overall. Many gospel seeds were sown and they relied on the Lord to water them. The people were friendly and invited Francis to come back the next dry season. This was the first visit of missionaries to Atsi-Kachin villages. Well over 100 villages remained unvisited by any preacher of the gospel.

In early 1938, the Fitzwilliams held the first Bible school training among the Kachin. The new book of Christian catechisms in the Kachin language they had prepared was a great help. Many Kachin had the book and came regularly to study. As February was a dry month (and, thus, suitable for traveling), Francis decided to visit more Atsi-Kachin villages. But when the summer rains began, many people returned to work in the fields. It was difficult to gather the Atsi-Kachin to listen to the gospel.

---

[3] *China's Millions* (North America edition), 1937, p. 59.

Despite the progress made, it seemed to Francis that most Kachin were willing to give up their idols only if they could keep their sins. Eleven Kachin families had recently professed to know the Lord, yet they were weak in faith and still somewhat bound to superstitions and the fear of demons. Francis sometimes asked himself, "Is it that we have not prayed enough?"[4]

First fruit among the Jingpo

On Christmas afternoon 1938, the missionaries and a large company of Kachin and Lisu Christians took a winding, bamboo-shaded path down to a clear mountain stream to hold the first baptism service among the Kachin in the area. Four Kachin men were baptized. More had come for baptismal examination, but did not seem to have a clear understanding of salvation and the principles of Christian faith, so they were asked to wait another year.

Still, the advance of the gospel persisted. New Kachin believers craved biblical teaching. One Kachin Christian told the Fitzwilliams that when he was in a nearby district teaching the Bible, people would not let him go to bed at night. When he said he was too tired to teach any longer, they still begged him to continue speaking. The Fitzwilliams, along with other missionaries and some of the tribal Christians in the area (Lisu and Kachin, especially), began organizing multiple Bible conferences and training times for the masses of new believers. At the same time, outreach efforts also expanded since many of the Kachin villages in Yunnan still did not have a Christian witness.

---

4   Ibid., p. 76.

Faithful to the end

In late 1939, the Fitzwilliams started to map out the next year's Bible training itinerary. Francis planned to hold a Bible school for the Lisu on February 2, followed by a few gatherings for the Jingpo Kachin. Before then, he went to visit villages and preached the gospel while the tribal people were at home celebrating the New Year.

At that time, two young Chinese evangelists from Hong Kong heard God's calling to join Francis. In mid-February 1940, four villages invited the Fitzwilliams to come and lead Bible studies. Francis, Jennie and the two Chinese evangelists each took a village and agreed to meet back in a week. At the appointed date, Jennie and the two Chinese workers returned, but there was no sign of Francis. Finally, the next morning, a few Lisu arrived, carrying Francis, who had contracted typhoid

Fitzwilliam family

and was in a coma. Even though he had been so weakened that he had to lie on a cot while preaching, the Lisu carrying him said he had continued preaching the gospel until he passed out.

A few days later, February 25, 1940, Francis passed away at age 38, leaving behind Jennie and their 11-year-old son. The old Kachin man who had first invited the Fitzwilliams to preach the gospel among his people comforted Jennie, saying, "Don't you worry, we'll take care of you. You just stay here and teach us. We'll take care of you." She was eventually taken prisoner by Japanese forces in China, before being repatriated to the United States in September 1943. She tried to return to China in 1949, but was prevented from doing so after the Communist takeover and subsequent expulsion of foreign missionaries from China.

Postscript

Francis J. Fitzwilliam's death made a great impact on one of the two Chinese evangelists who had joined him in Yunnan in 1940. At the 2001 Chicago Gospel Conference, Rev. Paul Shen shared the story of Francis' life and death and the impact on his life as a young Chinese believer:

Rev Paul Shen

> Fitzwilliam had chronic diarrhea for quite some time. Western and Chinese doctors could not find a way to heal him … in fact, after he left us in February 1940, his diarrhea flared up again. He did not stop working. Finally, he collapsed and fell on the ground. The next day, some Lisu carried him home.

His face was very pale and his whole being was very thin and skinny. He was in a coma. At that time, we could not find a doctor for him, as it would take a doctor two weeks' journey to come to our place. I knew he was seriously ill and I went to my room, knelt down and prayed for him earnestly. However, God called him home in the middle of the night.

In that mountain village, there was no coffin to be found and we wrapped his body with a blanket. My colleague and I dug a hole in the ground and buried him. Afterwards, we piled some pebbles and rocks on top of the soil . . . found some wood, made a cross and asked his wife to write his name, date of birth, and date of death on it. As the evening sun was setting in the west, the light shone through the tall trees. With the bright colors overhead, the trees looked like glorious pillars shining in heaven.

As I stood beside his grave, lifting up my head and feeling as if I was standing in heaven in front of God, I said, 'Father God, a white brother who traveled thousands and thousands of miles, crossed the seas, and climbed the high mountains to China, has just died for our countrymen. Dear Lord, his wife is so young that he should not die so early. Father, I am a Chinese, and even though I offered myself to you before, now I am now offering myself to you again. Please take me and use me. Wherever you want me to go, in life or in death, I will follow. I dare not to leave you or ignore your commands. Please accept my second offering and lead me to be a missionary for your purpose!'

Dear brothers and sisters, [Francis] Fitzwilliam's death became my spiritual turning point. By his graveside, I offered myself to the Lord again, and since then, there has been no turning back ... today, if you were touched by the Holy Spirit and want to be a missionary, please stand up. Please let this 80 year-old preacher pray for you.[5]

Inspired by Francis Fitzwilliam's death, Rev. Shen remained faithful to the Lord. After Francis' death, Rev. Shen served the Lisu in Yunnan for two years. Due to a serious ulcer condition, he left the mountainous area and began serving the Han Chinese. Over the ensuing years, God used him to establish and shepherd churches in Taiwan, Hong Kong and North America.

As for the Kachin people who Francis and Jennie served, they are now identified as a Christian people group.

Kachin girls

[5]   Shen Baoluo (Paul). "Working in Yunnan Province among the Lisu tribe." Christian Life Quarterly, Vol. 6, No. 1, March 2002, pp. 10-11.

Nearly two-thirds of the Kachin living in China and Myanmar profess faith in Christ. The joy of the Lisu—which was so attractive to the old Kachin man who first approached Francis Fitzwilliam at the Harvest Festival—is now the joy of hundreds of thousands of Kachin as well.

34. Sixty Years, Step by Step in Faith

When it became clear in 1951 that the CIM must leave China, there was deep sadness in leaving a land and people that were greatly loved. There was also urgent prayer by CIM workers and supporters around the world, seeking the Lord's direction for what should happen next. Already some workers, unable to return to China, had begun working in neighboring countries and were surveying needs and opportunities for future service. At first, those workers expected to start ministries to the Chinese diaspora throughout East Asia. Soon, the workers recognized the great need for ministry to numerous people groups who had never heard the gospel. One of those people groups was on the island of Mindoro in the Philippines.

Dr A. J. Broomhall

Dr. Jim Broomhall and his wife Janet gazed in awe as the island of Mindoro came into view. They had sailed from the main Philippine island of Luzon, and as their boat drew closer to their destination, it looked like a tropical paradise set in a shimmering blue sea: fishing villages all along the coast, lush green land beyond, and then, towering high above, range upon range of forest-clad mountains. It was those mountains, and the mysterious tribal groups known to live in them, that drew the Broomhalls there. God was guiding them to pioneer among the Mangyan people who, as far as anybody knew, had never heard the gospel.

The Broomhalls were no strangers to adventure and pioneering. They both came from families that had been closely involved in the CIM since its inception in 1865. Jim was descended from Hudson Taylor's much-loved sister Amelia. Jim himself had been born and raised in China and then with Janet had served there with the CIM. Before the final exodus of CIM workers from China, Jim and Janet had at last been able to go and live among a previously unreached tribal group, the Nosu (also known as the Yi), where Jim, a medical doctor, had built a simple clinic. After a few short years, the Broomhalls and their two colleagues were forced to leave again in 1951.

After a short period back in England to recover from some very difficult years, they arrived in the Philippines and tried to make contact with another elusive people group. Nobody was sure how many distinct tribal groups might be hidden away in those Mindoro mountains. The island might look like a tropical paradise from a distance, but the reality was rather different. The lowlanders, keen to harvest timber for which there was a lucrative market, despised the Mangyan and annexed more and more traditional tribal land. As a result, the Mangyan distrusted anyone not of their own tribal group and rarely let anyone catch a glimpse of them.

So dense was the jungle, and so difficult the trails, that only the Lord could arrange opportunities to find these people and win their confidence. Simply getting to the point of having conversations with them presented massive hurdles. How do you speak to people when nobody outside their own group knows their language? How do you learn a language for which there is no teacher? Pioneering can be very hard. Would it be faith or folly to venture far inland, up into those mountains, with only what could be carried on one's back and to try to live there and see what happened?

With the conviction that the Lord was guiding them, the Broomhalls began their task. Much of the time all they could do was pray and wait. As various colleagues came to join them, intrepid pairs would explore the trails in different parts of the island. For them, too, much of the time was spent prayerfully waiting. "Please, Lord," they prayed, "guide us so that we can meet these people and reach out to them with your love!"

Gradually, the increasingly international team discovered that there were six distinct Mangyan tribes, some with sub-groups, each with their own culture and language, although there was some overlap. Far north of Mindoro lived the Iraya. As one traveled south there were the Alangan, then the Tadyawan, then the Tawbuid, followed by the Buhid and lastly in the south, the Hanunoo. The growing team divided into six mini-teams. Each one focused on one tribe in particular, looking for ways to find them, to learn their unwritten languages and to begin the long task of Bible translation. Meanwhile, the Broomhalls provided wise leadership, encouragement and prayer support.

God answered prayer in extraordinary ways. Long before the arrival of the Broomhalls and the growing team, a Tadyawan leader named Aplaki had a vision and an encounter with a spirit sent from God. The Mangyan were all well-acquainted with the spirit world, living in constant fear of evil spirits and demons. This encounter was quite different, as Aplaki reported afterwards to his people. He was met by a shining being—a good spirit such as neither he nor anyone he knew had ever witnessed. The shining being told him that one day people from a far away land would arrive, bringing good teaching that would free the tribes from fear. It would be a long time yet before these people arrived, but Aplaki must tell his own people about the teachers that would someday come. Aplaki told them that they must listen and obey all that the strangers would teach. His people also needed to make their children aware of what was going to happen.

Many years later, in 1955, two OMF women, Hazel Page from Canada and Caroline Stickley from the U.S., had just spent three days trekking in the mountains, unsuccessfully trying yet again to find some Mangyan. The women, discouraged and disappointed, sat at a sawmill, waiting and hoping for a truck to drive by that could take them nine miles out to the main road and possibly back to the team's base in Calapan. To add to their misery, the odds of a truck appearing seemed increasingly slim, and they had just resigned to their fate of camping another night without food or water. Suddenly, to their absolute amazement, four tribesmen emerged silently from the jungle's edge. The women stared at the tribesmen in shock, mirroring only a fraction of the shock felt by the men, who had never seen white women before.

In faltering Tagalog, the language of the lowlanders, the women asked the men if they had ever heard of "Our Father in heaven"—the good God who loved them and wanted them to be his friends. Had they heard of the God who had created the whole world? The God who was more powerful than all spirits?

Caroline and Hazel had no idea whether the men understood any part of their message before they melted back into the jungle, nor did the women know of Aplaki's vision and the story handed down through the generations. All the same, Caroline and Hazel knew the encounter was arranged by the Lord and believed that one day there would be a believing community established among these hidden people. In fact, another five years would pass before Caroline, this time with Canadian worker Dode Pack, could at last live among tribal families and begin to see the Lord moving them to faith.

Meanwhile, the Broomhalls did not lose sight of the fact that there were at least six tribes to reach. Werner and Doris Demand from Germany were assigned to the Iraya, another group who lived in constant fear of the spirits. Somehow, without any direct encounters with missionaries, the little Mangyan groups had heard that the westerners carried medicines that could cure some sicknesses. In 1961, the Demands received a message about a man called Narding.

"Narding, our leader, has a bad wound. Can you help him?" some tribesmen asked.

Doris sent some medicine with the pleading men, but only two weeks later they returned. "Narding is even more sick," they said. "His wound is very bad. He thinks he is dying. Please come!"

Werner and Doris traveled up to where Narding was, a one-hour walk on the small dikes between the paddy fields. The men had carried Narding for four or five hours across the mountains from Mananao. The Demands found Narding, and they were thankful for Doris's skills as a nurse. She diagnosed Narding with blood poisoning and gave him penicillin. After a few days the Demands visited again to give him a second injection. "I had left a small Gospel of Mark with Narding," Werner recalled. "At that stage we didn't know that he was the only one of his clan who was able to read. He had attended a lowland school for two years."

A few months later, Narding appeared with a friend at the Demands' house in Paluan. Narding had brought along the small Gospel booklet and read it to his companion in the evenings on his sleeping mat. "We were surprised to hear him trying to explain what he read," Werner recounted. "We thought that he must already be a believer. He told us that at first he had hidden the Gospel in the thatch of the roof, but when he got sick again he asked his wife to take it down for him. It proved to be the start of the work in Mananao."

Some time later, Werner and Doris received an invitation: "We have built a chapel, now please come and teach us!" The Demands lived a five-hour walk away from Mananao, but they built a small bamboo house near Narding's village so they could live close by much of the time. In the years following the Demands' move, 80 or 90 baptisms took place in Mananao.

All the teams in this area of the Philippines had to cope with long hours of difficult hiking. They also had to be willing to live in utter simplicity without any amenities and with very restrictive diets. Further, they experienced intense spiritual warfare as they penetrated strongholds of the evil spirits. They needed incredible perseverance. For Russ and Barbara Reed from the U.S., they endured 10 hard years before they saw any response from the Tawbuid people or had any opportunity to live among them. Pioneer ministry among these unreached tribes was costly and faith-testing. There were many tears, mingled with the conviction that the God who had brought them there had eternal purposes for these people.

Gradually, as the gospel took hold, the Mangyan no longer had to move away after a death because of fear of the spirits (as had been the custom previously). They had been delivered from the bondage of fear and developed a pattern of settling

Russell Reed

Tawbuid group

down in one location. It became easier to live among them. Some OMF workers, such as Andreas and Ruth Fahrni from Switzerland, came from farming backgrounds and shared their agricultural knowledge with the tribespeople. The Mangyan learned how to grow food successfully without cutting down more and more trees for new fields. Food also became more varied and nutritious.

Each OMF team worked hard at learning a language that had never been written down before. Once the language was learned, they started on the long journey of scripture translation so that each tribe could hear God's word in their own language. Along with translation came teaching believers to read. It was a painstaking process to write down scripture passages, lessons and songs, and then to make many copies. (These were the days before photocopiers and computers.) Yet, as groups of believers were established in all six tribes, a hunger for God's word grew, and any written materials were highly prized.

By 1971 there were 120 scattered churches among the six Mangyan tribes. An effect of the gospel's presence among the Mangyan was a change in attitude toward other tribes. Historically, the tribes defended their own territory and were deeply suspicious of one another. Now as Christian believers, they wanted to relate to one another. From this spirit of unity the Mangyan Tribal Church Association was born, linking all the groups together. Several years before, a short conference and then a Bible school had been set up to give intensive training to emerging church leaders from the six tribes.

Those who attended needed at least basic skills in reading and writing and some ability to learn in Tagalog. There was no one tribal language that all could understand, and Tagalog would give them the opportunity to relate to the world beyond their mountain homes. It took great courage and dedication for these tribal men and women to master these skills. Yet, time after time, students testified to the Lord's grace in stretching their faith and providing them with the ability to learn.

Many of the small groups of believers, almost as soon as they came to faith, felt convicted by the Lord that they should carry the gospel to other small communities and extended families scattered over the hills. After all, other

Mangyan Bible School, Philippines

people needed to know that Jesus Christ could deliver them from bondage to the spirits. That missionary mindset had an extraordinary outcome.

In 1975, OMF was asked to start work in the southern island of Mindanao, particularly among the Manobo tribal people. Dave Fuller from Canada and Andreas Fahrni went to investigate. Dave and his wife Bev were leading the Mangyan Bible School at the time and felt greatly fulfilled in that ministry. However, Dave returned from the survey trip and showed some photos of the Manobo villages that had no one to teach them the gospel. The Manobo village leader had extended an invitation: "We know about the Father God, but we do not know how to find him. Will you come back to teach us?" The Mangyan leaders heard about the invitation and immediately responded: "We must go to tell them the way to find Jesus!" Addressing the missionaries, the leaders said, "Kuya (Big Brother) David and Ate (Big Sister) Bev, you should be the first ones to go. We will collect money from the churches here to send you." The Lord eventually provided workers, both expatriate and Mangyan, to respond to the Manobo leader's plea for a teacher of God. Today, there is a Manobo Church Association that carries on what began in 1975. When God calls, he also guides and provides. The pennies collected by the Mangyan churches bought the very first Cebuano language Bible used to teach the Manobo.

In 1978, word came of Negrito tribes in Camarines Sur, another Philippine island. Mangyan missionaries went there, too. Later, other Mangyan went to the Palawano tribes living on an island close to Mindoro. How much God was doing among the Mangyan, and through them, in such a short time! People who for countless generations had never lived outside their hidden mountain homes were now stepping way outside their comfort zones. They braved the sea, faced culture shock and homesickness, and learned another language—all to take the precious gospel to more unreached tribes.

Theo Herren from Switzerland, who with his late wife Maria worked for years among the Mangyan, went back in 2011 to share in the 40th anniversary celebration of the Mangyan Tribal Church Association (MTCA). It was a moving experience as some 1,800 Mangyan believers came from all over the island to gather together for four days.

Theo reflected on the powerful scene:

"I was sitting on a couple of rigged-together bamboo poles, surrounded by a vast crowd of Mangyan believers who sat shoulder-to-shoulder. We listened attentively to the report of one of the four Mangyan missionary families that had been commissioned by the MTCA to serve among a tribal group on the island of Palawan. Two additional Mangyan families worked among a remote mountain tribe on the main island of Luzon.

"Sitting on those poles I found my mind going back. Forty years ago I sat at almost the same spot with six rather shy Mangyan men, chosen by the churches in each of the six tribes to represent them on the Board of the newly-founded MTCA. At that time, such an association was an altogether new and rather strange concept for people who were not used to looking beyond the boundaries of their own tribe. Now, thinking of the future, they found it important to establish a body that would take care of the Bible school, send out missionaries and oversee the churches and the various projects that were developing. The association would also enable the Mangyan churches to take their place in the wider body of Christ in the Philippines.

"I was back, 40 years later, and could only marvel at all that had grown from those small, humble beginnings. While those original six men whom the churches had chosen were virtually without any formal education and had only learned to read and write as adults, they loved the Lord. Now their sons, able and well-equipped, faithful men, were heading up the Church Association and taking good care of it.

"We can never take for granted that second-generation believers can believe and trust God in the same way as their parents. There I was, witnessing mature and able men with hearts full of love for God and their fellow men, serving the Church Association in a spirit of grace and humility. My heart sings as I pause to thank God for his goodness, faithfulness and grace. It makes me confident to trust God for the future."

As you sail to Mindoro on a calm day, the sight still strikes you as amazingly beautiful as it was when the Broomhalls arrived in faith some 60 years ago. Yet, spiritually, everything is different. The Mangyan are still often shy and most comfortable in their mountain homes. The difference is that, instead of chants to the spirits, the hills often resound with praises of the living God. Now, numerous Mangyan declare themselves disciples of the Lord Jesus. Many OMF men and women have invested years of their lives in taking the gospel to these formerly unreached people. The Mangyan church stands as testimony to God's faithful, guiding hand.

35. Getting the Message Out

> Decades spent striving to get the word of God into the hands of an unreached people group in Southeast Asia were not in vain. But the path to doing so was full of unexpected turns, setbacks and much waiting.

Jim[6] first arrived in East Asia in 1952 at the age of 23. He spent the next several years crisscrossing Southeast Asia to record Bible stories in various languages, many of which did not yet have a written form. Presenting the gospel in people's native language was one of Jim's lifelong passions.

One day, Jim came upon a celebration unlike any he had ever seen. He inquired and found out that it was a wedding party for a couple from a certain minority people group in the area. Thus began his love for this group who had little access to the good news of God's grace. Numbering several million, the group was largely closed off from outside influences.

While working in other areas from 1952 to 1957, Jim tried unsuccessfully to find a speaker from the group to help him record the Bible in their language. On two occasions he thought he had someone, but no one turned up for the meeting. During this time, as he was mulling over the setback, the Lord spoke to him through Isaiah 49:

> I will also make you a light for the Gentiles, that my salvation may reach to the ends of the earth … this is what the Lord says: 'Yes, captives will be taken from warriors, and plunder retrieved from the fierce.'

---

[6] Names have been changed.

Could God rescue these people who had long been closed to the gospel? Although Jim spent the next five years in South America seeking out overlooked people groups and recording Bible stories in their languages, he never stopped thinking about the unreached group in Southeast Asia. How would they hear about Jesus?

After his time in South America, Jim began seeking ways to reach them. Because of political turmoil in parts of Southeast Asia in the 1960s, he took a "detour" to the University of California at Berkeley for graduate study in Linguistics. While there, he ministered to international students and also met Betty, his future wife. On their first date, Jim picked up a globe, spun it around and pointed to the people group's homeland, saying, "This is where I'm going." Growing up in a missions-minded home, Betty had also sensed a calling into missions, but had not felt led to any particular group or ministry until that point. Jim and Betty were married the next year (1967).

By 1969, Jim had completed all the requirements for a doctoral degree in Linguistics, except for his dissertation (which he completed later). Along the way, he continued to ask mission organizations about the possibility of ministering to the people God had placed on his heart. All the inquiries were met with a resounding "No." This included his first inquiry to OMF.

But God's ways are not our ways. More than five years after contacting OMF, a letter came in the mail with news of a possible sponsorship under one of the local churches from a nearby area, on the same island where the group was located. Providentially, a local church leader had sat next to one of OMF's field directors at an ecumenical conference. In the course of conversation, the local leader said that a young man from the group Jim was interested in had just been baptized. "Could OMF send a missionary to work with pastors and begin translation work on the Bible in this group's language?" the leader wondered. Remembering Jim's inquiries, the field director said he knew someone who might be a good fit for such a job.

Translation work begins

In 1970 – 18 years after Jim had first encountered the group – he, Betty and their young son sailed to Southeast Asia for language and culture study. In March 1971, the family settled into a small city south of the area where the unreached group lived. Jim started working with a recent convert, John, translating portions of the New Testament. John, one of the first Christians from this group, had come to Christ after studying in another area, where he met some Christians and heard the gospel.

Another native speaker, Paul, helped as well. He was not a member of the people group, but grew up in the area because his father worked for the government. The team of three began their research into the written language of this people group. It was difficult work. The team found very little in writing and also some differences in dialect. They mainly had an oral language, but at the end of three-and-a-half years, the Gospel of Luke was finally ready. Two hundred copies were printed. The problem was how to distribute them.

Several creative and some rather unorthodox ideas for getting the Gospel into the hands of this people group were explored (including using a "Gospel blimp" to drop the Gospels into the province or putting the books in bottles that would float down the coast), but nothing worked out. The distribution problem was rooted in ethnic tensions in the area.

Several churches had been burned by this people group. No local Christian living in the area dared to even have the Luke translation (of the unreached people's language) in their homes and would certainly never give it to anyone. Also, although this unreached group was known for being "curious and gregarious," said Betty, they would not let outsiders get too close. The translations had to be stored until a later time.

Prayer and local mobilization

In the mid-1970s, Jim and Betty went on home assignment to the U.S. Their time back home allowed them to rally greater prayer support for this unreached group. According to Betty, they may have been the first Westerners to focus prayer on the group. The couple knew how important prayer was for their ministry endeavors. Many of their prayer partners had been praying for them even before they joined OMF. The prayer group organized by Jim and Betty was not concentrated in a central location, but spread throughout the country and included several churches and family members. "The key to the commitments [to prayer]," said Betty, "was people just being obedient to persevere in prayer, while also having clear goals in prayer." Prayer letters were sent almost every month. God called and entrusted this work to a band of committed prayer partners. Spiritual warfare was often intense and faithful prayer was the weapon needed to overcome, especially as the wait to disseminate the written Word of God lingered for quite some time.

It was not just in the U.S. that Jim and Betty mobilized prayer for the group. During the 1980s and 1990s, Jim and Betty formed a prayer team of local Christian students and teachers (in Southeast Asia) who focused on prayer and ministry to this group as well. The team met weekly at Jim and Betty's home to pray. They also worked to support Christians of other ethnic groups who were placed in the area by the government.[7] Many of these workers were nominal Christians and afraid of being placed in such a "hostile" area. Others had a vibrant faith and understood their "calling" to this people. Jim and Betty's prayer team would take trips into the area to provide encouragement and support to these Christians. The group sometimes gathered in locations remote enough to be able to sing and pray together without being heard. For many of the small towns in the area, these Christians were the first evidence that believers could be decent and kind, even as the overall atmosphere was still hostile to believers and remained so for some time.

In the mid-1980s, due to tightening visa restrictions, Jim applied to a local university to teach Linguistics. Betty also worked at the university, teaching conversational English and Western culture to staff preparing to go abroad for further study. The family lived half a mile from the campus and had continual contact with a Christian fellowship group for college students. Their home was the site of an informal "Bible institute" attended by a cadre of enthusiastic students who studied the scriptures with Jim, who focused his teaching and mentoring on the mission of the church to reach unreached people groups. The family prayed that these students would catch the vision for their unreached neighbors.

---

[7] The government would assign jobs to teachers, government employees, policemen, and army members throughout the country, regardless of ethnicity. Thus, Christians who were not members of this group could be working in the province.

The "Skinny Bible"

In 1989, Mark, a native member of the group Jim was trying to reach, became a believer in Jesus Christ. He had heard radio programs from the Far Eastern Broadcasting Company (FEBC) while working on a boat in the Straits of Malacca. He had also read a book about the end times and seen a movie about Jesus. All of this led him to Jesus. After Mark's commitment, his whole family—a wife and eight children—followed him and came to Christ as well.

At the time, there were three churches in the area for Christians from other islands and ethnic groups. Mark, however, was not welcome in the congregations. In fact, they begged him not to come to their churches for fear that their buildings would be destroyed. Mark finally traveled to another area in order to be baptized by John, the man who had worked on the translation with Jim (and had since gone to seminary and was ordained.) The following week, John was picked up by the military police and put in jail for a year, even though he was never charged with a crime.

Meanwhile, Jim continued his translation work and in 1996 completed four small booklets, which, when compiled together, were dubbed "the Skinny Bible." Selections from various books of the Bible were included: the Pentateuch, Psalms and Prophets, parts of the Gospels, Acts, Paul's letters and Revelation and a revision of the Gospel of Luke. When Jim looked for a publisher, he found none willing to risk publishing Christian scriptures in this people group's language. Finally, another missionary led Jim to a small Christian publishing house where the owner accepted the request. The Skinny Bible was bathed in prayer for several years. Every step had challenges. And once again, they were faced with the distribution question.

How could they give the books to the local people? Most copies were (once again) put in storage. Jim often pondered over the persistent barriers to get the scriptures into the hands of the people he loved. Focused prayer continued.

In recent years—after Jim and Betty had retired and left the country—a natural disaster near this unreached people group's homeland opened the area to outside help. A pastor remembered the Skinny Bibles translated by Jim and his team, retrieved them from storage and sent them with Christian relief volunteers and others going to the area. Each booklet was torn into sections and offered to people in an acceptable way. A large church in a nearby area also distributed these portions to refugees whom they housed after the disaster.

Due to Christians' immediate response to the crisis, some of the prejudices and superstitions the people had long harbored toward Christians began to dissipate. Relief efforts allowed local Christians an opportunity to show love and allowed the people to receive it from them. It broke through stereotypes on both sides.

As for Mark and his family, the impact of the gospel on his and his family's life persisted through the 1990s and early 2000s. His eldest son, Alan, attended seminary on another island and then returned to work in his homeland with his wife and children. The family continued to struggle living as followers of Jesus in a hostile environment. Then the disaster killed Mark, Alan's wife and kids and his other siblings. Alan, of course, was devastated at the loss of his family. He eventually re-married a friend from seminary and now lives and ministers with his new wife and children. God's work continues through many faithful people. Reliable sources say that there are small groups of believers in various places in the previously unreached area.

"In spite of our weaknesses and failings, God moves in his way his wonders to perform," reflected Betty. "Vision and persistency are essential both in the goers and the senders. Results may be very slow and inconsistent, but that does not alter the call."

36. First Year Challenges

Most people find it difficult to leave the familiar comforts of their homeland to live in a new country with a different language and culture. Crossing cultures can be a bewildering and painful experience, even for the person who believes that the Lord has called them to go. Eilish Agnew, an OMF worker from Ireland, describes with great honesty the difficult but productive pruning that God worked in her life during her first years as a missionary.

Back in 1974, a few months before leaving for Asia, I stumbled across an article on cross-cultural service called "Culture Shock, Language Shock, and the Shock of Self-Discovery" by William A. Smalley.[8] I do not remember very much about the actual content, but the title stayed with me. It turned out to be a very accurate summary of my own experience in my early years in the Philippines.

First of all, there was language shock. In all my anticipation of missionary life, for some reason I had totally failed to account for the frustration caused by an inability to communicate with the people God had called me to love. In my late teens, while running a Good News Club in my parents' home in Ireland, one of the songs I loved to sing was a chorus that began, "Untold

---

[8] William A. Smalley, "Culture Shock, Language Shock, and the Shock of Self-Discovery," *Practical Anthropology* 10 (1963): 49-56.

millions are still untold." Those words filled my youthful heart with missionary fervor. Now that fervor began to evaporate as I grappled with the intricacies of Tagalog (a language of the Philippines) and struggled to say even the simplest of Tagalog phrases such as "Good morning! Good afternoon! How are you?" I began to think that, given my present rate of progress in Tagalog, the untold millions might have to wait a very long time indeed before (if ever) they were to benefit from the mature spiritual wisdom I had so blithely assumed I could share.

Communicating even the simplest of truths was beset by pitfalls, as I discovered during my first attempt to teach a Sunday school class of six- and seven-year-olds. My adolescent dreams of sitting under a palm tree, surrounded by wide-eyed, brown-skinned children drinking in every word, came true—but not quite in the way I had anticipated. I was using *The Wordless Book*—a book of colored pages illustrating simple gospel truths: black for sin, red for the precious blood of Christ, white for cleansing and so on. You would think that even with my limited language I could not go wrong with that. Unfortunately I confused the Tagalog word for "heart" (*puso*) with the word for "cat" (*pusa*). As a result, I informed my wide-eyed audience that the Lord Jesus could make a black cat white (true enough, I am sure, but not the point I was trying to make). I did not realize my mistake until the lesson was over and the children were on their way home. I wonder what they told their parents?

Halfway through what should have been a full year in language school, I was asked to move to field headquarters in the capital, Manila, as secretary to the Field Director. At the time, it felt like a most welcome reprieve from the challenges of language learning, as most of my work from then on, both in the field office and in weekend church activities, was in English. Even though I could get by when it came to casual chat in Tagalog, I continued to feel a deep sense of failure.

What then about culture shock? I did not realize I was experiencing culture shock when it was taking place; this realization came in retrospect. I only knew that I was desperately missing familiar things—home, family, favorite foods, the Irish landscape, the changing seasons and Ulster *craic* (an Irish expression meaning good company, fun and enjoyable repartee). I had not yet discovered that wonderful Filipino equivalent, *pakikisama.*

For perhaps the first time in my life, coming as I did from a large, close-knit family, I felt desperately alone. I was surrounded by many kind, caring and hospitable people: missionary colleagues, national co-workers, Filipino neighbors and fellow church members. Yet I felt I did not truly belong. I felt that I was always on the outside looking in, as it were, reflecting wistfully on what appeared to be the much more satisfying friendships and family relationships of others.

This longing for depth of relationship translated, at times, into unreasonable emotional demands upon more than one of my fellow workers, so much so that finally the missionary colleague with whom I was sharing a home asked the field leadership to move me elsewhere. That was really a blow to my already crumbling sense of identity and began a downward spiral of depression that ultimately ended in a near-breakdown.

Next I will explain the shock of self-discovery. The opening words of Calvin's famous *Institutes* read as follows: "Nearly all the wisdom we possess, that is to say, true and sound wisdom, consists in two parts, *the knowledge of God and of ourselves*" (emphasis mine). Looking back, I can see only too well how, prior to the experience I have been trying to describe, I did not truly know myself. Over the years I had developed a persona to fit my own and others' expectations of what a Christian, and especially a Christian ministry worker, should look like. Now in the crucible of service I began to find that my true self was very different from the ideal I had tried to portray and live up to. I suppose I was experiencing what some might call an identity crisis.

However, as I began to discover the depths of my own inadequacy and need I also began to discover, as Calvin believed, that the knowledge of God and of ourselves are intrinsically linked. In my brokenness I was cast upon God as never before, and in that process found a faithful God whose resources of mercy, grace and covenant love were, and are, limitless.

Then I found God's loving answer. God's faithfulness to me during this painful self-discovery was mediated through a number of channels. First and foremost, he communicated his love and compassion through his word. Although for months on end I found it impossible to have a regular and disciplined daily time of personal devotions, through many a sleepless night my mind would be flooded by verses of scripture learned in childhood. Favorite passages from the Psalms or parts of Isaiah brought great comfort and the hope that beyond this present darkness there might be a new beginning.

Many of my OMF colleagues were also sources of help and strength. One of these was Dr. Monica Hogben, who at the time was the Mission Medical Officer. With godly wisdom, she refused to give in to my pleas to send me back home to Ireland and insisted that I work through this emotional and spiritual crisis right where I was. Later I discovered that she prayed for me every single day. Theo Herren, the gentle, godly Field

Director, was also a tremendous encouragement, both in prayer and in practical support. He realized it was best to release me from the pressures of working in the Field Office and gave me the opportunity for some time out with a delightful Mennonite family in a beautiful rural area some miles from the noise and pollution of Manila.

Among the fellow missionaries who were of particular help to me during this dark period was one of my Northern Ireland colleagues, Edna Ashton, who with her husband Alan invited me to come and live with them and their two children. Edna, along with Indonesian colleague Hannah Handojo, listened, prayed and counseled with me over many hours. How grateful I was for these friends standing by me when at times they must surely have been even more bewildered than I was by my emotional and spiritual anguish.

One of the promises God gave me in the very depths of despair was from Isaiah 43:18-19: "Forget the former things; do not dwell on the past. See, I am doing a new thing! Now it springs up; do you not perceive it?" At the time, the fulfillment of such a promise seemed impossible, as it must have seemed to the people of Israel in its original context. Another promise, that God "will make the Valley … a door of hope" Hosea 2:15, was a text that I turned to again and again.

In time, largely through the channels I have already described, God did indeed do something new, not only in my inner life, but also in opening up new opportunities in terms of ministry. One of these involved a complete change of direction, moving from office work to church planting, when I joined a team pioneering a new work in a large suburb of Metro Manila. The Tandang Sora Team, as it was known, was ultimately responsible for planting the Cornerstone Bible

Christian Church in Quezon City. My years with the team and the church, flourishing to this day, were among the happiest and most rewarding of my 16 years in the Philippines.

Sometimes, being broken and put together again by God's loving hands is the best thing that can happen to a person. C.S.Lewis once compared our lives to a building which the owner sees must be demolished as opposed to simply being refurbished – but only because he plans to rebuild something better. I firmly believe this is a part of what God was doing in my own life during those early years in the Philippines. That's not to say he has not had a lot more work to do since. But, as the apostle Paul assures us, we can have confidence that the one who has begun a good work in us will bring that work to beautiful completion one day. He who called us is faithful, and he will do it (see Philippians 1:6 and 1 Thessalonians 5:24).

37. From Japan with Love

In 1965, 100 years after Hudson Taylor had trusted God for "24 willing skillful workers" to begin the China Inland Mission, OMF leaders took another new step forward. For the first time, Asians would be welcomed as members of the organization, not just as national colleagues. This decision was made early in the life of the Asian church's fledgling missionary movement and showed that God was making the church global as never before. Today, on some field teams, Asian OMF members are in the majority. Among the first Japanese members were Makino and his wife Izu.

Japan was a difficult place in which to grow up in the years following World War II. Most Japanese were hungry and struggled to survive. The Japanese suffered from deep confusion and trauma as a result of their defeat in the war and from the horrors of the atom bomb. No family remained unscathed. It is one thing to rebuild broken infrastructure, but quite another to repair families and to rebuild a national psyche and identity.

The Japanese church was—and remains—numerically small. Many Japanese never had any opportunity to hear the gospel. They saw Christianity as the religion of the Western world that they resented. If you lost faith in traditional Japanese religions, where might you turn? For Makino's father it was to Communism. Izu's grandfather was a Shinto priest. In fact, Izu was born at the shrine where he officiated, but her father had turned to atheism, while her mother put her hopes in Buddhism.

Despite this background, God had his hand on both Makino and Izu. In middle school, out of curiosity, Makino went to an evangelistic meeting organized by a small Christian club. Makino heard the gospel there for the very first time. Fascinated, he started attending a Bible study group. A few months later, he accepted Jesus as his Lord and Savior. That little group of believers set him on the path of lifelong discipleship and also convinced him of the importance of working with young people and students.

Meanwhile, Izu, six years younger than Makino, moved with her family away from her hometown. Her grandfather died and the family could no longer live at the Shinto shrine. Their new home was close to a church that had been started by a female American missionary. Extraordinarily, Izu's grandmother, the wife of the late Shinto priest, decided that four-year-old Izu should go to the church's Sunday school. "She will get some good moral teaching there!" Izu's grandmother said. Thus Izu's journey to faith began. Years later, as a high school student, she was stopped in her tracks as she read her Bible and came across 1 Corinthians 1:18: "For the message of the cross is foolishness to those who are perishing, but to us who are being saved it is the power of God."

"God opened my heart to understand the meaning of the cross," Izu said, "and I put my trust fully in the Lord Jesus."

The same Lord who had given faith to both Makino and Izu was guiding them to a shared future. After graduating from college, Makino worked among high school students. During that time he met Izu, who was then a university student. Izu went on to become a staff worker with Kirisutosha Gakusei Kai (KGK), the Japanese InterVarsity movement, while Makino headed for Singapore to attend the Discipleship Training Center (DTC). Suitable Christian marriages are very important in Japanese Christian culture, and watchful Christian leaders like to help things along. While Makino was at DTC, he contacted Pastor Kondo to ask whether Izu could be a good partner for him. Since Professor Baino and Pastor Kondo had their eyes on Makino and Izu, they recognized that Makino and Izu had similar ministry aspirations and were ideally suited to one another. "We think you need to pray about this," the professor and the pastor told Izu. Step by step, both Makino and Izu knew God was leading them to marriage.

Meanwhile, Makino was having great adventures at DTC. He was a passionate evangelist and quickly gained the reputation of jumping over language and cultural barriers to share the gospel. "Even if he had only half-a-dozen words in a language, he would eagerly point to Jesus and offer some Christian literature!" said one friend. On a short missions trip to Turkey, where distribution of Christian tracts was strongly discouraged, Makino and four friends went door-to-door at midnight to hand out gospel leaflets. Leadership had repeatedly told the young evangelists that by no means should they go back along the route where they had been distributing tracts. In a particular situation, Makino and his friend followed the orders, but eventually found themselves on a road with no exit. They stared at the wall in front of them. What should they do? Makino opted to vault himself over the high wall. To his alarm, he landed on his feet inside a police compound. "Lord, how do I get out of this?" he prayed. The answer came: "Use your Japanese." The Turkish people had a fondness for Japanese people and their language. Makino launched into a long stream of Japanese while handing the Turkish officers his passport, which contained a mix of Turkish and Japanese words. Upon realizing Makino's Japanese nationality, the officers eased up and released him and his friend. Makino knew that the situation could have ended far differently, but the Lord had delivered him from harm.

Undeterred, and even more motivated after the incident, Makino enthusiastically continued in street evangelism. While he was at DTC he prayed persistently, "Lord, where do you want me to go? What ministry do you have planned for me?" DTC had close ties with OMF, having been founded by veteran OMF missionaries David and Ruth Adeney, and with students regularly attending weekly prayer meetings at the organization's international headquarters in Singapore. OMF had also just opened up the opportunity for Asians to become field workers. As Makino prayed, listened and sought advice, he knew the Lord was saying, "My child, come to Thailand with me!" Izu, too, was open to going wherever the Lord led her. So, with DTC training completed, Makino and Izu married, were accepted by OMF's Japan office and arrived in Bangkok in September 1974.

It was a difficult time for the team in Thailand. Two nurses, Minka Hanskamp and Margaret Morgan, had just been kidnapped one morning in South Thailand as they arrived to open their leprosy clinic. OMF received a ransom demand for a huge sum. In line with organizational policy, ransoms could not be paid, because paying would put all other workers at risk of abduction for ransom. "The Land of Smiles" could be a dangerous place. It was a sobering introduction to missionary service for Makino and Izu. In the end, the two women were executed. In 1975, the neighboring countries of Vietnam, Laos and Cambodia all fell to Communism. Would Thailand be next? In days of such uncertainty, should missionaries spend time in language study, or in discipling believers in-depth, or in anything other than urgent, widespread, pioneer evangelism?

Passionate evangelist though he was, Makino also firmly believed that the gospel needs to go deep as well as wide. For a person raised and steeped in Buddhism, the process of coming to faith in Jesus often requires much time, faithful prayer and patient teaching. Once someone puts his faith in Christ, he needs careful nurturing if he is to stand firm in his faith. As much as they appreciated colleagues who were engaged in widespread scattering of the seed of the gospel, Makino and Izu knew they wanted to be able to engage in intensive discipleship. They were thrilled when God guided them to join the staff of Thai Christian Students (TCS), so closely related to the high school and university students' ministry they had been involved in back in Japan.

TCS was still comparatively young, but had some good Thai staff and a growing number of groups of Christian students in various universities. Some of these young people were the children of first generation believers; some were themselves the first in their families to believe. Makino and Izu were in their element as they nurtured these young people, many of whom were eager to take every opportunity to study the Bible. In return, the Thai young people taught Makino and Izu a great deal about Thai culture and helped them as they tried to become increasingly proficient in the Thai language. Years later Makino could say, "We worked under the leadership of Tonglaw Wongkamchai. He and our other Thai colleagues taught us so much. It was an enormous spiritual blessing to us."

Sometimes people argue that all mission effort should be focused on church planting, and that engaging in student ministry, for instance, is to deflect limited resources. However, the TCS students were active members of church youth fellowships and many went on to leadership in the churches. Some became pastors and theologians; some carried their faith into a variety of professions. Others became valued staff at the Bible Society, World Vision, Scripture Union and other Christian organizations.

During the time that Makino and Izu served with TCS, church planting had largely been concentrated on rural areas and small towns or among tribal groups. The TCS ministry provided a crucial balance, reaching the growing community of university-educated and professional people. When Makino and Izu were invited back to a TCS reunion in 2013, they were not only joyfully greeted by many staff, but they also met many of their former students who now have significant roles in church and society. "We were overwhelmed with their warm welcome and their testimonies. To our surprise they are between 45 and 62 years old now! We were so happy to see that most of their children are also active in their local churches. The biblical faith they live out has passed on to the next generation, which

Rev. Naoyuki & Mrs. Izu Makino

we have been praying for. We had similar reunion meetings in Chiang Mai as well as in Bangkok. We have sung, 'How good is the God we adore' in our hearts!"

In 1988, Makino and Izu were asked to take responsibility for OMF's orientation courses for new workers as they arrived in Singapore. The courses provide an important introduction to OMF's structure, field ministries and leadership for new workers. The role was a great responsibility, but one for which Makino and Izu were ideally suited.

In 1994, Makino was asked to serve as Home Director for OMF's Japan office. For the next 10 years, Makino and Izu encouraged Japanese churches to have a deeper vision for world mission, to care for Japanese workers coming home from the field and to help those sensing God's call to overseas service to find their role, whether with OMF or elsewhere. Finally, at the age of 60, Makino believed he should step down so that a younger colleague could bring fresh energy to the role.

Makino and Izu by no means sat idly with nothing to do. After some months of waiting on God for guidance, they stepped in to pastor a small and struggling congregation in Tokyo. A visiting friend commented on how simply and prayerfully Makino and Izu lived for the sake of the gospel. It was to be another ten years before the Lord said, "It is now time for you to pass on the baton!" The ministry of prayer and of sharing the gospel continues.

Reflecting on his life, Makino says: "When I became sure of God's call to be a full-time Christian worker, I believed the Lord would take care of me, whatever I did and wherever I went. He has been faithful in providing all of our necessities, as well as spiritual riches. In Thailand, he kept us safe when we went to evangelize in dangerous villages. Often it was not until afterwards that we realized how much he had protected us. He healed us when we became sick. He has given us many friends, through whom we have learned many precious lessons. During these past years pastoring a little church, in answer to prayer and without open appeal even to church members, God has supplied us with the half million U.S. dollars to pay off the church's debt."

Makino and Izu's friends would say that their joyful, prayerful faith and their undiminished passion for sharing the gospel and nurturing believers has been inspirational. Makino and Izu themselves would simply say that God has been faithful, and that the praise belongs to him.

38. Searching for the Open Door

> Obtaining visas can be a lengthy and complex process. This is especially the case for countries that, for any number of political or religious reasons, do not permit church-related work by expatriates. One worker tells of his and his wife's experience as God opened the way for them to serve in their desired destination.

The driving rain of the typhoon pressed against us as we waded through the raging waters surging over the concrete footpaths. By the time we reached the visa office that could issue our hoped-for visa, we were soaked through and through. As we dripped our way into the entrance foyer, our hungry one-year-old daughter was not pleased to have her food and drink confiscated by the over-zealous security guards. Somewhat soggy and clutching a grumpy child, we finally reached the visa counter and handed over our paperwork. What we heard next were the words that strike terror into the heart of every cross-cultural worker: "We cannot accept your visa application." We were not having a good day.

Visas are a constant headache for those who work in some East Asian countries. Since these places do not grant missionary visas for traditional church planting or church-related work, expatriate Christians have to find another legitimate and acceptable means by which to live in the country. We all need to find and sustain visa-granting employment (sometimes referred to as a "vehicle"), most commonly as students, teachers or business people.

OMF takes these visa vehicles seriously and seeks to fulfill them with integrity. We are not "undercover missionaries" who say one thing and do another. If we have a student visa, then we go to our classes and study hard. If we teach, then we are the best teachers we can possibly be. If our business produces soap, then we make sure it gets you clean. Our ministry duties must be performed in addition to our professional work, or ideally should flow out of our professional jobs.

When my wife and I first arrived in our country of destination at the start of 2007, we were given three-year student visas. If only three years was long enough to master the country's beautiful but difficult language! We were blessed, though, as it is now extremely rare for visas to be granted for more than a year at a time in the place we settled. The long and complicated process of renewing visas, together with the uncertainty as to whether they will be granted at all, is highly stressful. The stress increases as one's current visa edges closer and closer to expiring. This pressure can often result in attrition, with workers deciding to give in and return to their home countries.

As we neared the end of our formal language study period, we talked and prayed a lot about where exactly God wanted us to be next. We felt drawn to one particular people group and place, but it can be a tricky business to figure out where God is guiding you. For a long time, we did not seem to have any confirmation, at least in terms we recognized. Then, unexpectedly, in our final semester of language school, my new teacher came from the area we were considering, and we were able to learn much more about the culture and needs of the people who lived there. We also heard of others who were thinking of going there. Our friends encouraged us. We experienced peace in our hearts. There comes a point in discerning God's purposes for you when you just have to commit to the course you think is right and trust that he will open or shut the door accordingly.

Initially, after moving to our new location, things seemed to be going really well and we settled quickly. There remained, however, the issue of visas. What should be our visa vehicle? Having recently had our first child, we knew that the onus for professional work would have to fall on just one of us. We decided that I would be the one to get out and job hunt.

Teaching is one of the more stable visa options available, but I really did not want to teach English. Despite having some lovely English teachers among our friends, I have to say that it is not a line of work that would make me want to get out of bed in the morning. Besides, I am Scottish, so I speak questionable English anyway. I had two criteria for finding a job. The first was that I could teach from my professional background. It seemed a real waste to have studied and worked in one particular subject for many years, only to let that knowledge go unused. The second criterion was that I wanted to be able to do some teaching in the language I had been struggling so hard to learn. I did not want it all to drop out of my head again.

Unfortunately, teaching jobs for foreigners seemed pretty scarce where we were, let alone with the characteristics for which I was looking. However, we continued to trust. If God had really guided us to this place, then surely he would provide the job and the visa we needed.

It was not long before I found a suitable position available in a local university. I went in for what had been described as an informal interview, only to find 12 teachers around a boardroom table interrogating me. After demonstrating my best, but still flawed efforts in their language, I was offered a job exactly like the one for which I was praying. Theologians need look no further for proof of the existence of a miracle-working God.

So far, so good. Next began the long wait for visa paperwork that I would need to take outside the country in order to apply for a work visa. The start of the teaching semester crept closer and closer, as did the expiration date of our current student visas, but still no paperwork emerged. It turned out that the university department had agreed to employ me without the authorization of the central management who oversee all foreign teachers. Worse still, the central budget for foreign teachers was already exhausted for this year, leaving me stranded in some sort of academic limbo.

Was the job and visa going to come together? Had we misheard what God was saying to us? Was this the result of spiritual opposition? Should we persevere? Should I start looking for another job? Should we pack up and head home?

By this stage, the school term had already started and we had been granted non-renewable 30-day visa extensions to remain in country. The uncertainty of not knowing whether we were coming or going was eating away at us. There seemed to be growing evidence that the job had fallen through.

Frustrated and confused, I went prayer walking around the university campus and surrounding area. God had guided us so far. Would he not show us what to do next? As I walked it seemed as if God was reassuring me. In the midst of a dark and shadowy day, the gate to the university was lit up with brilliant sunshine, as if God were saying, "Yes, this is the right way." As I met students coming and going, I was reminded of how much I enjoy chatting with people at this stage of their lives and felt God telling me that I still had a role to play in working with students. As I walked around a lake in the middle of the campus, I had to push my way through overhanging willows: difficult but not impossible. It was as if God reminded me that he could deal with far more difficult problems than this and make a way through.

I would love to say that all of this encouragement helped me to persevere in trust and to keep patiently waiting on the promised paperwork. Unfortunately, as we so often do, I felt that I had already given God enough time to act and so I put my plan B into action. I re-enrolled in language school and paid my fees for another semester, safe in the knowledge that they could grant me another student visa. This would solve all of our immediate problems, although not the long-term ones.

The very next day I got a phone call from the university saying that the issues with my job had finally been resolved. The department would cover my first year salary from their own budget rather than from the central one. The visa paperwork was ready for collection! In a wonderful parallel to this new breakthrough, I discovered that the hanging willows around the university lake had now all been chopped down, reminding me of God's faithfulness in making a way where the path seems difficult. I felt more than a little bit rebuked for not having been more patient and trusting in the direction God seemed to be leading us in.

It appeared that our visa struggle was at an end. Imagine my disappointment when I saw that the visa paperwork had been prepared for processing in our home country rather than at the center closest to us, as we had requested. Daunted by the expensive and inconvenient prospect of taking our young child halfway around the world, which would delay the start of my teaching further, we went to the closer center anyway to see what would happen.

At this point in the story, we have come full circle to the dramatic scene recounted at the beginning. Tired, wet and worn down, we were completely dismayed that our application was being rejected: the paperwork needed to be processed in the U.K.

Thankfully, that was not the end of the story. Knowing that rules and regulations are sometimes more fluid in East Asia than in Western countries, we asked politely if there was a supervisor that we could appeal to. With some insistence and much impatient waiting on our part, the requisite person was finally found. He eyed the soggy and trouble-making foreigners suspiciously, his exterior gruff and unmoved. Our prospects seemed hopeless.

It was at this point that his gaze fell upon our secret weapon: our starving and grumpy one-year-old. The possibility of us taking a distressed child on more international flights seemed to invoke his sympathy. Whether driven by his ability to relate as a father or the fear that he would someday be punished for inflicting such misery upon us, he granted us mercy.

After calling the university to verify our situation, he told us that our visas could be processed as long as my wife passed a local medical examination first. She passed the examination and, true to their word, the work visas were handed over. Praise the Lord!

I am now teaching my subject bilingually in an East Asian university and living for Jesus among the people around us. Our journey is not unique to us. Stressful job searches and visa obstacles are part of the spiritual opposition to keep us from sharing the love and grace of the Lord Jesus with those who do not know him. God, however, is faithful to guide us to jobs and visas that allow us to serve and minister to his people. As we see God remove obstacles, our faith grows. He lovingly invites us to trust him more. After all, he is the faithful one.

39. Divine Appointments in Africa

In recent decades, huge migration movements have taken place, including those from East and Southeast Asia. These moves have been driven by many complex factors, including temporary migration for education or jobs, long-term migration in the wake of war or persecution, or searches for a better life somewhere else. OMF has responded to the Asian diaspora with ministry in many countries, partnering with churches and other agencies to support those in need, and to share the love of God with them. Hans Walter and Sabine Ritter were disappointed that health problems prevented them from going where they had initially hoped to go, but trusted that God knew what he was doing. Instead, they served on the home staff of OMF Germany, where Hans Walter was National Director. In 2012, they were asked to head up a new initiative in Africa.

Hans Walter and Sabine studied the invitation from OMF's international leadership in Singapore with growing excitement. They both had special links in Africa: Hans Walter was born in Ghana, they had both lived in Africa for a while, and many of Sabine's family members were still in South Africa. Now, with up to 2 million Chinese working in Africa, African churches were asking OMF for help to reach this huge diaspora.

It was not that the African churches wanted an army of foreigners to come and be the ones to reach the Chinese. No, African churches are full of evangelistic fervor, and there are large numbers of Christians in sub-Saharan Africa. What they needed was help to set up training systems: in order to learn how to understand Chinese culture and how to learn some Chinese language. Would OMF partner with them in responding to this great opportunity to engage in cross-cultural mission? Could OMF set up a reproducible language- and culture-training platform that could then multiply, blessing both African churches and the Chinese people?

It was an invitation that delighted the Ritters' hearts. They were glad, too, that it would provide an opportunity for their children to spend some time in the continent that was so dear to them. They would go, probably for two-and-a-half years, and trust that they could lay the foundations that the African churches were asking for during that time. The Lord helped them bypass the medical issues and the family was off to Africa. By late 2012, they were settling into life in Nairobi, Kenya. They found that the Lord had prepared other people—Africans, a Taiwanese and a Chinese person—to have the same vision. The team was forming.

Within weeks of their move, in January 2013, the Ritters wrote:

"It is quite exciting to see God's master plan in action. The other day another family from the Southern Baptists in the U.S. arrived in Nairobi with the same calling to bless the Chinese in Africa. They seem to have a similar vision and want to work with us. We are hoping to get together tomorrow morning before the Chinese service.

"When we are not busy getting settled in some way, we are very much involved in Swahili language study. It is really opening up many doors to the local people. Their eyes start shining when we stumble out our imperfect sentences. Kenyans are such welcoming and gracious people. It is great to be able to love them more as we learn to understand their culture and language. After two or three months of Swahili study we would like to focus on Chinese language and culture."

The Ritters' prayer that God would bring to them a growing network of other people who shared their vision was being steadily answered. In March they wrote, "In early January we went to a church service and spotted an ethnic Chinese family. When we went to talk to them we learned they had arrived just two days before. Guess what—they had come to work with the Chinese! A few weeks later they were at our house when the phone rang. 'Could we come and see you?' asked the person calling. 'Sure,' we said. Half an hour later, a young Kenyan couple rang our doorbell. They shared that they had just both finished their engineering qualifications, but believed God was

Three couples from three continents who independently received the call to reach the Chinese in Africa.

calling them to focus on reaching Chinese. So, imagine that, we are not alone. God has prepared others to work with us."

China's relationship with Africa is not new, but has grown steadily closer. From an economic standpoint, China has many reasons for befriending Africa. The booming economy in China demands many raw materials that are abundantly available in Africa. China has invested heavily in many African states, and there are large numbers of Chinese migrant workers everywhere. It makes sense that African Christians are eager to learn about this new culture that is expanding in their midst. How could OMF best help them?

There were already Chinese language schools springing up in many African cities. Many of these were even supported by the Chinese government. However, the schools usually emphasized learning a great number of Chinese characters. Knowing the characters is important, but a curriculum focused on spoken communication skills and understanding culture was most needed. OMF already had experience in this approach and a practical program was soon developed. "We hope this will help good communication between Chinese and Africans and enable Africans to show the Chinese that God's love has hands and feet," wrote the Ritters.

A program was only the start. "The next step," wrote Hans Walter, "is to train Chinese teachers to teach this specially-designed curriculum at churches and other central venues. We have met a few Africans who have very good Chinese already; they could be a vital help. Could we partner with a Christian university?" A partnership with a university would extend the reach of the program way beyond anything a small team could achieve and would ensure that the program was firmly in the hands of African Christians themselves.

The first step, though, was to try out some training with local church leaders. The opportunity came to spend a day with a group of 25 pastors in the biggest slum of Nairobi. The subject was basic and very practical: "How to befriend Chinese." The response was warm. Many of the pastors already had personal links with Chinese people.

One Wednesday, Sabine joined the newly-started Moms and Tots group at the little Chinese church. When she shared about the love of God, one Chinese woman started to cry. Sabine discovered that she was a medical doctor and a specialist in her field, but she had never experienced real love. The Chinese woman cried for a long time, amazed that there could be a God who loved her.

God continued setting up divine appointments. In India, a Japanese OMF member shared a taxi with an African man on the way to the airport. The man turned out to be the bishop of a large denomination based in Nairobi. He shared that he was eager to welcome the many Chinese arriving in his city and to bless them with the love of God. As a result, the Ritters were introduced to him and within weeks were able to introduce an intensive training course for the people in the bishop's churches.

By October, the Ritters had arranged a partnership with Daystar University to train teachers through an intensive three-month Chinese language, culture and ministry course. "We are praying that one day it will be available all over Africa," Hans Walter said. "The university will offer to train teachers from nations all over Africa so that many will know how to teach this course." The Ritters praised God for another answer to prayer—a university partnership had developed.

By April 2014 God answered the Ritters' prayers yet again: two new Chinese-speaking families were on track to move to

Nairobi, with one of them scheduled to take on leadership of the project when the Ritters return to Germany in 2015. "It will be hard to leave," Hans Walter and Sabine said, "but we trust God for whatever the future brings."

It will be exciting to see how the Lord brings blessing to China through the African churches. The growth of the Chinese church in Africa marks a fresh chapter in the amazing story of the sovereign grace of God as Asian people move around the world. It also marks another chapter in the story of OMF's Diaspora Ministry.

An outing to Mt. Suswa, bringing different cultures together in God's creation.

God's Faithfulness to All Generations

Some of the stories that follow tell of God's grace cascading down the generations through a family. Others show God's grace at work in individuals and in his church. Some of the stories cover many years, even decades; some trace God's ultimate unconquerable goodness and mercy for the church in an entire country. All of these stories remind us that it is God himself who is sovereign over the affairs of all humankind, in all eras and through all generations.

As we have traced CIM and OMF's 150 years of existence, we have learned of missionaries who have answered God's call to be the "hands and feet " of Jesus in the communities where they live. Their legacy lives on in many different ways: through the vital medical facilities they have established, schools they have set up, churches they have planted and helped to develop. They blessed their communities by organizing relief efforts during times of natural disaster or by providing care and training for the poor and marginalized. God sent each one to serve "in their generation" and also to impact the generations that would follow.

40. The Inheritance of Faith

> Hebrews II is a wonderful roll call of men and women who trusted God. The chapter begins, "Faith is being sure of what we hope for and certain of what we do not see" (Hebrews II:I). The story of the church has been one of passing down the baton of faith in the Lord Jesus from Pentecost to the present, generation to generation. Sometimes, families have the joy of successive generations following the Lord. In this story, we trace one family whose journey of faith began in China in the 1890s through the work of the CIM, and another family who has been part of OMF for four generations. There are many similar stories that could have been written, including that of Hudson Taylor's own family, reaching down to Jamie Taylor, his direct descendant, who still gladly serves the Chinese people.

One day in the 1890s a Chinese grandmother watched anxiously as her oldest grandson became increasingly ill. The child was the oldest son of her oldest son, and in the culture of that time such a child held a special place in the family. The grandmother was a respected matriarch in both her family and her village, so when she saw her precious grandson growing weaker, she who decided to take him to the CIM hospital several miles away. She had heard that the doctors there could do wonderful things, though nobody in her family or village had ever been there.

As the doctors cared for the child, they also spoke to the grandmother of the living God to whom they looked for healing. "We are here in the name of the Lord Jesus Christ," they said to her, "and so we pray to him for healing for your grandson, as well as using medicine." The grandmother had never heard of this God before, but she thought, "If he can heal my grandson, when nobody else has been able to save him, then I will believe in him." The little boy was cured, and the grandmother kept her word. She went back to her village and family, and told them that because this God had healed her grandson, she was going to follow him.

She probably did not understand very much about following God, and some villagers resisted this strange new religion of which she spoke. However, little by little her status in the village led to one and then another being first curious and then convinced. A growing number of people from the village started going to the church near the hospital, even though it meant a long walk or a bumpy cart ride. In addition, three generations of the women of the family attended a school established by the CIM close to the hospital. They each embraced the faith for themselves.

In time, one of the grandmother's sons became a pastor. When his son grew up, he worked for an airline stationed in Hong Kong (after World War II). Later, others from the area where he had grown up also moved to Hong Kong. Since they had a different dialect from the Cantonese used there, they established a network of churches in their native tongue. Two generations later, Anna was born in Hong Kong.

When she was 20, Anna met Joe, then 24, when the company for which he worked sent him to Hong Kong for training. Joe himself was born and raised in Singapore, but his grandfather had been a well-known doctor in the same area of China as that from which Anna's ancestors had come.

After that first meeting in Hong Kong, Joe and Anna kept in touch, though at the time Anna was not interested in marriage. It was to be another seven years before Joe and Anna married, during which time Anna's family had emigrated to the United States and Joe had gone to New Zealand for further study. It was there that Joe gave his life to Christ.

Soon after their marriage, Joe and Anna settled in Singapore. They felt that their calling was to engage in business, and through that to provide jobs, serve the community and share the gospel whenever possible. They did so in Singapore until 2011, when their attention was captured by the work of a non-government organization caring for orphans in Cambodia.

The Foursquare Church Children of Promise runs over 100 homes for some 3,000 children. Using their business skills, Joe and Anna have been able to contribute significantly to the work. They are helping with a rice production facility in Banteay Meanchey to produce rice for the needs of the orphans. Anna has set up sewing projects in Siem Reap (in Northwest Cambodia) to teach Cambodian women how to sew clothes and handicrafts. These products are then sold in other places, providing employment, serving the community and giving many opportunities to share the gospel, according to Joe and Anna.

Though not members of OMF, Joe and Anna are part of the fruit of the gospel enduring through the years. The legacy of that CIM hospital and the faith of a Chinese grandmother long ago continues today.

On January 24 1902, a young man from Tasmania, Australia, arrived in China. His name was Douglas Pike, and he served through 27 turbulent years in China until his murder at the hands of bandits in 1929.

When Douglas first went to China, the CIM—and indeed China itself—was still recovering from the traumas of the Boxer uprisings in 1900. Although many missionaries returned to the field after the Boxer Rebellion, some CIM workers could not return due to health issues caused by events of that year. In Australia, as in other countries from which CIM personnel came at that time, there was a huge response to the call for men and women to take the place of the martyrs and other casualties of the Boxer uprising. This was not the time to retreat, the leaders said. There was still so much to be done.

Within months of arriving in China, Douglas was assigned to the province where he would serve until his death. His service included just two home leaves, as well as a short period in 1926 when he led the transport department of the CIM's Shanghai headquarters. This latter assignment was a complex task as around 1,000 CIM workers and their children frequently made journeys, some lasting many weeks. In addition, many supplies arrived in Shanghai to be sent out around the whole country. The role needed a person with a deep understanding of different local conditions and a clear head for detail. Douglas was the ideal choice. Still, he could not wait to return to church work.

Douglas's main love was sharing the gospel with those who had not yet heard it, and then patiently teaching those who came to faith. This ministry occupied almost all of his time in China. In 1906 he married Mary Louisa Boulter and they made an

Douglas and Louisa Pike

effective team, with Louisa working primarily among women and children. They themselves had five children, of whom the eldest, Allison, and the third, Walter, followed them into service with the CIM. Their fourth child, Faith, died at the age of 10 following an operation; she was at the CIM school at Chefoo at the time. Amidst their pain and grief, it was some comfort to Douglas and Louisa that this little girl loved the Lord and that during her illness, they learned later, three people came to trust the Lord as a result of her bright testimony.

As the years rolled by, Douglas and Louisa saw growing responsiveness to the gospel. Often they traveled around their province to share in a week of meetings at a particular location. Increasingly, the main speaker was a Chinese evangelist or pastor, but Douglas and Louisa often taught as well. Much of their time was filled with examining candidates for baptism to ensure understanding of the gospel and commitment to follow Christ. In 1922 they could write of 116 women and 145 men baptized at the end of one such week. In 1923 they wrote of 1,100 men and women attending meetings in one place and of 261 baptisms. There was, they said, a spiritual awakening from the Lord and they rejoiced in it.

Douglas, Louisa and many others had written for years about the problem in China of bandits and groups of brigands who attacked people as they traveled. The problem was partly the result of poverty, partly of lawlessness and partly because of competing local warlords. Many roads passed through isolated areas vulnerable to attack, but even areas close to towns were not always safe. In September 1929 Douglas was attacked by a group of 14 armed bandits, stripped of his outer garments and possessions and bound. His Chinese companions were also stripped of their outer clothing and threatened when they tried to help Douglas. The bandits demanded a high ransom, which could not be paid. A little later, they murdered him. He was last seen fearlessly sharing the love of God with the bandits. He managed before his death to scribble a postcard to Louisa. "The Lord is on my side; I will not fear: what can man do unto me? Psalm 118:6," he wrote. He hoped he might return to Louisa soon, but he was also ready to go to his Maker.

Ten years before, Louisa had written in the autograph book of a child at Chefoo School the following verses:

"God hath not promised sun without rain,
Joy without sorrow, peace without pain,
But God has promised strength from above,
Unfailing sympathy, undying love."

Then, above her signature, she had written "Philippians 4:13," which says "I can do everything through him who gives me strength." How often after Douglas' death she must have returned to that truth from God's word.

Six months before Douglas died, the General Director of the CIM, D.E. Hoste, had issued an appeal for 200 new workers. It seemed an impossible goal, but the high number reflected the needs as they were perceived at the time. Within three years, the 200 had come. Among them were Allison and Walter, two of Douglas and Louisa's children.

Allison by now was a trained nurse; she arrived 13 months after her father's death. Two years later, in 1932, Walter arrived; he was a qualified pharmacist. They both were assigned to the province where their parents had served so long and where Louisa still bravely lived. In fact, Allison was able to live with her mother, and together they had a special ministry to children and young women. Often, there were 80 or more children coming several times a week for Bible instruction, which gave opportunities to visit the children's families at home, too. It was a busy and fulfilling life.

By then a young man named Rowland Butler was working in the same area. Eventually, he and Allison were married. They continued serving the CIM (and later, OMF) until Rowland's death from leukemia in 1971. In 1933, Rowland had his own brush with brigands. A band of 20 men accosted him and stripped him, but he managed to persuade them that the money he was carrying was all they would get and that no ransom would be paid. Was it really worth keeping him—or killing him? They would get no more if they did and risked punishment if they were caught. They let him go—but not before Rowland had told them they needed a Savior.

A few years later, Rowland was one of the leaders seeking to discern the Lord's guidance for the CIM following the departure from China. He later became one of the international directors based in Singapore, where Allison was renowned for her warm hospitality, listening ear and wise counsel.

Allison and Rowland Butler, 1954

Even after becoming paralyzed from the waist down as the result of a freak attack by a swarm of hornets in Malaysia while on holiday, she had a full and active ministry. Perhaps she inherited some of her mother Louisa's rugged determination. She never lost her love for China. Following her accident she could no longer travel with Rowland as he visited the fields, but she would brightly say that the Lord had given her a precious ministry of prayer, which could take her anywhere.

Among those Allison prayed for were her family, including her great niece Anna (her brother Walter's granddaughter). Today, if you were to go to OMF's headquarters in Singapore, you would find Steve and Anna Griffiths living in one of the flats that Anna's Great Uncle Rowland designed in the 1950s. In fact, says Anna, they continue to sit on some of the furniture Rowland and Allison bought to furnish the new homes all those years ago.

Steve and Anna met in Africa, where Steve had grown up and where Anna went to visit. After some years working there with the Leprosy Mission, they joined OMF in 2000 to serve in Cambodia. Following the terrible years under Pol Pot and

Anna Griffiths, daughter Aimee and her Cambodian friend

the genocide he and the Khmer Rouge unleashed, the task of rebuilding the country was enormous. OMF has been able to play a small, but significant part in that rebuilding. Steve's experience as a doctor and Anna's as a Bible teacher were invaluable. They both loved sharing the gospel with people, pointing to the Savior who could heal the unspeakably deep wounds so many bore.

Later, they were appointed to an international leadership role based in Singapore, where they still carry major responsibilities. They are thankful for their heritage, from Steve's family as well as Anna's. The baton of faith has been passed down through the generations.

41. A Pioneer Surgeon

A mother's prayers and example helped set the course for her young daughter's life. That daughter was Jessie McDonald, who became the first woman surgeon of the China Inland Mission, arriving in China in 1913.

A young girl listened spellbound to a visiting missionary, on home leave from China, describing the sad fate of many Chinese women with little or no access to medical care. "Lord Jesus, when I grow up I would like to help those women," she prayed.

The child was Jessie McDonald, and her prayer would be answered beyond anything she could have imagined. Born in 1888 in Vancouver, Canada, Jessie grew up in a Christian home where her mother prayed earnestly for the gospel to take root in China. Jessie's mother was not able to go herself, but there were Chinese— at that time mostly men—arriving in Vancouver in growing numbers. She could at least reach out to them.

She started teaching English to the new arrivals, hoping to bless them as they struggled to find their way in a new and strange environment and to tell them about her Savior. By age seven, Jessie had joined her mother; she had her very own Chinese pupil to whom she could teach English. No, he had never before heard the name of Jesus, he told her. Jessie was so distressed that she vowed to go to China herself one day. When she heard the missionary speak a few years later, she knew *how* she would go: as a doctor.

The plan of going to China as a female doctor was in itself a commitment of faith. At that time, there were very few female doctors in the Western world. Prejudice against the medical profession being an acceptable sphere for women was common. By the time Jessie entered medical training at the University of Toronto in 1905, she was still one among just five women in a class of 350. Not content with qualifying as a physician, she went on to Europe to study tropical medicine in Vienna and then surgery in London. Finally, knowing that she needed theological study as well, Jessie spent a year in Glasgow, Scotland

CIM hospital in Kaifeng

at the Bible Training Institute. She applied to the China Inland Mission and sailed for China in September 1913. She was just 26 years old.

The CIM sent Jessie to the city of Kaifeng to join the veteran doctor Whitefield Guinness. She was to remain there for 26 years. The CIM hospital was the only medical facility in the near vicinity, and patients often endured days of difficult travel to reach it.

Sometimes they were so sick by the time they arrived that nothing could be done for them, especially since few were brought to the hospital until local remedies had been tried and failed. Yet many patients did survive, and they and their families were grateful. Some listened gladly to the gospel, some did not. Most of the patients were men, since local custom did not approve of a woman being treated by a male doctor or in a hospital for men, and in any case in the culture of the time women were considered to be more expendable than men.

Jessie immediately tried to change the situation for women in the area. Not only would she treat male patients, but she would also ensure that, as far as was possible, the barriers to women accessing medical care would be removed. She had hardly settled in at Kaifeng before she designed and oversaw the construction of a building for female patients, financed by a generous gift from the United States for that specific purpose. Word quickly spread. In 1915 she treated 299 women, many as inpatients; by 1917 the number had risen to 698. She was still treating male patients as well. Many of them suffered from infectious diseases such as diphtheria, scarlet fever or tuberculosis, but others came to the hospital after having been stabbed or shot, or needing surgery for the removal of neglected tumors.

Jessie's wisdom in getting training in surgery as well as in medicine was soon apparent. She also treated very large numbers of patients with eye problems. Constant exposure to wind-blown dust affected everybody as they traveled or worked in the fields. Dust and grit quickly damaged unprotected eyes, especially when few people bothered to waste precious water on washing their faces.

Opium addicts were also treated at the Kaifeng hospital, which earned a good reputation for helping these needy people break their habits. Addiction could be tackled when a patient cooperated with extended treatment, but a common problem was patients leaving the hospital before treatment was complete and then returning to their old ways. Among the women who came for care, attempted suicide was a major issue, especially when a woman was treated badly by her husband or his family or when a young woman was forced into a marriage against her will. On one occasion, Jessie removed at least 50 needles

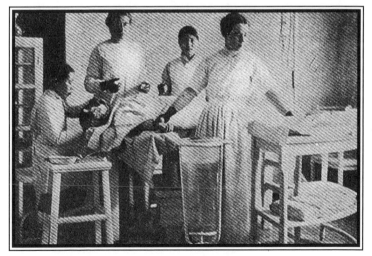

Dr Jessie McDonald – Kaifeng hospital, Henan, 1916

from the stomach and intestines of a young woman who had swallowed them in despair.

Her skill as a doctor and surgeon, as well as her capacity for developing facilities, won the respect of men and women alike, whether among foreign missionary colleagues or the local Chinese community. This latter group included patients, patients' relatives and a substantial number of local officials with whom she had to deal. Few Chinese in any category were Christians, making her acceptance all the more remarkable. Jessie was always adamant, however, that while she must treat equally all patients regardless of their social or religious standing, the task of her medical work was not only to bring healing to bodies and minds but also to point to the Healer of souls. Her great joy was when a patient or someone else she met came to faith in the Lord Jesus.

In order to improve and increase the hospital's staff, Jessie started training local Chinese nurses. Women's role in Chinese society was gradually changing at the time. Over the years, Jessie saw a large number of women trained to become skilled nurses, much sought after by other hospitals.

However, China was often in turmoil at the time as well, and in 1927 it became necessary for most CIM personnel to withdraw to the coast. It was three years before Jessie could return to Kaifeng, where to her distress she discovered that the hospital's buildings and equipment had been greatly damaged. Despite the setback, Jessie—now the hospital's senior doctor and in charge of the whole work—gathered a team around her, rebuilt the buildings, tracked down trained staff and bought new equipment. The hospital once more served the people of Kaifeng.

In 1939, Jessie faced another crisis. The Japanese had invaded parts of China, and even before Pearl Harbor brought them formally to war with the United States and Great Britain, they were hostile towards most other foreigners working in the areas they controlled. As a Canadian, Jessie was unwelcome. The Japanese tolerated her for a while, as she scrupulously treated anyone of any nationality who was sick (sometimes she even found herself saving the lives of Japanese wounded soldiers alongside her Chinese patients). By late 1940, however, it was clear that she could no longer stay. Her continued presence might cause trouble for her Chinese friends. Sadly, Jessie left Kaifeng for good.

The CIM had decided to open a new hospital in Southwest China, where the Japanese were not in control, and asked Jessie to oversee its establishment. She accepted the task and in 1941, moved to a new area and began all over again to shoulder the chief responsibility for building, equipping and staffing a hospital. She was now 53. She steadily brought together a fine team of doctors and nurses, and the hospital quickly earned its reputation for being a good place to go for skilled and loving care. In particular, those too poor to pay for treatment and who would otherwise suffer needlessly or die, found they were as welcome at the hospital as their wealthier neighbors. The hospital was also in an area where opium addiction was even more of a scourge than it had been in Kaifeng.

With a strong team of doctors in place, Jessie no longer felt that she had to stay at the new hospital all the time. What about those still too far away to access help? In 1948 she opened a branch clinic of the hospital 150 miles away, far from the rest of her team. Yet, before long, Jessie was again engaged in medicine and surgery in a busy town with no other medical facility. She divided her time between the hospital and the clinic, in the process traveling hundreds of miles each month.

Jessie would gladly have stayed in China until she was too old to hold a surgeon's scalpel or diagnose accurately. Instead, she reluctantly left China with her colleagues in the exodus of 1951-52 and returned to North America. She was by then old enough to begin a peaceful retirement. Instead, she joined the faculty of Biola School of Missionary Medicine in California. If she could not be in China, at least she could help train a new generation of men and women for medical service in many other countries. She urged her students to strive for two things: to provide the best medical care in a variety of contexts, as the resources could be very basic at some facilities, and to prayerfully depend on God as the true Healer.

It was not only China that changed much in Jessie's lifetime. So had Western medicine. Indeed, most of the world saw immense political and social change. But the gospel remained as it always had been, and the desire planted in Jessie's heart as a small child that people should hear about the Savior remained a constant in her life. She saw God at work through good times and bad. She continued to inspire others, not with her own adventures but with the faithfulness of God, when she died at the age of 92.

42. I Will Build My Church

> When the CIM left China in the early 1950s, there was much prayer and discussion as to where else they might serve God's purposes most effectively. At the time, Korea was engulfed in civil war that developed into an international war, and it was decided that the CIM should not try to work there. A survey in 1954, after the war ended, recommended that there were less evangelized places than Korea with greater claims on the Mission's resources. Service there was once again set aside. However, a little more than a decade later, the situation changed.

Sometimes the Lord's apparent "No" becomes "Not yet." Such was the case when the fledgling Overseas Missionary Fellowship was deciding whether to send personnel to Korea. There were good reasons for deciding in 1951 (and then again in 1954) that Korea would be outside the organization's sphere of ministry, especially while there were so many unreached parts of Southeast Asia. In any case, there were other mission groups already working in South Korea. It was not the OMF's desire to duplicate or compete.

Then in 1965, when the organization's International Council decided the time had come to welcome Asian applicants to serve as members, the first to apply was a Korean couple, John and Susan Kim. They were studying in the United States at the time and were accepted there, since there was no mechanism for them to be interviewed in Korea. However, it was important for them to reconnect with their church in Korea before going to the field, so they went back to Korea to prepare, they hoped, for service in Japan. As it happened, however, they were unable to obtain visas for Japan. After several years in Korea, the Kims eventually returned to the States to pastor a

Korean congregation there, but they were an important link in the chain of events.

The Kims' application raised once more the question of the organization's connections to Korea. Michael Griffiths, shortly to become General Director, and Arnold Lea, then Overseas Director, went to investigate. Two of Korea's largest Presbyterian denominations declared themselves keen to receive OMF workers. In particular, there were invitations to help with youth and literature ministries. The organization's leadership decided to trust the Lord to send the right personnel to meet the Korean churches' needs.

Almost immediately, the U.K. National Office inquired about the possibility of placing personnel in Korea. Two couples and a single woman were all asking. One couple, Peter and Audrey Pattisson, had already spent two years in Korea with Save the Children Fund on the staff of a hospital treating tuberculosis patients. They believed the Lord wanted them to return to Korea, but they preferred to do so under the auspices of OMF and as part of a team. They already knew another couple, John and Kathleen Wallis, and the single woman who had inquired, Margaret Robertson. All five were sure the Lord was calling them to Korea and wanted to do so with OMF. Surely this must be God's confirmation.

In 1969 the five workers arrived together in Korea, where they were met by John Kim. He had been greatly disappointed in not being able to go to Japan, but that meant he was able to provide invaluable help to this new team as they began the task of language study and finding their particular niches for ministry. John's commitment to OMF and his unexpected stay in Korea were evidence of God's loving sovereignty. By the time the new team arrived in Korea, John was teaching at a seminary in Seoul. He quickly introduced the group to some of his students.

It was to be these students who helped guide the OMF team to their particular contribution to the Korean church. Years later, Peter Pattisson wrote, "We found some real friends among these seminary students. They had great warmth and enthusiasm, considerable theological knowledge and, like students everywhere (especially theological ones), an intense concern for orthodoxy, but, all in all, a surprising lack of personal devotional life centered around the word of God. It was a clue to a situation we were to find repeated far and wide."

At that time, many Korean churches gathered for early morning prayer meetings. The meetings had multiple purposes:

1. Give the first part of the day to the Lord.
2. Intercede for the nation, the church and the pastor.
3. Have group devotional time. For some people, it was not easy to understand the Bible; some people were illiterate until they became a Christian.
4. Give a daily offering and sometimes give a tithe of farm produce.

The meetings were still attended by a number of older believers, but the majority of younger Christians rarely went.

All five members of the small OMF team had personal experience with the ministry of Scripture Union (SU), both in its work with children and young people, and in their literature. In particular, they had all found the Scripture Union Bible reading system had nurtured their personal Bible study and prayer life. An Australian couple had hoped to start SU work in Korea a few years earlier, but due to health reasons had to return home after a short time. Nonetheless, they had shared their vision with the leaders of a student ministry in Korea. One of the leaders had already written some Bible study notes for use among the students. Upon meeting the new OMF workers, he told them it would be really helpful to have the team help establish SU work in Korea, and to take its ministry into the churches as well as among young people.

Over the next several years, along with the Pattissons' ongoing work at the tuberculosis hospital, the main focus of OMF's efforts in Korea was to encourage personal engagement with the scriptures, as well as discipleship in order to supplement and personalize what believers were being taught at church meetings. Step by step, many Korean students and church members discovered more deeply what it means to have direct access to our heavenly Father through personal Bible study and prayer, expecting God to speak to them as they studied and prayed. The team grew and began work with churches and student groups in an increasing number of cities.

As they gained the confidence of church leaders, ministers asked for help in improving their preaching so that it better engaged the day-to-day life of their members. Willie and Katie Black from Scotland were among those who helped in this ministry. Willie, an ordained Presbyterian minister, was warmly welcomed by the Korean pastors. At one time, he met with 100 pastors each week, in 10 different groups, to help them with sermon preparation. Other workers, such as Cecily Moar from Australia, worked alongside the student movement.

Much of the history of OMF has been focused on pioneer evangelism and church planting, but that was not the case in Korea. The church was already well established, although with a disturbing tendency to fragment. OMF ministry in

Korea was low profile, seeking to serve in the background. The goal was always to serve through the churches already there and to ensure that Koreans took the lead in any further ministry or organization that emerged. From the start, when Scripture Union was formally constituted in Korea, it was led by a Korean, Yune Zong-Ha. It was not easy to establish an interdenominational ministry, since most denominations in Korea preferred to operate separately, but gradually SU and the student ministry modeled the importance and blessing of cooperation across denominational boundaries. Church leaders saw that SU was not competing with the churches, but assisting them.

During the 1980s, Korean churches began to take world mission seriously. Today Korea is home to one of the largest mission movements in the world. Many Korean missionaries are willing to go to some of the hardest places in the world and to live simply. At the request of Korean church leaders, in 1980, OMF established the Korean Home Council, which shortly afterwards became a full national office. In order to help those wanting to join the organization, some native English speakers helped Korean workers learn English, the common language of OMF and of working teams, and helped prepare them for the challenges of cross-cultural life. Cross-cultural living can be especially demanding for Koreans, as their country remains strongly homogeneous in language and culture. Other Koreans have come from Australia, North America and Europe (to which their families had emigrated) and brought more diversity. The churches of the Korean diaspora have shared the South Korean churches' desire to reach the world for Christ.

Since 1980 OMF has been blessed by a swelling number of Korean members. Many of them live in difficult ministry contexts. They are often able to go where Westerners are no longer welcome. Many Korean co-workers testify to the way in which the work of Scripture Union in Korea and other ministries to which God led OMF members have enriched their love of God and of his word. God's work through that initial team continues to bear fruit.

By 2004 it seemed that the contribution of OMF expatriates (non-Koreans) in Korea—though certainly not of missionaries from Korea—was complete. The Lord's "No" that became a "Not yet" and then a "Now," had become a "Your role is finished." But that is not the end of the story, for along with many other networks around the world, OMF is committed to pray for the whole Korean Peninsula. Where we can no longer go, or where our work is done, the ministry of prayer remains. For God, there are no borders. Times change, generations come and go, but God remains faithful to his eternal purposes.

43. Justice for the Poor

In the late 1960s and early 1970s, student protests and politically radical movements took place in many countries. The unrest had different immediate causes in different places, but many claimed to seek greater justice for the poor and marginalized. Most were inspired by idealistic political ideology. Campuses in the Philippines were no exception.

Manila, capital of the Philippines, was an uneasy city in the late 1960s and early 1970s. You could set out from home along a busy but peaceful street, turn a corner or two and suddenly find yourself in the middle of a battle. Students armed with large stocks of Molotov cocktails and ping pong balls filled with dynamite and shrapnel faced police and military armed with guns and grenades. Sooner or later, one side would start firing, and bloodshed ensued.

The New People's Army calculated that if they could win the hearts and minds of students, especially those of the prestigious University of the Philippines in Manila, they would be able to oust the President and take over the country. It was not always difficult to gain student sympathy. The President and his wife had become obscenely wealthy while swelling numbers of Filipinos were desperately poor and hungry, the slums places of despair with appalling conditions. Unless you had money to offer as a bribe, the forces of "law and order" were not on your side, however innocent you might be. A growing number of those who dared to question the status quo mysteriously disappeared, never to be seen again.

The dominant Roman Catholic Church seemed to enjoy its wealth and had no prophetic voice (with some exceptions). It did not look as if traditional Christianity had any answers. It was easy to see why idealistic young people might see revolution as the only solution.

It was the InterVarsity Christian Fellowship (IVCF) group on the campus that started to offer an alternative vision. IVCF workers believed that the Bible had answers, both for the needed transformation of the human heart and also for ways in which to pursue justice for society. They set to work not only in urgent evangelism, but also in combing the scriptures for answers to difficult but urgent questions. They realized that the gospel is about more than personal piety and a ticket to heaven; authentic discipleship must impact every dimension of life, individual and corporate.

Their courage in asserting a well-reasoned alternative to the revolutionary ideology was costly. Some Christian student leaders were targeted, attacked or intimidated, or their families were threatened. The difficulties produced a cohort of young people dedicated to following Christ through thick and thin.

A Filipino youth named Marlon Roldan entered this intense context as he enrolled at the University of the Philippines. Although his parents were committed members of their respective churches and had taught him to pray, Marlon did not at this time have a lively personal faith in Jesus. He was, however, troubled by the social injustices in his country and, wondering how he could make a difference, decided to follow a path that focused on community development. He was well aware of the ideology of the protest groups competing for his allegiance, but sensed it could not bring justice and peace.

God had his hand on Marlon. While searching for life's purpose and some ideals worth living and dying for, Marlon was invited to join a small IVCF group that was discussing the Bible and what it taught about the concerns that were so important to him. "In the midst of the turmoil the words of Jesus came through: 'I am the way, the truth and the life,'" said Marlon. "I told him, 'I want these. Please show me the way to live. Teach me the truth behind all my problems and difficulties. I want to have a meaningful life. Please come into my life. I surrender, I am totally yours.'"

Marlon was one among a key group of students who came to faith around that time. Many of them like Marlon were deeply concerned for the well-being of their countrymen. They had numerous questions for which they sought God's answers. Several of them later became members of OMF, serving in several different countries. Others became strategic leaders in their churches and professions at home. One foreign missionary couple, seconded by OMF to work with students, found the group immensely stretching and stimulating. They freely admitted to learning alongside the students as they searched God's word together, even as they tried to be faithful mentors. Many of the students became lifelong friends. There were many shared tears and many shared joys.

During Marlon's last year at the university, he was assigned to do part of his training in a Mangyan village in Mindoro. The Mangyan were a group of six tribal minorities, among whom OMF missionaries had worked since the early 1950s. In addition to teaching the Bible and translating it into the six languages, OMF personnel acted as catalysts to establish an extensive development program, in partnership with a group of Christian lawyers. The program aimed to address physical, social and economic issues that often negatively impacted ethnic minorities and (especially) tribal groups.

After graduating, Marlon and his wife, Yoyit, worked for six years leading the community development project among the Mangyan.

The project included programs for adult literacy, primary health care, legal assistance, establishing cooperatives and trading and agriculture. It also involved working together in close partnership with the OMF missionaries who were still serving the minority groups. Marlon and Yoyit also acted as dorm parents for a number of Mangyan children who came to the lowlands for elementary schooling. Theirs was a full life, but one in which they grew to love the Mangyan people and be loved by them. At the end of the six years, Marlon had trained a Mangyan church leader to take over from him. This was the kind of social change he had dreamed of from even before he came to faith.

Marlon & Yoyit

In the mid-1980s Marlon sensed the Lord calling him to pastoral ministry. He was able to study both within the Philippines and in London, and then pastored two churches over several years. During this time, Yoyit developed her ministry in university teaching.

However, Marlon could not quite shake off his deep commitment to community development, particularly for the marginalized, and for church planting that was committed to social transformation in the name of the Lord Jesus. So, from 1996 to 1999 he worked with an organization, the Asia Evangelistic Fellowship, where his role involved extensive travel throughout the country.

On one of his journeys he visited the island of Palawan in the western part of the Philippines and was distressed by the neglect of the tribal minorities there. A year later, Marlon took a group of lowland pastors from Palawan to Mindoro to show them what was being done among the Mangyan, coordinated

Marlon & Yoyit Roldan & family

by the Mangyan Tribal Churches Association working on behalf of all six tribal groups. The work was then firmly in the hands of the Mangyan themselves. "Well," said Marlon, "do you not think you could help the minorities on Palawan develop something like this?" At the same time, he asked the Mangyan church leaders, who were already sending their own missionaries to the Negrito people of Southern Luzon, "Would you pray about sending people to Palawan, too? You know how your lives have been transformed through receiving the gospel. You could help these people, too!"

Marlon repeated the challenge to the Mangyan while back in Mindoro for a visit. He met one of the Mangyan church leaders, Peter Mayut, whose arm was in a sling. "What happened?" asked Marlon. "I was with the principal of the Mangyan Bible School, looking to see whether we could send some of our people to minority groups somewhere else," replied Peter. "We were on a motorbike and an OMF couple was on another bike, too, when we were ambushed. The OMF couple and their driver were all injured. I felt something like a red hot charcoal passing through my hand between two fingers—it was a bullet, and it went on to kill the driver in front of me. It was a terrible experience."

Marlon gently said, "Why not come to Palawan and see for yourselves what you could do there? I promise nobody will ambush you there!" Almost at once, the Bible school principal and some of his students set off across the water to see for themselves. They talked with Palawano church leaders and even showed lowland pastors how to do the chronological Bible storytelling that had helped them so much, especially with oral learners. As a result, the next year Marlon found himself accompanying four Mangyan families on the boat to the village in Palawan where they were to work in partnership with lowland pastors.

Marlon & Andrea Roldan

In 2001, Marlon became the community development advisor for the OMF Serve Philippines team. The Philippines, scattered across hundreds of islands, is home to numerous distinct ethnic groups and languages. The Serve Philippines program enables Filipinos to serve cross-culturally, but within their own country. Often, workers are engaged in quiet initiatives in Jesus' name to improve the lives of the poor and neglected or those suffering in the aftermath of natural disasters such as earthquakes, typhoons and tsunamis, all of which frequently afflict the country. Marlon's experience in development work is an invaluable help to many projects.

Marlon and Yoyit are also delighted that their daughter, Andrea, joined OMF. After working in another country with a minority group, she first coordinated short-term mission teams for OMF's office in the Philippines and later became the international facilitator for all of the organization's short-term openings. While OMF mainly looks for people committed to long-term service, with time spent learning a language and beginning to understand a culture, there are significant opportunities for short-term service, too.

With Marlon and Yoyit as her parents, Andrea knows that the best short-term mission works in conjunction with sustained long-term ministries. She also loves to see people being transformed through coming to know the Lord for themselves, but also by working to transform the lives of those around them.

As a young man, Marlon searched for answers to life's big questions and sought ways to improve the lives of the poor and neglected in the Philippines. In Christ, Marlon found the answers he sought and God has used him to bless many in his country and beyond.

44. A Catalyst for Mission

In 1973, Kunimitsu and Hiroko Ogawa became the first Japanese OMF missionaries to Indonesia. Why would the Lord take them from their home country where the church is so small to Indonesia where many churches are quite large? In 1984 the Ogawas were asked to go to Singapore to lead a training center preparing believers (Asians and Westerners) for cross-cultural ministry. Their experience in Indonesia brought great depth and wisdom to this ministry.

"Ever since I was called to overseas mission work in 1969, I have had a God-given hope and a question. Why is it that, although less than one percent of the total population of Japan is Christian and therefore Japan perhaps needs the gospel more than other countries, that my wife and I have had to go and work overseas? I do not believe there are mistakes in God's plan, but what sort of answer would God give to this question? Believing that he will surely answer it, we have earnestly continued to walk the missionary path."

So wrote Kunimitsu Ogawa a few years after going to Indonesia. He and his wife Hiroko discovered that God has purposes far beyond our understanding when he calls us to obey in faith.

The Ogawas were convinced as they read the scriptures that all Christians are called to be globally minded and involved in cross-cultural mission in some way. When the strong sense of call to serve among the Javanese of Indonesia came to them, they left behind successful careers in research and academia, applied to OMF in Japan and were accepted. Together with their baby daughter they set off for Indonesia. The Evangelical Free Church of Japan that sent the Ogawas out only had about

800 people (nationwide) at the time. It was an adventure of faith for the church as well as for the Ogawas.

After some initial Indonesian language study, the Ogawas began working with the Muria Church in Central Java. Their early years were far from easy and included the death of their third child a few hours after her birth. Later Kunimitsu wrote, "My wife and I often pondered on the word of God, 'For we know that all things work together for good to them that love God, to those who are called according to his purpose' (Romans 8:28). Now as we look back, we realize that by passing through these experiences, we touch the loving heart of the people among whom we live. It was a new challenge to us to continue believing in God's loving purposes for us, and a warning that we did not have enough love towards the people to whom we had been sent. I think we could say that this was one of the chief causes for the subsequent blessing on the Salatiga Church." Their baby was buried alongside the baby son of their Indonesian pastor. Here was deep identification.

The Ogawas needed to learn Javanese as well as Indonesian, but at the same time they were engaged in a variety of ministries: evangelism, teaching at a Bible school, discipling university students. By the time they began their second term of service in 1979, they were working in a team with a local pastor. In addition to the main congregation, there were three smaller village churches to teach and encourage. Yet right from the very beginning of their time in Indonesia, the Ogawas felt burdened to see Indonesian Christians become involved in cross-cultural mission.

"Even while I was still studying Indonesian I began preaching around the churches, and in almost every sermon I used to introduce the subject of mission," said Kunimitsu.

"However, there was never any positive response. On the contrary, there was opposition. We heard comments like 'Japan is Japan, Indonesia is Indonesia. It's too early to think about sending missionaries to foreign countries. In Indonesia itself there are many areas that need gifts and workers.' Whatever I said, there seemed to be no realistic thinking about it, and so I lost hope."

The one thing the Ogawas could do was pray. They started a small prayer group in their home to pray for the world. When, after home assignment, they went to work with a church in Salatiga, they started a prayer group again focused on looking at the need for the whole world to hear the Good News of Jesus Christ. At first, the church's deacons disapproved, but gradually they came to accept mission to other parts of Indonesia as something they could support. It was an important first step.

Later, the Ogawas were visited by Hanna Handojo. In 1978, Hanna had been the first missionary to go out with OMF from Indonesia (she went to the Philippines). After Hanna spoke at the missions prayer meeting at the Ogawas' church in Indonesia, the church decided to start financially supporting both home and overseas missions. Prayer for missions was included in the regular services, not just in the missionaries' prayer meeting. The vision for engaging in mission steadily grew and became a normal part of believers' lives in the church. Teaching on world mission was included in the twice-yearly believers' training courses. No longer was mission something other people brought to them, but something that the whole church was to be committed to.

Today, a growing number of Indonesians serve Jesus Christ cross-culturally, both within and beyond their home country. Among those who have worked with OMF from Indonesia are Andersius and Ratna Namsi, who served in Thailand from 1999 to 2008.

In 1992, the Namsis applied to OMF through its Indonesia Home Council. They applied to go overseas, but were unable to do so at that time because they could not raise the needed funds. Instead, they served with a national church in its cross-cultural outreach. They enjoyed serving in Indonesia and did not think too much more about going overseas, since the financial issue seemed such a high barrier, impossible to overcome.

In 1998, Indonesia and much of Southeast Asia was badly affected by a financial crisis. Yet it was then that the Lord again convinced the Namsis that they should go to Thailand. In 1999 they left for Thailand in obedience to the Lord, even though they had only enough funds to stay there for six months.

Suddenly the Lord then provided the funds for them to stay in Thailand long-term and enabled the Namsis to become full members of OMF. "It was a miraculous and amazing thing that God has done for us and for our ministry, especially in light of the major economic crisis back in Indonesia," said Andersius. "The Lord himself made something impossible become possible."

Andersius and Ratna learned that a church in another Asian country had been praying for two years to be able to support an Indonesian missionary. Someone from that group had heard Andersius' testimony shortly before he went to Thailand. Then another church also decided to support the couple. God provided.

The Ogawas wondered why the Lord would take them from the small church of Japan to Indonesia. Perhaps the answer lies here: they were to be part of the story—one significant catalyst among others—to encourage Indonesians to take their place in world mission. Their story became part of the far larger story of God's purposes of grace for his people.

A few years ago, after the Ogawas had retired, the Lord called them to plant a new church in Tokyo. Around that time, the Ogawas returned to Indonesia to visit the church they had served for so many years in Jakarta and share their vision for the church plant in Tokyo. The church held a special commissioning service for them. One of their former students —now a successful businessman—gave a significant financial contribution to help with the work in Tokyo. Their efforts at cultivating a heart for the nations among Indonesian believers had not been in vain. The "missionary path" that Kunimitsu spoke of has come full circle: As the Ogawas plant a new church in Japan—where less than one percent of the population knows Jesus Christ—they do so with the support and prayers of their Indonesian brothers and sisters. God will fulfill his purposes.

Afterword

The Next Story

Now that you have read these stories, how can you respond? We hope that you will join us in praising God for his faithfulness and for his compassion and power in bringing hope, truth and peace to the peoples of East Asia. We pray that you will be moved to worship God for his amazing ability to work through normal people.

Is God prompting you to join us in other ways? There are still peoples and places with insurmountable obstacles (humanly speaking) to the gospel. What will it take to see God's church begin and grow in every people group in East Asia?

Is God calling you to PRAY? You can pray in response to missionary prayer letters, the news or tools such as *Operation World*. Some people pray best in community and like to gather some friends together. Find a prayer guide or a regular prayer update to help focus your prayers in specific areas.

Is God leading you to GO? You can serve for two weeks, two months, two years or two decades. We see short- and medium-term placements as a great opportunity to explore cross-cultural ministry while contributing to the long-term needs.

Is God showing you how to WELCOME? How much time have you spent with international students, immigrants and foreign visitors living right in your city? East Asian governments send many of their best future leaders to study overseas. Can you join or start a ministry to befriend and love these guests in your country as you share your life with them?

Is God compelling you to MOBILIZE? If you have already been on a short-term mission trip, you can lead the next one or find three friends to go on a team next year. You could serve as a volunteer with an OMF mobilization team. How can you help others see the vision God has given you?

Is God inviting you to LEARN? Use every available resource to grow and prepare yourself for the next step God is preparing for you. Read missionary biographies and news about the places God has put on your heart. Take a course such as *Perspectives or Kairos*. Connect with cross-cultural workers whenever you can and ask them as much as you can about their experiences.

Is God asking you to SEND? Missionaries need lots of practical support and encouragement at every stage of their ministry. Start or join a missionary's support team at home to be part of the work they are doing. Give sacrificially of your time, money, creativity and encouragement to move the ministry forward.

We want to help you explore these opportunities. Even if you never set foot in East Asia, God has opportunities for you to follow in the footsteps of the pioneers whose stories have been told in these pages. Many of us started our journey with God's prompting in these simple questions and opportunities. Please get in touch with us today and let us know how we can pray with and encourage you on your journey.

OMF International
www.omf.org

Bibliography

150 YEARS OF GOD'S FAITHFULNESS

- Broomhall, A. J. *Hudson Taylor and China's Open Century.* Sevenoaks, Kent: Hodder & Stoughton and the Overseas Missionary Fellowship, 1981-1989, 7 vols.
- Huntley, David Alan. "From Shanghai to Nanyang—and back." Unpublished article, 2013.
- Huntley, David Alan. "The Withdrawal of the China Inland Mission from China and the Redeployment to New Fields in East Asia: An Understanding of the Methodology and Decision-Making Processes." PhD Diss., Trinity Theological Seminary, 2002.
- Steer, Roger. *J. Hudson Taylor: A Man in Christ.* Singapore: Overseas Missionary Fellowship, 1990.

Various editions of CIM and OMF magazines; titles have changed numerous times in the organization's 150-year history:

China's Millions 1875 - May 1952
The Millions June 1952 - 1964
East Asia Millions 1965 - 1996
East Asia's Millions 1997 - 2011
East Asia's Billions 2000 - 2011
Millions 2012 -
Billions 2012 -

To Strengthen the Weak

5. The Pilgrim Life
- David Huntley's Thesis, "The Withdrawal of the CIM from China; and the Redeployment ...etc." (2002), p. 72

- "Fields for Reaping, Malaya" by Anne Hazelton (Pub.by CIM OMF in 1957) p. 17
- China's Millions 1946 - 1952, The Millions 1952 - 1964, East Asia Millions 1965 - 1968
- Unpublished material by Mary Welander
- Reflections of OMF Malaya/Malaysia workers
- Welander, Mary. *I Was a Rebel.* London: OMF International U.K., 1962.

6. Let the Little Children Come

Grace Harris sources:

- Harris, Grace. "Round the Camp Fire." East Asia Millions December 1977.
- Other articles from China's Millions 1946 - 1952; The Millions 1952 - 1954; and East Asia Millions 1952 - 1980.
- Recollections of OMF workers in Thailand
- Brief notes from Grace Harris

Erwin Groebli sources:

- Story submitted by Erwin Groebli
- Background from East Asia Millions 1965 - 1996, East Asia's Milions 1997 - 1999, East Asia's Billions 2000 - 2008.

7. Church Growth in Borneo

- Stories submitted by Brian and Esther Newton.

8. A Sudden Boldness

- Article submitted by Robert Erion.

9. His Eye is on the Sparrow

- Article submitted by Beth McFarland.

10. Learning to Trust: Marginalized Women in Cambodia

- Story submitted by Elisabeth Hirschi
- Hirschi, Elisabeth. *Gottes sanfte Berührungen* (God's Gentle Touch). OMF Books, 2013.

11. Beyond Our Strength

- Interview with a worker in a creative-access country.

From Darkness to Light

12. Fertile Ground
- Interviews and emails with current and retired OMF workers who cannot be named due to security reasons.

13. The Power of Touch
- Bell, Roland. "Flood fighting at Manorom." East Asia's Millions February 1976.

Articles by Anne Townsend:
- "Teach Us at Dawn." East Asia's Millions September 1966.
- "Of Such is the Church." East Asia's Millions November 1967.
- "That's not missionary work, is it?" East Asia's Millions June 1968.
- "Metamorphosis of Paddy Field Hospital." East Asia's Millions October 1968.
- "Cultural Comprehension." East Asia's Millions December 1968.
- "Moving – Where?" East Asia's Millions September 1969.
- "In medicine." East Asia's Millions October 1970.
- "Impossible." East Asia's Millions April 1976.
- "A need to be met." East Asia's Millions June 1976.

Articles by John Townsend:
- "Speaking of Medical Work." East Asia's Millions June 1971.
- "I wish you could come." East Asia's Millions March 1972.
- "Why Mission Hospitals?" East Asia's Millions February 1976.
- "Why Medical Work?" East Asia's Millions August 1979.
- "Many Members – One Body." East Asia's Millions August 1979.
- Unpublished autobiography (used with permission).

14. Light Shines in Mongolia
- Article submitted by OMF worker Kirk Matthews.
- Cable, Mildred and Francesca French. *The Making of a Pioneer*. New York: Frederick A. Stokes Co., 1935.

15. From Tragedy to Faith
- Article submitted by OMF worker Matthias Holighaus.
- OMF Thailand Field prayer letters, 2004.
- Emails from other OMF members present at the time.

16. Seek the Truth from Facts
- Article submitted by a worker in a creative-access location.

17. The Pearl Family Garden
- Twillert, Tera van. "Serving those on the street." East Asia's Billions October 2009.
- Twillert, Tera van. "Promised Land: The birth of a new ministry." Billions January 2014.
- Emails with Tera van Twillert.

To Provide

18. More than All We Ask or Imagine
- Frame, Raymond. "CIM Story of the Year 1948: Friend, I do thee no wrong." 1948.
- Other articles from *China's Millions* (1948) were also consulted.

19. A Bible College for North Thailand
- Davis, John. Unpublished memoirs.
- Interviews and correspondence with David Pickard (former Thailand Field Director and former General Director of OMF)
- Other articles from *East Asia's Millions* (1975 - 1995) were also consulted.

20. Enduring Power of Print
- "OMF Book Boom in Indonesia." East Asia Millions June 1972.
- Dainton, Martin. "Coffee into Books." East Asia Millions April 1968.
- Dainton, Martin. "Milk for Babes." East Asia Millions June 1969.

- Dainton, Martin. "Through Communication." East Asia Millions October 1970.
- Merle Grigg. "Tracts for the Times." East Asia Millions October 1966.
- Russell Grigg. "Indonesia Flash." East Asia Millions November 1965.
- Leatha Humes. "Texbooks for a Nation." East Asia Millions December 1967.
- Longley, Guy. "Christian Literature in a Muslim Land." The Millions November 1961.
- Ruck, Anne. *God Made It Grow: OMF Indonesia, the First 50 Years.* 2003.
- Steed, George. "Proceed to Indonesia." The Millions April 1960.
- Other issues of East Asia Millions and East Asia's Millions
- Correspondence with Leatha Humes and Jack Largent
- Recollections of retired OMF members.

21. Foxes Have Holes, Birds Have their Nests

- Article submitted by Averil Bennett
- Bennett, Averil. "The Church along the Mekong." East Asia's Millions August 1991.
- Bennett, Averil. "There's Power in Praise." East Asia's Millions December 1992.
- Other articles from East Asia's Millions (1983-1993) were also consulted.

22. A Misunderstanding—and God's Answer

- Article submitted by Son Chang Nam.

23. A Huge Gift in Japan

- OMF Japan field records and correspondence
- Personal correspondence and conversations with John Taylor, former Japan Field Director, and Naoyuki Makino, former National Director of OMF Japan.

24. Loved into the Kingdom

- Article submitted by Sin Ee Teo and other OMF workers in Taiwan and Singapore

25. Typhoon Blessing
- Article submitted by Wendy Marshall

Through the Fire

26. The Boxer Rebellion of 1900
- "The Beginning of the Boxer Trouble in North China." China's Millions September 1900.
- China's Millions October and November 1900
- China's Millions November 1900.
- Other memorial editions of *China's Millions* until 1901.
- Broomhall, A J. "The Boxer Madness, 1898-1900." In *Hudson Taylor and China's Open Century*. Vol. 7, *It Is Not Death to Die*, 291-434. Sevenoaks, Kent: Hodder & Stoughton, 1989.
- Broomhall, Marshall. *Martyred Missionaries of the China Inland Mission, With a Record of the Perils and Sufferings of Some Who Escaped*. London: Morgan & Scott, 1901.

27. For Love of Children
- Various articles in China's Millions 1887 - 1918.
- Personal correspondence with Mary Searles, a surviving relative.
- Thompson, Phyllis. *A London Sparrow*. London: Word Books, 1971.

28. Wheelchair Evangelist
- Articles by Jean Anderson:
- "Booked to Sail for Southeast Asia." The Millions January 1953.
- "A First Glimpse of Thailand." The Millions March 1954.
- "A Spirit at Work in Central Thailand." The Millions April 1954.
- "Opportunities Through Leprosy." The Millions April 1956.
- "Missionary on Wheels." The Millions March 1964.
- "Hope for the Hopeless." East Asia Millions October 1965.
- "Beauty for Ashes." East Asia Millions November 1966.

- "Wheels within Wheels." East Asia Millions October 1968.
- "Manorom Convert." East Asia Millions December 1977.

Other writers:
- "Miss Jean Anderson." The Millions April 1960 and January 1961.
- "He Maketh My Way Perfect." The Millions June 1961.
- Wibberly, Gerald. "Bible Study and Rubber Shoes." East Asia Millions June 1976.
- Reflections from OMF workers in Thailand.

29. A Heart Prepared by God
- Unpublished manuscript by Gillian Orpin.
- Other issues of East Asia Millions, East Asia's Millions and East Asia's Billions.
- Correspondence with Leatha Humes and Jack Largent.
- Personal recollections of other retired OMF International members.
- Bottom of Form
- "Tragedy in Tribesland." The Millions July 1962.
- "Laos." East Asia Millions September 1968.
- "Abroad," East Asia Millions January 1970.
- Orpin, Gillian. "The Leading of Love." The Millions March 1963.
- Whitelock, Doris. "What Makes a Translator?" East Asia Millions November 1970.

30. From Killing Fields to the Love of God
- Article submitted by Solina Chy

31. Suffering Can Open Doors
- Article submitted by Irene McMahon.

32. Life-changing Illness
- Article submitted by Steve Paterson

To Teach and to Guide

33. Joy, Suffering, and the Awakening of the Kachin

- Sik Pui Wong, Sheming de ai: Zhongguo Neidihui xuanjiaoshi xiaozhuan 捨命的愛：中國內地會宣教士小傳 (Sacrificial Love: Portraits of CIM Missionaries), CCM Publishers, 2006. English translation by Greta Y. Wong.
- "Papers of Jennie Kingston Fitzwilliam - Collection 272." Billy Graham Center Archives. http://www2.wheaton.edu/bgc/archives/GUIDES/272.htm.
- Shen Baoluo (Paul). "Working in Yunnan Province among the Lisu tribe." *Christian Life Quarterly*, Vol. 6, No. 1, March 2002.

34. Sixty Years, Step-by-Step in Faith

- Barham, Marie. "The Mangyans of Mindoro." China's Millions April 1952.
- Brown, Morven Cree. "Responsive Tribespeople." The Millions December 1955.
- Page, Hazel. "In Search of Words." The Millions November 1953.
- Reed, Barbara Flory. *Beyond the Great Darkness: Modern Missionary Pioneering in the Jungles of the Philippines*. Singapore: Overseas Missionary Fellowship, 1987.
- Stickley, Caroline. *Broken Snare*. London: Overseas Missionary Fellowship, 1975.
- Williamson, Francis and Marie Barham. "Reaching Mangyan Tribespeople." The Millions November 1952.
- Williamson, Francis. "Into the Philippine Islands, Mindoro." The Millions June 1952.
- Williamson, Francis. "The Tribes Wait to Hear." The Millions June 1952.
- Williamson, Francis. "Seeking the Mangyan," The Millions July 1955.
- Information submitted by Theo Herren.
- Personal correspondence with OMF workers to the Mangyan, 1968 - 2014.

35. Getting the Message Out
- Personal correspondence with retired OMF workers.

36. First Year Challenges
- Article submitted by Eilish Agnew.
- Smalley, William A. "Culture Shock, Language Shock, and the Shock of Self-Discovery." *Practical Anthropology* 10 (1963): 49-56.

37. From Japan with Love
- Correspondence and prayer letters from Naoyuki and Izu Makino.
- OMF Japan Field prayer letters
- Various articles from East Asia's Millions (1974 - 2002) were also consulted.
- Reflections of various OMF members.

38. Searching for the Open Door
- Article submitted by a worker in a creative-access nation.

39. Divine Appointments in Africa
- Prayer letters from Hans-Walter and Sabina Ritter

To All Generations

40. The Inheritance of Faith
- Various issues of China's Millions 1902 - 1952; The Millions 1952 - 1964; and East Asia's Millions 1964 - 1971.
- Story of Douglas Pike submitted from family archives
- Personal interviews with OMF workers in Cambodia and Singapore

41. A Pioneer Surgeon
- Various issues of China's Millions 1913 - 1951.
- Kelman, Georgina "'Jessie Mac,' A Missionary Doctor in China." Georgina Kelman: Works on Paper. June 11, 2012. Accessed May 18, 2014. http://georginakelman.blogspot.com/2012/06/jessie-mac-missionary-doctor-in-china.html.

- McDonald, Anne. "A Missionary in China: Dr. Jessie Mcdonald." Lecture, Proceedings of the 16th Annual History of Medicine Days, Calgary, Alberta, March 2007.

42. I Will Build My Church
- Pattisson, Peter. *Crisis Unawares*. London: OMF International U.K., 1981.
- Various issues of East Asia's Millions 1965-2004.
- Prayer letters and correspondence with Peter and Audrey Pattison and John and Kathleen Wallis, 1968 - 2014.

43. Justice for the Poor
- Correspondence with Marlon Roldan
- OMF Philippines Field prayer letters
- Unpublished personal records of Dick and Rose Dowsett

44. A Catalyst for Mission
- Ogawa, Joshua K. *Unlimited Purpose: An Asian Missionary Tells His Story*. Singapore: Overseas Missionary Fellowship, 1986.
- Letter submitted by Andersius and Ratna Namsi.
- Reflections by OMF members in Indonesia and Japan.
- Various articles in East Asia's Millions (1973 - 1997), East Asia's Billions (1997 - 1999), East Asia's Billions (2000 - 2012) and Billions (2012 - 2014).

Historical Markers in the CIM/OMF journey

A.D. 635 - 1839
The early attempts to evangelize China

Early attempts to evangelize China, such as those by Nestorian Christians in A.D. 635, were often met with persecution. By 1839 the Opium Wars had broken out and Protestant missionaries entering China in the 19th century found evangelization work to be restricted and slow-going. In 1853 the Chinese Evangelisation Society (CES) sent Hudson Taylor to China.

1865
The founding of the China Inland Mission (CIM)

Taylor served six years in China, during which time he married Maria Dyer, another missionary in China. During this time, God began burdening his heart for the millions yet to be evangelized inland. This sense of direction was not endorsed by CES and Taylor decided to resign.

He and his family returned to England for a while for health reasons. On 25th June 1865, he was walking on Brighton Beach praying about China and its spiritual needs—God revealed that he would be the one to lead a new foreign mission to China. Taylor prayed for 24 willing and skillful workers—two for each of China's 11 provinces and also Mongolia. He deposited £10 in the bank—the "China Inland Mission" (CIM) was born.

1866
Early days of the CIM

Taylor left England for China with his family and 16 workers aboard the Lammermuir. CIM missionaries visited China's provinces dressed in Chinese clothing, preaching the gospel with the desire to start churches. By the end of 1866, 24 workers were active in four stations across inland China.

1870 - 1875
Early advances despite hardship

The years following 1870 were some of the darkest in the history of CIM due to low finances, political upheavals and poor health of the missionaries. A call for 18 more workers was made. A period of expansion followed as 18 new workers, two by two, took up residence in nine new provinces.

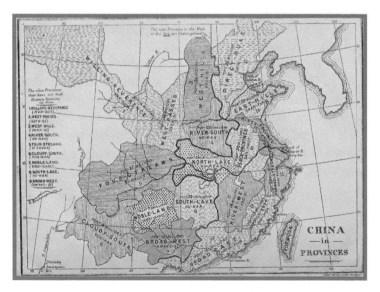

1881 - 1886
Two calls for advance

With the total number of missionaries at barely 100, a call to pray for 70 new workers went out. God provided 73 new workers within three years. The Cambridge Seven went out during this period. After a call for 100 went out in 1886, 102 workers sailed for China within the year.

1900
Boxer Rebellion, a reign of terror

In a reign of terror, the Boxers set out to exterminate all foreigners in China. Hundreds of missionaries and thousands of Chinese Christians were put to death. The CIM alone lost 58 missionaries and 21 children. During this period, the work force of the CIM increased to 933 people.

1905
Hudson Taylor dies

After over 50 years of active service for China, Hudson Taylor died on 3rd June 1905 in Changsha, and was buried in Zhenjiang next to his first wife, Maria.

1915 - 1934
Years of growth for the CIM

Early ministries of the CIM involved starting churches, supporting literature work, doing evangelism and running hospitals and schools. By 1915, 1,063 workers were located at 227 work stations throughout China. By 1934 the number had risen to 1,368 missionaries were serving in 364 stations.

1927
Darkness reigns, but the CIM calls for 200

A tumultuous political situation resulted in Christians across China being persecuted, tortured and put to death. Half of the overall missionary community left permanently. In the midst of darkness, the CIM issued a new call for 200 new missionaries over two years. By 1931, another 203 new missionaries had arrived in China.

1939
Continued growth and many baptized

Almost 200,000 Chinese and minority people had been baptized by 1939. During World War II and the years that followed, missionaries shared the gospel among university students and professionals, even government leaders.

1949 - 1954
The "reluctant exodus" from China

Mao Tse Tung and his Communist Party took power in China in 1949. Many mission organizations pulled out, but CIM issued a call for missionaries to stay and then brought 49 more new workers in 1948 and 1949. In 1950 the CIM General Director deemed that further work in China was impossible and instructed all missionaries to leave.

1951
The future of the CIM decided

The CIM decided that, rather than dissolve, it would continue and expand to new fields: Thailand, Malaysia, Japan, Philippines, Indonesia and Taiwan. A new headquarters was established in Singapore. At this time, it was decided that the name should change to the "Overseas Missionary Fellowship of the China Inland Mission" (CIM – OMF)

1964
Expanding the identity of the mission

CIM-OMF changed its name to Overseas Missionary Fellowship (OMF) in 1964 (and in 1993 to OMF International). At this time, the mission began accepting Asians into membership and set up home offices in eight regions of East Asia.

1964 - 2006
Growth and expansion throughout East Asia

During this time, OMF discovered great pockets of need, including totally unreached people groups in the countries surrounding China. They knew that God wanted them to move forward  in faith. Home councils were formed in Japan, Korea, Singapore, Hong Kong, Malaysia, the Philippines, Taiwan and Indonesia. Beginning in the early 1980s, Christian professionals were sent into China, and during the 1990s outreach began to six more creative access nations. At the same time, teams were deployed among the Asian diaspora in a number of Western and Asian countries. The name was changed again to OMF International.

2006
The continuing legacy

Dr. Patrick Fung became the General Director and the first Asian leader to hold this position in OMF International. The OMF International leadership sought God and a call for 900 new workers was issued. 499 new workers were added between 2006 and 2010.

2015
OMF International today

OMF International currently has 1400 members from over 40 nations. They serve among 100 people groups in East Asia, as well as among the Asian diaspora in the USA, Canada, Europe, Africa, Australia and New Zealand.